Understanding School Transition

What happens to children and how to help them

Jennifer Symonds

Routledge
Taylor & Francis Group

LONDON AND NEW YORK

First published 2015
by Routledge
2 Park Square, Milton Park, Abingdon, Oxon OX14 4RN

and by Routledge
711 Third Avenue, New York, NY 10017

Routledge is an imprint of the Taylor & Francis Group, an informa business

British Library Cataloguing in Publication Data
A catalogue record for this book is available from the British Library

Library of Congress Cataloging-in-Publication Data
Symonds, Jennifer.

Understanding school transition : what happens to children and how to help them / Jennifer Symonds.

pages cm

1. Students, Transfer of–Psychological aspects. 2. Transfer students–Services for. 3. School children–Psychology. 4. Student adjustment. 5. Students, Transfer of–Great Britain. I. Title.

LB3064.S96 2015

371.2'914–dc23

2014042639

ISBN: 978-0-415-67663-2 (hbk)
ISBN: 978-0-415-67664-9 (pbk)
ISBN: 978-1-315-71438-7 (ebk)

Typeset in Bembo
by Cenveo Publisher Services

Printed and bound in Great Britain by
TJ International Ltd, Padstow, Cornwall

Contents

Foreword

Life, from birth to death, is full of transitions. These can involve changes in personal lifestyle, in family relationships, in the workplace, but most attention has been given to those transitions which take place during the compulsory phase of schooling. In most Western and developed countries, starting with entry to kindergarten or nursery, and depending on the type of system, it can involve a minimum of one and, in rarer cases, up to four further moves during the compulsory period of schooling before the young adolescent emerges into the workplace or proceeds to some form of further or higher education. In the UK, for example, a pupil may go to separate infant and junior primary schools before moving to a secondary school at the age of 11 years. In other cases, after moving from the primary first school at 8 or 9 years of age the experience consists of four or five years in a middle school before moving to a high school. Further complications exist when the secondary school has no sixth form, so students again have to move for two further years to a sixth-form college. In the USA, a similar plethora of organisational arrangements (elementary, middle/junior high/high school/all through secondary school) give a slightly less complex series of transitions, although it is true to say that in both countries the majority of students now only move once or twice during their school careers. For a variety of reasons, mainly because the transition covers the start of major biological and emotional changes associated with the onset of puberty, most research has focused on the move from primary or elementary schools, to secondary, middle or junior high schools, at around 10 to 14 years of age.

In the UK, interest in transition (also referred to as transfer) began in the late 1960s. The shift away from a selective system at secondary level and the establishment of all-ability comprehensive schools over the next decade raised questions about how best to use existing school buildings to accommodate the new arrangements. In some cases pupils moved from their first (elementary/primary) school at either 8, 9, 10 or 11 years of age, depending on the type of secondary provision. Thus, early research interest was directed towards questions regarding the advantage and disadvantage of these different arrangements.

These early studies were mostly quantitative, because the success of a particular transition arrangement was mainly judged in terms of pupils' attitude and enjoyment of school and in the amount of academic progress recorded by the end of the first year after the transition.

One of the earliest findings concerned the 'hiatus' or dips in academic progress during the first weeks in the new school. For most pupils it was easily overcome, but for around 12 per cent it remained a serious problem, particularly in situations where the new comprehensive school deployed setting and banding to cope with its mixed ability intake. Research has subsequently shown that such pupils, particularly when poor performance is linked to some form of learning disability, are much more likely to be excluded on the grounds of bad behaviour. This minority of disengaged pupils can have a profound effect on the overall school and classroom environment.

Initially, dips in attitude and attainment were put down to a lack of continuity, particularly with regard to the curriculum and teaching. Secondary school teachers tended to ignore the subject matter that had been covered in primary school and, instead, made a 'fresh start' in their respective specialisms. Pupils said they spent a lot of time during the first half-term repeating work they had already done in the final year of primary school. Teachers also tended to do more talking and pupils did more writing. Some secondary schools attempted to deal with the continuity problem by instituting a special 'transition' year whereby the curriculum and teaching was modelled on best primary practice. There was a special teaching area, a form teacher who took most lessons, and the curriculum was based on an integrated topic rather than a single subject approach. In some cases, pupils had their own special designated play area, toilets and separate lunch provision so that there was very little mixing with older pupils. Other schools took the opposite stance and attempted to 'throw the newcomers in at the deep end'. Few concessions were made after day one. First-year pupils had a similar timetable, the same teachers and play areas, and shared the same facilities as every other student. After the first three days, it was no longer deemed acceptable to be late for a lesson because one couldn't locate the classroom or to forget to bring the necessary books or the right PE kit or to fail to hand in homework on time.

Gradually, however, more 'mixed' and qualitative studies began to emerge. These suggested that the conclusion that the hiatus caused by transition was a relatively brief affair was based on a false premise. While there were short-lived minor traumas such as finding one's way around the school, remembering to bring the right sports equipment and finding out how to pay for lunch, other issues, such as relationships with teachers, friendships with one's peers and coping with the academic work, were a continuing source of anxiety. Out of these studies emerged the idea of transition as a *status passage* with its own rituals and myths. Generations of new secondary pupils believed, for example, that the older pupils would push their heads down the lavatory and pull the chain. In Australia, this myth was referred to as 'the royal flush'. The advice thus shifted to the effect that too great a degree of continuity was undesirable, because if pupils found their first year of secondary school much the same as their last one at primary, there would be little evidence to suggest they had made a successful passage from child to young adult or from being a pupil to becoming a student.

When children were interviewed prior to transition, they tended to support the view that, while a degree of continuity was important, so too was an element of discontinuity. Thus they worried about coping with the work, but nevertheless were excited to have a wider range of subjects to study, particularly those involving doing and making, such as science, art and design and technology. They bemoaned the loss of their primary teacher but looked forward to being taught by a range of subject specialists. They worried about losing their old friends from primary school but were excited about making new relationships.

By the beginning of the millennium, much had been done to effect a balance between the two contrasting viewpoints. Feeder primary and the secondary senior management teams met regularly to smooth the administrative difficulties involved in the transfer of pupils' records and the provision of additional support for pupils with learning disabilities. Special induction days were organised during the summer term prior to transfer, and in some cases carried over into the summer vacation. On these days the primary pupils were able to meet the teachers and experience some lessons, have the opportunity to bond with future form-mates from other schools, eat and pay for a school dinner, receive next year's timetable and question pupils who had moved from their school in the previous year. The teacher in charge of the transfer year, together with the special educational needs coordinator (SENCO), made visits to the primary school Year 6 class to get to know the pupils and answer their questions. All these activities were designed to reduce initial psychosocial stress associated with the move to the 'big school'. Efforts were also made to develop some degree of curriculum continuity by introducing *bridging units*. These small-scale projects, mainly in English, mathematics or science, were started in the primary school and completed in the first few weeks in the secondary Year 7 classes. In an effort to reduce disparities in teaching approach, primary and secondary teachers visited each other's classes. Lastly, some schools introduced post-transfer induction programmes. These were designed to introduce students to the demands made on them in their new school, particularly the need to develop as autonomous learners. Certain local authorities, particularly Suffolk, were designated 'beacons' because of their exemplary practice and charged with helping others to rethink their transfer strategies.

However, many of these initiatives came under pressure in the late 2000s, when the decision was taken to allow all schools, and not just those in inner cities with serious weaknesses, to opt out of the mainstream state sector and reinvent themselves as independent Academies. This programme, based on similar ideas and principles that had spawned the Charter School movement in the United States, not only took these schools out of Local Authority control but reduced the financial resources available to support those establishments that opted to remain within the mainstream sector. The decision to allow parents to create 'free schools', and more recently the new special needs provisions which allow parents to opt out of mainstream and take their money with them, has led to further financial reductions. The recent recession and the consequent cutbacks have added to the problem and schools have struggled to maintain their existing transfer arrangements. While there are still pre-transfer induction days and coordinators, and SENCOs still visit the main feeder primary schools, teacher exchanges have ceased, the use of bridging units declined and post-induction sessions have become a rarity.

The publication of Jennifer Symonds' book is therefore timely and to be welcomed. It is thoroughly researched and comprehensive in its coverage of the issues. It offers something for everyone involved in the transition process: teachers, administrators, parents and hopefully politicians. It is the latter's decision to adopt a competitive market approach to education, in an attempt to drive up standards while at the same time making efficiency savings that has been the main reason for the reduction in support of vulnerable students during the transition phase. This book reminds us all of the important part that school transition plays in the wellbeing of future adults and, hopefully, will rekindle enthusiasm for and interest in the transfer problem.

The author adopts a clear logical structure in organising the material into 13 succinct chapters. In the first two of these, she uses the idea of transition as a significant status passage and the theory of person-environment fit, derived from the psychology of 'basic needs' to situate the move from primary to secondary school within the context of students' psychological wellbeing. She then deals with sources of stress and anxiety (or, more accurately for most pupils, apprehension tinged with excitement and anticipation) over the transition period, and offers teachers ways of helping to reduce negative feelings. Several chapters then deal with specific topics such as the role of parents, teachers and teaching, the nature of peer relationships among young adults, questions of identity and self-esteem and specific problems to do with dips in attainment and the decline of positive attitudes towards school in general and certain subjects in particular. The text contains copious illustrative examples drawn from her previous research and that of others. There is a great deal of sound, practical advice in every chapter.

There is a special chapter on vulnerable pupils, those with complex learning or behavioural needs; another on the 'five bridges', the administrative, social, curriculum, pedagogical and personal developmental aspects of transition designed to make the move from primary to secondary school as stress-free as possible. Another chapter looks at the ways in which teachers can adapt the methods and techniques used by researchers in order to monitor the transition process and take appropriate action where the data suggest that some form of intervention or change in the current procedures is necessary.

The concluding chapter is devoted to examining the coordinating roles of the teacher responsible for overseeing and managing the transfer process and also that of the SENCO. Again, all these chapters offer much practical advice.

I first met with Jennifer Symonds when, after completing her doctorate at Cambridge, she joined a small team investigating, among other things, the possible impact of transition on students' wellbeing. She at once struck me as an outstanding researcher. Not only was she highly capable of the normal 'everyday' aspects of research (identifying sources, gathering and making sense of data and summarising findings, etc.), but she demonstrated a distinctive capacity to think 'outside the box' and stimulate new lines of enquiry. In this way, for example, we explored new ground in the study of the links between the biological features of young adolescents and the part these play during transfer, and we examined the ways in which transitions were managed in the workplace. This led us to form the view of transfer as a continuous process, sometimes resulting in a move between schools and sometimes occurring within schools as pupils moved to the next year group. Contexts were different, but the issues and their treatments were similar.

The same qualities can be found within the chapters of this book. The use of the research on developing qualities of resilience in young adolescents in drawing up advice for parents is one instance. I particularly liked the treatment of identity in Chapter 7 and the use of optical analogies to explore the linkage between certain personality traits and the process of transition. The interactions and the possible consequences are compared to the passage of light through a prism, where the rays are diffracted into a variety of coloured strands while at the same time a lens enables each of these strands to be brought into sharper focus.

Research on transition will continue. Currently, a major concern among the Western-developed countries has to do with the wellbeing of their young people. This is not surprising, given that the UK and the USA are at the bottom of the international league tables on this measure. Given that certain situations, such as the move from primary to the much bigger secondary school or the onset of key public examinations, can also produce anxiety and stress among a sizeable proportion of the student population, and more severe symptoms leading to depression in a minority of cases, the need for more research in this area can easily be justified. According to Hagell (2012),[1] in the UK alone, during the 25-year period from 1974 to 1999, the numbers of young people reporting frequent bouts of anxiety or depression has doubled, particularly significantly for girls, where it has risen from 10 to 20 per cent. Parents have also reported that behavioural problems have also risen from 7 to 15 per cent during the same period.

More recently, increased concerns about young adolescents' use of drugs, tobacco, alcohol, junk foods and their sexual habits have led to a number of interventions underpinned by various psychological and psychiatric clinical approaches. Schools do quite a lot to ensure that their students feel safe, happy and are generally satisfied with life within their institutions. There are protocols for dealing with bullying, supervision of play areas, the use of student monitors to ensure that no student is left isolated, bored and lonely when not attending lessons. All these measures are designed to improve *hedonic* aspects of wellbeing concerned with feeling good about oneself.

More important, however, are the *eudemonic* or functioning aspects of wellbeing that not only produce positive feelings but enable young people to act out these sentiments in ways that allow them to live a 'satisfying' life. Schools that promote the functioning aspects of wellbeing do not need to introduce preventative measures to reduce incidents of bullying or to stop individuals from feeling lonely and at odds with rest of the school community. Instead, there is a sense of 'connectedness' within the school that ensures that, as part of acting in ways that make one feel good about oneself, students seek to promote similar reactions in other individuals within their peer group. Intuitively, it would seem reasonable to surmise that what happens at the transition stage is an important determinant in the promotion of school connectedness and the development of this functioning (eudemonic) form of wellbeing, but the necessary research to establish such links still needs to be done. This book provides a vital starting point for this experimental voyage of discovery.

Professor Maurice Galton
University of Cambridge, UK,
Faculty of Education

Note

1 A. Hagell (ed.) (2012) *Changing adolescence: Social trends and mental health*. Bristol: The Policy Press.

Introduction

School transition is a life-changing event. Especially for children. Although children go through other important changes, such as moving house, experiencing their parents' divorce, or welcoming new siblings into the family, those transitions are not about them alone. In comparison, when they change schools, *they* are the sole focus of the experience. *They* are the people who are changing. It is up to them, to adjust. Although many children relish this challenge, it makes others worried and nervous. This is augmented by the fact that moving schools is also intensely social. There, children move into a new forum of peers, teachers and other educational professionals. Within this network, personal and social issues bounce off each other, drawing the child's attention to their self-management (i.e. coping skills), achievement, reputation and relationships. This stimulates their identity development so that children change as people, just as they change schools.

This book focuses on children's wellbeing at this pivotal time, for wellbeing underpins whether children adjust well or poorly to the changes they experience at school transition. And children's adjustment is important not only for them, but also for the mental and social health of the student year group and teachers. This is why educators have paid more attention to transition in recent eras, both as a professional activity and as an ethical one. Researchers are interested in transition, too, for it is a window into how children develop when they experience sudden environmental changes. This is essentially a harmonious marriage of interests, for what researchers uncover can be used by educators wishing to employ intelligent transition management that helps children adapt.

Part II of this book, 'What happens to children', makes this evidence base available to educators in review chapters dedicated to central topics in school transition psychology. These chapters (Chapters 3 to 10) are preceded by a discussion of the historical emergence of school transition as a status passage and its implications for adolescent development (Chapter 1), which is followed by a chapter in which I give my perspective on wellbeing and explain the nitty-gritty mechanisms of how children adapt to new environments (Chapter 2). You can use this information in your classrooms to help you understand why children behave the way they do. The bottom line is that knowing more about children's psychology at transition will make you a better educator.

Part III of the book changes tack, to explore what you can do for your students, i.e. 'How to help them'. There are many methods of coordinating transition, including providing children with interventions designed to support their move, improve their attitudes and school outcomes. Now, although the consensus is that any effort towards helping children at transition will do them some good, the success of individual interventions is less clear. And when a lot of planning and resources are involved, you might want to know whether these are being put to good use or whether you might do something differently. That is why, after reviewing transition interventions, I have dedicated a chapter to methods of evaluating them that you can easily employ in your school.

The book concludes with a chapter on effective transition leadership. Here, six educators speak about how they coordinated transition in their schools. It became obvious from their accounts that managing transition well is good for your personal development as an educator, for children, and for the entire school when your actions pave the way for happy, well-adjusted new cohorts who help define the school's social and academic cultures. So the question is, really, 'Why wouldn't you pay attention to transition, and do everything in your power to improve it?' Hopefully this book can provide you with some ideas on how to do exactly that.

Before we begin, I must announce a few caveats. First, the research underscoring the chapters mainly represents schools and students in the United Kingdom and the United States, where the bulk of school transition research has been carried out. Second, the majority of this research has involved schools that children transition into ('transfer schools') rather than the schools they transfer from ('feeder schools'). On this note, readers interested in feeder schooling will find dedicated information in Chapter 3 on anxiety and stress, and Chapter 4 on hopes, fears and myths. The successive chapters also consider how children fared before transition compared to afterwards. Third, the conclusions in this book are drawn mainly from the evidence surrounding transition at age 11 or 12 years old, into secondary schools in the UK, and into middle or junior high schools in the US, although the reader will find some instances where I have dipped into the literature on transition to high school.

My final point regards terminology. Although Maurice Galton and others (see Galton, Gray, Rudduck, Berry et al., 2003) prefer using the term 'transfer' to describe moving between schools, and 'transition' to indicate moving years within a school, I have used the word 'transition' as my main descriptor, given that, to me, it reflects the slower process of *becoming* a transfer school student. With respect to Galton et al. (2003), as discussed, I have used the term 'transfer' to differentiate between transfer and feeder schools. And, finally, I referred to children in those schools as adolescents or children, depending on whether I focused on adolescence as a cultural and biological state (spanning the ages of 9 or 10 to 18 years; Eccles, 1999), or on children as a group of similar-aged people (under the age of 18 years; United Nations, 1989).

References

Eccles, J. S. (1999). The development of children ages 6 to 14. *The Future of Children: When School is Out,* 9(2), 30–44.

Galton, M., Gray, J., Rudduck, J., Berry, M., Demetriou, H., Edwards, J., & Charles, M. (2003). Transfer and transitions in the middle years of schooling (7–14): Continuities and discontinuities in learning. *Research Report RR43.* London: Department for Education and Skills.

United Nations (1989). *Convention on the rights of the child.* Office of the United Nations High Commissioner for Human Rights. Available at: www2.ohchr.org/english/law/crc.htm#art12

Part I

Foundational Knowledge

Chapter 1

School transition as a status passage

Chapter overview

When 10- to 14-year-old children change schools, they *become* a secondary, middle or junior high school student. This requires them to master new skills – such as commuting to school alone and managing their own school equipment – which necessitate increased responsibility. In tandem with these personal experiences, teachers, family members and peers can expect children to behave more like adults. And, at the same time as they progress personally and socially, many children are going through puberty, which can mark the end of physical childhood. This sets up school transition as a status passage, akin to the adolescent initiation ceremonies of pre-industrial cultures. Many of its features are determined by the historic emergence of primary and secondary phases of education, while others are contrived by children and adults in a bid to increase children's independence. This chapter reviews these defining features of school transition, setting it in the social historical context of human and educational development.

How school transition acts as a status passage

Every year in England, around half a million children become secondary school students (DfE, 2013). Some might share Matthew's opinion, that at primary school 'you just feel like you're too old, there's thousands of young kids underneath you' and are ready to move on. Others may prefer the security of their primary school classroom teacher and classmates to a larger school with different teachers for each subject. Either way, the majority report settling in well to their new school after the first term (Gray, Galton, McLaughlan, Clarke & Symonds, 2011), despite having to adjust to different teachers, new peers, additional subjects and more complex timetables, buildings and grounds. Each of these changes in school environment marks a new area of experience that children utilise when constructing their identities. After transition, Ruby reflected that 'when I was in primary school, if I fell over they'd come running to me like they're my mum. But here I fell off my stool and the teacher just shouted at me.' She then described how the 'tougher' attitude of secondary school teachers made her feel more responsible for her own behaviour. Children can also feel more mature simply by leaving primary school, as Billy explained to me in his third term post-transition: 'I was excited that I was moving and growing up and stuff ... cause it's secondary school and there's more older people. I think that as there's older people, I'm more older as well.'

If we consider how same-aged children develop in non-Western cultures, we can see that many features of school transition are similar to those of adolescent initiation ceremonies that signal the end of childhood. These ceremonies or rituals are conducted in over two thirds of pre-industrial societies (Schlegel & Barry III, 1991) and usually require children to undertake a rite of passage in an area valued by that community such as sexuality, fertility, valour, wisdom or responsibility (Schlegel & Barry III, 1979). In order to complete the rite of passage, children must experience some type of physical or mental change. Ndembu boys in Africa are circumcised at puberty, which qualifies them to take part in hunting ceremonies (Turner, 1967), while Micronesian Butaritari girls have their skin oiled and stomachs bound at first menarche (Brewis, 1996). After the ceremony is complete, children are awarded a new role of being a responsible member of adult society.

In many ways, school transition serves the same purpose for children in our communities. Although it is not officially linked to puberty, transition occurs at or around the same time as the average child (age 11.5 years) experiences their first outward pubertal changes, such as growing pubic hair, breast buds and first menarche or ejaculation (Coleman & Coleman, 2002). When they think of secondary school, children and adults note that 'school takes on the quality of a training centre for their future adult role' and that it is time 'to get down to business ... to take one's education seriously' (Higgins & Eccles, 1983, p. 35). Making new friends, being taught by subject specialist teachers, learning new subjects and being part of an older peer group all serve to convince children that they have acquired the characteristics of a secondary school student, and this is often followed by a change in their behaviour and expectations as I discuss later in this chapter.

The term 'status passage' was first applied to school transition by researchers Linda Measor and Peter Woods in their book *Changing Schools* (1984). Glaser and Strauss (1971) define it as an event where people change into a different social role that appears more or less responsible, mature or demanding. Besides school transition, there are many other status passages in Western culture, including learning to drive, getting married, and retiring from work. However, school transitions in state education systems are perhaps the most ingrained, as they occur for a majority of people in each developed country, at a set time in the lifespan. Although headteachers and teachers can control certain qualities of this status passage, such as whether children move into classrooms that are more or less demanding, many significant features of the passage are cemented in school structures. The change from a smaller to a larger school, for example, is typical of middle and secondary school transition in the UK. Below, I explore how these characteristics have emerged historically, in a bid to better understand how a national status passage with widescale implications for children's psychological wellbeing has developed.

Why does school transition as a status passage exist in England?

The dominant age of transfer at 11 or 12 years to secondary school is a relatively recent phenomenon in English educational history. During the late Victorian era, a series of Elementary Education Acts (1870, 1880, 1891) established the first national school leaving ages: 11 years in 1893 and 12 years in 1899.[1] However, most children lucky enough to complete elementary schooling transferred to the workforce, where they toiled as farmhands, in small workshops, as domestic servants and, in fewer cases, as factory labourers (Frost, 2009). These positions often involved long hours of work for little pay.

Over the next 40 years, a flurry of school types emerged for older working-class children, enabling children to avoid entering the workforce before age 14 years. An early version was the 'higher grade' schools, which offered two or three more years of education in elementary school buildings. Often the curriculum of these extra years geared children towards entering trade or industry (Howe, 2011). In the early 1900s, these schools were grouped together with junior technical schools and public grammar schools by the 1902 Education Act under the first national system of secondary education. This system was divided internally by the curricula of these schools, with some preparing children for entry to working-class jobs and others promoting entrance to liberal professions (Richardson & Wiborg, 2010). The latter type based their curriculum mainly on that of grammar schools, by teaching more academic and less technical subjects. As such, they were the archetype of the secondary school curriculum today (Chitty, 2002), and of many of its differences to primary schooling.

This confusion of secondary school types in the early 1900s resulted in the existence of a range of ages of transfer from elementary to secondary education in the first few decades of the 20th century. In a report on adolescent education (1926), Sir William Henry Hadow (1859–1937) recommended that children transfer from primary to secondary education, preferably in a different school, at age 11 years. This was so that 'at the age of 11 children are beginning a fresh phase in their education, which is different from the primary or preparatory phase, with methods, standards, objectives and traditions of its own' (p. 89). Hadow rationalised that a clean break in education would fit well with the transition to adolescence, which he described as 'a tide which begins to rise in the veins of youth at the age of eleven or twelve' (p. xix). Hadow's vision of transition at age 11 years was based on matching educational phases to children's developmental stage, following the popularisation of the notion of adolescence by G. Stanley Hall in the early 1900s.

It was another 18 years before Hadow's recommendation on the age of transfer was formally recognised by the 1944 Education Act. In the winter of 1940–41, the Educational Reconstruction Committee met in Bournemouth to discuss how to further nationalise the education system, and as part of these discussions the committee debated whether children should transfer at the age of 11 or 13 years. The majority of board members supported the later transfer, based on the grounds that children were better equipped to choose a vocation at this age (Richardson & Wiborg, 2010). However, the Education Secretary went against the majority by setting the age of transfer for 11 years, in order to keep the standard grammar course for 11- to 16-year-olds intact. Essentially, this move cemented the view that children need a clean break in education as they enter adolescence.

Over the next 20 years, English secondary schools became more specialised – as either technical schools offering vocational education, modern schools with a mixed academic and vocational curriculum or academic grammar schools. Entrance to a specific type was decided by children's results on the 11+ examination sat at the end of elementary school. Because of this, school transition in early adolescence became a formal marker of whether children would go on to have an academic or vocational occupation in society. In this era, the concerns voiced by advocates of a later transition at age 13 years became a reality.

For years there was dissatisfaction with the social inequality imbued by the tripartite system. This spurred further reorganisation in the early 1960s to a comprehensive curriculum for all children, introduced by the 1964 Education Act. The backdrop to this Act included a review on the state of primary education (CACE, 1967), conducted by Central Advisory Council for England led by Lady Plowden, commissioned by the then Education Secretary, Sir Edward Boyle. Popularly referred to as the 'Plowden Report', this review recommended that children aged 8 to 12.5 years be educated separately from their younger and older peers, in order to allow them the benefits of specialist subject teaching without exposing them to the larger, adult-oriented environment of the secondary school. Referring to the child development research of the time, Plowden concluded that because most children would experience puberty after age 12 years, it was advisable to have a higher age of transfer to secondary education. This advice echoed Hadow's vision of educating children of pubertal age in different schools to their younger peers.

Around the same time, an independent review on the age of transfer was conducted by researchers John Nisbet and Noel Entwistle for the Scottish Council for Research in Education (Nisbet & Entwistle, 1966). These researchers disagreed with Plowden by concluding that the age of school transition should not be dependent on puberty, as puberty occurred over a number of years and was not consigned to any one event. However, neither recommendation had much bearing on the eventual common age of transition that emerged from the educational restructuring in the 1960s.

The 1964 Education Act sparked a period of experimentation, modelled on the efforts of Sir Alex Clegg, the then Chief Education Officer of the West

Riding of Yorkshire. In the period leading up to the Act, Clegg trialled schools for 9- to 13-year-olds based on the idea of middle schools in the United States, following requests for secondary reorganisation from local school governors and divisional executives (Hargreaves, 1986). Clegg's middle schools capitalised on the use of existing school buildings, which were designed for moderate populations of secondary modern and technical school students, and therefore were a good alternative to building new comprehensive schools for 11- to 18-year-olds. Clegg's efforts were successful, and his three-tier system became one of several options listed by Circular 10/65 (DES, 1965) for how Local Authorities could reorganise to comprehensive education.

On receiving the circular, many local authorities followed Clegg's lead and reorganised to a three-tier system of elementary, middle and high schools, with the early adolescent transition placed at the ages of 10, 11, 12 or 14. Within a period of five years, there were 1,690 middle schools in England (Hargreaves & Tickle, 1980). Many of these schools embraced the notion of middle years education that softens the transition from childhood to adolescence by offering increased social support, a more personalised curriculum and relationships and sex education specific to this age group (e.g. Brown & Saltman, 2005). Indeed, my recent study of adolescent development in a typical middle school versus a typical secondary school found that children did feel better supported and were more engaged personally and emotionally in the middle school because of this provision (Symonds, 2009).

However, despite middle schools being good for children's wellbeing, the majority of local authorities have reorganised back to a two-tier system, with the age of transfer firmly placed at 11 or 12 years of age. Although it has been argued that this is to improve test scores, as with each transition comes a dip in progress (Suffolk Local Authority, 2006), there is little evidence to support this, with the GCSE results of children in the three-tier system being similar to those of children in the two-tier system, once schools are matched by socio-economic status (Symonds, 2007). More probably, the driving force behind reorganisation and the decline of the middle school is to keep all schools in line with the national Key Stages of education that issue a change in curriculum between Years 6 and 7. The decisions made by the 1944 Education Act live on, despite there being little evidence that these support children's wellbeing. Importantly, they create a striking difference between one type of school and another, requiring a significant adjustment from children who are going through a vulnerable developmental period. I shall now explore these differences, so that we can see what children must adjust to.

What are the main features of school transition as a status passage?

Table 1.1 outlines these differences using data gathered from Department for Education statistics (DfE, 2011, 2014), a national survey of break and

Table 1.1 Key features of primary and secondary school environments

School characteristic	Primary schools	Secondary schools
Age range (1)	5 to 11 years	11 to 16 years
Roll size in per cent of schools nationally (1)	500 students or under in 94 per cent of schools	1,500 students or over in 91 per cent of schools
Average class size (1)	27 children in KS2	20 children in KS4/5
Average student–teacher ratio (1)	21 students per teacher	16 students per teacher
Main type of teaching	Single classroom teacher	Multiple subject specialists
Examinations	End of Year 6	End of Year 11
Typical calendar (3)	Three terms	Three terms
Typical weekly timetable (3)	Five days of five lessons	Five days of eight lessons
Typical lesson length	1 hour	35 minutes
Combined length of breaktimes (2)	77 minutes	69 minutes

Notes
1 DfE (2011)
2 Blatchford and Baines (2008)
3 Symonds and Hagell (2011)

lunchtimes (Blatchford & Baines, 2008) and a review of school time (Symonds & Hagell, 2011). Focusing on the differences, we can imagine children's typical expectations of transition, as captured across studies (see Chapter 4; also Gray et al., 2011). Before they change schools, children may wonder how they will cope with a peer group roughly three times larger than what they are used to. Will they keep their friends from primary school? Will they make new friends? Will they encounter danger amongst these peers? And what about new teachers? Children fret about adjusting to multiple teaching styles and new classroom rules, after having had the same teacher for most subjects. Furthermore, their new timetables look confusing. Will they ever manage to get to all those lessons on time? Those concerned about maturity status fear becoming the youngest students, especially if they have heard rumours about the nasty things that older children do to new arrivals. Finally, there are many practical things to worry about. Will they be able to organise their own equipment? How about getting lost in the larger school grounds? And what will the commute to school be like, especially if this involves catching a school bus for the first time?

In mind of these changes, it is perhaps logical that many children expect their new schools to offer a radically new experience to primary school. However, they also encounter similarities between school tiers. School calendars look much the same, with the long summer holiday and breaks for Christmas and Easter. This design traces back to the Victorian era, with the break in July and August meant for children to help with the harvest at home (Sharp, 2000). The national curriculum has also created similarities between tiers, for on both sides of transition children learn a mixture of core (English, mathematics and science) and enrichment subjects (i.e. music, fine art, drama, physical educa-tion), which echoes the curriculum of grammar schools (Chitty, 2002). Although there may be a public perception that primary schools offer more exploratory learning than secondary, this is more myth than fact, as teaching styles (Galton & Pell, 2002) and patterns of lesson activities (Galton, Simon & Croll, 1980) are relatively similar in both school types. In other words, the days of the primary school 'wild men²' are long gone, if they were ever there to begin with (Galton et al., 1980).

What are the effects of the status passage?

For a moment, allow me to digress into my personal experience. A few years ago I stood in a jewellers' shop waiting for my watch strap to be fitted. A mother and son came into the shop: he looked about 9 or 10 years old. Although the son was interested in obtaining a heavy-weight silver chain, his mother said no. She explained that 'You can't have one of them, you're not old enough.' Then she continued, 'You're still a boy, not a man. You don't want to grow up too fast!' This logic seemed to appeal to the boy, who appeared to quickly lose interest in the chains.

Just like the boy in the jewellers' shop, children of all ages look around them for indications of how mature they are. Often these are signs and symbols, such as wearing particular jewellery or clothes, or a certain haircut (and we all know how long a 12-year-old boy can spend getting those spikes in his hair just right!). In previous work, I have described these symbols as maturity status markers (Symonds, 2009). Conceptually, these markers are similar to the ritual elements of adolescent initiation ceremonies discussed earlier. In both cases, children use the markers/ritual elements to symbolise their graduation to a more adult role. However, maturity status markers are not necessarily deter-mined by adults, and can be scattered throughout the lifespan with no steady route to progression. Also, they act as markers only when they are conveyed as such by others, or interpreted as markers by children themselves. Essentially, anything can be a maturity status marker as long as it is connected by some person to growing up. This might lead you to think about how we can moti-vate children using this method, about what types of markers you can create in schools to make a difference to children's lives.

When children perceive school transition as a status passage, they interpret many of its features as maturity status markers. Aspects of school organisation may stand out especially if they require more independent behaviour from children. After transition, Christine in Measor and Woods (1984, p. 97) reflected that, at primary school, 'they used to ring a bell, and you had play-time, and they used to blow a whistle or ring a bell, you know a handbell, but they don't have one here'. For Christine, the hand bell took on symbolic importance as a marker of immaturity, which was not needed at the more 'grown-up' school. In the same study, Ruth (1984, p. 97) noted that 'at dinners here you are responsible for your money', whereas lunch money at primary school was cared for by classroom teachers. By noting this difference, Ruth conveyed a sense of moving towards adult independence in her new school.

The more teenage behaviour of an older peer group can also be translated into specific maturity status markers, such as wearing jewellery, talking in cliques, and dating. Many children aspire to achieve this teenage standard once they change schools, which can involve sloughing off childish behaviours from primary school. In the first term post-transition, Ruby in Symonds (2009) criticised members of her year group for calling people silly derogatory names: 'They're in Y7 now, they shouldn't be acting like they're in reception, they should be acting like they're part of grownups and they're becoming younger when they do that.' She then explained that 'Cause in Y6 they are still young and when they come to Y7 it's like a big step. Growing up' (Ruby). In this statement, we can see how Ruby regulates her own sense of maturity and imposes her expectations onto her same-aged peers. Another issue of maturity status is that often, after transition, children stop playing games at lunchtime and instead stand around talking in cliques (Kvalsund, 2000; Measor & Woods, 1984; Symonds, 2009). Although this can stem from a lack of recreational equipment at secondary school (Symonds, 2009), it also relates to children's reluctance to engage in activities that become prescribed as childish, for example, playing 'stick in the mud' or 'tag' (Measor & Woods, 1984). Although it can be a good thing that younger children act more socially mature after changing schools, it can also mark the end of childhood and the developmental benefits of play (e.g. Whitebread & Basillo, 2013).

Indeed, by seeking to become more socially mature at transition, some children catapult themselves into a downward spiral of disengagement and antisocial behaviour. In an American study, girls perceived that others in their year group were more socially mature based on whether they smoked cigarettes and associated with boys (Merten, 2005). In the UK and US, children have developed anti-academic identities after transition (e.g. Hargreaves & Pell, 2002) to signal a break from their previous identities as compliant children (Merten, 2005) and to obtain social status by displaying deviant behaviour that is associated with strength (Measor & Woods, 1984). These changes in academic identity are discussed in detail in Chapter 9.

Children have also looked to teachers for signals that they are more mature, and have found these conveyed explicitly and through tacit expectations. As mentioned, Ruby noted that her secondary school teacher was less inclined to help her after falling over than her primary school teacher would have been (Symonds, 2009). This experience took on deep significance for Ruby, as she repeated the story in detail in each of three interviews held across Year 7. Twenty years prior, Carol told a similar story in Measor and Woods (1984): 'What I like about the senior school, they trust you, don't they? In the other school they wouldn't hardly give you a pencil, because they said, oh you lose that, it's the end of you.' Unfortunately, although teachers often expect children to be more mature at secondary school, they can award very little responsibility or agency in learning. This lack of autonomy can be at odds with children's expectations for more independence after transition, and can be at the heart of children's ensuing dissatisfaction with school, as I discuss in Chapters 2 and 9.

Parents also play a part in creating the status passage, when they change home routines and rules in order to support children's autonomy at transition. For example, parents can encourage independence by tutoring their children on how to get to school safely when they take a new route or catch public transportation for the first time (O'Brien, 2005). Following this, some children use public transportation to socialise with new friends who live throughout the catchment area, which brings a host of new, unsupervised activities, such as going shopping or to the movies (Symonds, 2009). Other markers set by parents are the move to regular chores and the trade of chores for pocket money (Symonds, 2009). This plethora of maturity status markers in home, school and peer environments combines with the differences in school structures to create the basic qualities of the status passage, which, as I explore throughout this book, shapes children's psychological wellbeing.

Conclusions

In an ideal world, the status passage of school transition should encourage positive attitudes and behaviour. Some maturity status markers have this effect, when children become more socially responsible, learn to manage their own equipment, adapt to complex timetables and new teaching arrangements, commute more independently and help out at home. However, other markers have negative consequences. The change to socialising in cliques can encourage bullying and prejudice within a social pecking order, while copying older teenage behaviours can lead some children down a risky pathway. Furthermore, although school transition encourages children to 'grow up', many school practices do not support this. Year 7 children can feel at the bottom of the heap next to their older peers and have few opportunities to take on responsibility in their new schools. The answer for some children is to use what happens outside of classrooms as a blueprint for how to mature. This can lead to an overemphasis on appearances, social identities (such as being deviant or conformist) and teenage activities for children who are concerned with growing up quickly. In turn, children can begin to disengage from education.

So what can educators do to prevent children from dismissing school in their search for a more mature identity? My suggestion is that we provide clear maturity status markers for children's intellectual *and* social progression in everyday school practice. If these can tie in with children's expectations for

Turner, V. (1967). *The forest of symbols. Aspects of Ndembu ritual.* New York: Cornell University Press.

Whitebread, D., & Basillo, M. (2013). Play, culture and creativity. In D. Gauntlett & B. Stjerne-Thomsen (eds.), *Cultures of creativity.* Billund, Denmark: The LEGO Foundation.

Chapter 2

Psychological wellbeing

Chapter overview

This chapter outlines what psychological wellbeing is in my perspective, so that readers can consider how it develops at school transition. I conceptualise wellbeing as our basic psychological needs for identity, self-esteem, competence, autonomy and social support. I describe how these facets of wellbeing manifest during adolescence, as children begin to focus on age-related issues. Then, I explain how wellbeing alters at school transition through the process of person-environment fit. Finally, I offer readers insight into how wellbeing changed for two children who held divergent attitudes to school. Readers are encouraged to use this chapter to understand the building blocks of wellbeing and its development, before reading more about it at transition in Chapters 3 to 10.

What is psychological wellbeing?

In the late 2000s there was growing concern that objective indicators, such as personal income and rates of illness, did not sufficiently represent a population's wellbeing; there had to be consideration of how people felt about life (McLellan, Galton, Steward & Page, 2012). UNICEF (2007) made this distinction when they ranked 21 industrialised countries on six dimensions of child wellbeing: material goods, health and safety, education, family and peer relationships, behaviour and risks, and subjective wellbeing. The first five dimensions mostly concerned objective indicators – that is, factors external to the child. This angle was taken when measuring relationships by family structure and number of shared family meals. However, the sixth component (subjective wellbeing) was entirely children's personal ratings: of their physical health, enjoyment of school and satisfaction with their lives. Although there was some consistency across measures within countries, the United Kingdom and United States, for example, were last on nearly every measure. However, in Greece children had comparatively poor education, material wealth and health and safety, but high subjective wellbeing. This demonstrates that feeling positive about life is not necessarily connected to how well resourced children are; rather, it is a psychological issue.

When parents and children were asked what wellbeing meant to them, they mostly spoke about happiness (Department for Children, Schools and Families, 2008). They acknowledged that happiness was a temporary state that people strove towards, and that happiness was a deeply personal thing. One parent remarked that some children were just going to be miserable, despite having all they needed for happiness in their lives, echoing the variation of rankings in the UNICEF report. Using the phrase 'a good childhood', put forward by other government reports to describe wellbeing, made parents feel uncomfortable, as this suggested a moral judgment about what was good, such as having more money or belongings. Rather, some parents preferred 'a content childhood'. This encompassed times when children were happy, but also when they were less happy, as they learned to cope with not having everything they wanted, which parents felt was a necessary component of positive development.

The notions of happiness and being content, or satisfied with life, are often taken to be the pinnacle of children's subjective wellbeing (McLellan et al., 2012). They are the cornerstone of authentic happiness theory, which for years dominated the field of positive psychology, which is a mode of research and thinking on what makes an optimal personal state (Seligman, 2011). However, the inventor Martin Seligman recently criticised his own theory for not considering other types of positive experience. In his book *Flourishing, a visionary new understanding of happiness and well-being* (2011), he replaced authentic happiness with wellbeing theory, which considers happiness as part of positive emotion, one of five factors that constitute wellbeing. The others are: having positive relationships, personal accomplishment, being engaged in things and experiencing meaning in life. This definition blurs the distinction between objective indicators and subjective perception by stating that lived experience, such as achievement, is part of wellbeing, so long as it facilitates wellbeing for the individual. It also brings us closer to a definition of wellbeing that more holistically covers the types of positive experiences we have every day.

However, there is one critical part of being alive that Seligman's theory did not cover: the experience of being *you*. Although character strengths such as grit are considered in wellbeing theory (Seligman, 2011), they are but one element of what makes up our psychological selves, our identity, our awareness of who we are. This is an important aspect of wellbeing, as we can see by the intense and widespread work of therapists and psychiatrists. Often, therapists treat disorders of the self, such as having a low sense of self-worth, or discrepancy between one's ideal and actual identities, that can underpin depression and anxiety (Higgins, 1987). And, oddly enough, these types of disorders ignited the field of positive psychology, which was originally a stand against psychology being too focused on mental illness, rather than positive virtues (McLellan et al., 2012). In my perspective, the self is at the heart of wellbeing, for it is the self that holds attitudes, becomes engaged in things and experiences meaningfulness and satisfaction.

As Seligman pointed out (2011), wellbeing is a construct – or, in other words, an idea – rather than a discrete entity existing in its own right. Because, as an idea, wellbeing has no agreed definition (McLellan et al., 2011); it shifts in focus depending on the interests and beliefs of who is discussing it. This freedom to define wellbeing leads me to posit a slightly different perspective to Seligman's. The foundation of my perspective is Deci and Ryan's theory of self-determination (1985), which sets out competence, autonomy and relatedness (having positive relationships) as basic human needs for motivation. I have an open view on *competence*, seeing it as the actual and perceived effectiveness of our physical, mental and social activity. Competence is central to wellbeing, as it allows us to feel good about our achievements and abilities. Having *autonomy* is also important, as without freedom to think and do we cannot develop or maintain wellbeing. And, good-quality relationships and in particular *social support* underpin wellbeing, as we develop in interaction with other people who are therefore key to our happiness. I also believe that another basic human need is to develop our *identity*, which, as I shall describe later, is our salient conception of our psychological self. When people are held back from developing and expressing their identity, they become frustrated and maladapted. With identity comes our need for *self-esteem*, which is our emotional evaluation of ourselves. Self-esteem is critical to wellbeing, for if you feel negative about yourself then subjective wellbeing is impossible. Although our wellbeing is enhanced when we are engaged and motivated, I see these constructs as antecedents of activity surrounding our basic needs (such as being motivated to engage in learning science, because one is encouraged by social norms and evaluations of competence to locate one's future identity in the scientific industry). Together these five factors form my toolkit for understanding how children's wellbeing can alter during school transition (see Figure 2.1).

Self-awareness

Before discussing these five factors, I turn to the psychological self and its ability to be self-aware, for this is the house in which identity and the other factors take on meaning. Psychologists have long thought that our minds generate an I self and a Me self (e.g. James, 1890/1950). The Me self, also known as the self-construct or *self-concept* is the system of self-related information that we store

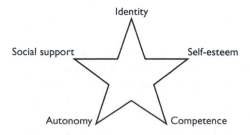

Figure 2.1 Five-point star of psychological wellbeing

be motivated and mentally healthy. The notion of competence is similar to Seligman's idea of accomplishment, that we can be more or less capable of doing certain things, and achieving in certain areas. This brings to mind our actual and perceived skills that are an important component of identity development in early adolescence (Erikson, 1968). According to Erikson, we have reasonably good ideas of what we are good at by the end of childhood. We refer back to these skills when matching ourselves to an appropriate adult career, during the pivotal period of early adolescence. This makes for a time of intensified interest in what we are good at, and what we can do, as we navigate our way through the adolescent identity crisis (Erikson, 1968).

When people think about competence, they might tend to focus on academic and practical skills such as mathematics and carpentry, especially in an educational setting. The UK national curriculum also prioritises transferable skills such as problem solving, leadership and self-management. However, I extend competence to the very far reaches of human ability, including our ability to regulate ourselves, cope, reason, create, imagine and sustain social relationships. The connection between competence and wellbeing is a very personal matter, as people give priority to different competencies depending on their values, beliefs and goals, which works into how they fuel their self-esteem. For example, I might believe that building a snowman with my children is one way to demonstrate my love for them, which is a behaviour that I value above all others, therefore when I do a good job on the snowman, I feel good about myself. How we prioritise competence can also be socialised, according to our ethnic culture, gender and age. In adolescence, being competent at adult behaviour, such as driving can hold more importance than it does in adulthood, as this marks a progression from a dependent to an independent role. Unfortunately, competence at antisocial activity such as smoking and drinking can also be understood as a maturity status marker, encouraging perhaps millions of teenagers to engage in substance abuse.

Our perception of our competence is formed by gathering information from our environment and from our internal experiences of emotion and cognitive functioning. Children's perceived competence changes rapidly at school transition, as they encounter novel self-related information stimulated by new relationships with teachers and peers, and work experiences. This can have a powerful influence on their identities, as was the case with Roxanne, in our study of musical identity at school transition (Symonds, Long & Hargreaves 2011). Roxanne was denied a place in the school musical because she failed to pass the audition. Although she had dreamed of being a singer throughout primary school, Roxanne was so disillusioned by this rejection that she relinquished her musical aspirations in the first term of secondary school, and turned her mind to journalism after being encouraged to think about realistic jobs by a career intervention program. This example illustrates how perceived competence is a powerful determinant of actual competence, and I explore the wellbeing of this important self-perception in the section on academic identity in Chapter 8.

Autonomy

The second basic need proposed by Deci and Ryan (1985), and that I have included in my definition of psychological wellbeing, is to have appropriate autonomy in our lives. Having freedom to control our actions and environments allows us to create conditions that support our personal development. Sometimes, freedom is necessary for us to try and fail, which helps us build resiliency. Autonomy is important during childhood, but takes on a new meaning during adolescence as children strive to become more independent of their parents and carers. Autonomy is no longer just about doing things by yourself, like swimming without help; it becomes a part of adolescents' identity – and almost a right – to be more independent from adults and to be free to choose who one wants to be. In adolescence, autonomy is necessary for developing a unique personal identity through discovery, experimentation and practice.

Children of transition age are awarded autonomy at school by making decisions about how and what they learn, when they take on leadership roles and have free time to do what they please. After they transfer schools, many children have reported wanting (Midgley & Feldlaufer, 1987) and expecting (Symonds, 2009) more autonomy as they become a more mature student. However, some children don't desire more freedom, and some even desire less (Mac Iver, Klingel & Reuman, 1986), perhaps as they expect to be confronted by more rules and restrictions, or don't want complete freedom in a context they are unfamiliar with. We observed this phenomenon in the Learning Futures project (Deakin Crick, Jelfs, Symonds, Ren, Patton & Grushka, 2010), where we spoke to children who were given freedom to do their own research in their first term after transition, by a school who wanted to foster their metacognitive skills through discovery learning. Although many children enjoyed this activity, others felt lost and incompetent, and preferred to have more direct instruction. These issues present a challenge for educators, as too little autonomy can turn some children off learning, but too much can have the same outcome. Like competence, children's perceptions of autonomy are integral to wellbeing, for it is these that motivate children more than their actual experience of autonomy (Ryan & Deci, 2000).

Social support

The last of my five points of wellbeing, social support is a broad term that encompasses many types of relational activity. The term that Deci and Ryan use for this is relatedness, which refers to having good-quality relationships such as appropriate attachment with parents. In my view, social support *underpins* the other four areas of wellbeing. As mentioned, people in relationships contribute to the health of each other's identity when they confirm their companion's attitudes, beliefs and decisions. They can also encourage each other to re-evaluate negative aspects of identity and make a change for good.

When children make new friends and meet different teachers at transition, they encounter many novel types of information that can spur identity development, such as being introduced to classical music. Friendships become increasingly important as a forum for testing out identity and for developing it away from adult control. Self-esteem also develops in interaction with other people, who provide us with signals that we are worthy people, and give us opportunities to feel good about ourselves. Having social support is part of developing competence, as friends, teachers and parents help children evaluate their competence, set joint goals for becoming more competent, and teach necessary skills. Finally, relationships support children's autonomy. Parents and teachers can be gatekeepers to free time and expression, while friendships allow children to develop social skills and identity away from adults. Even the search for independence is a relational matter, for as I see it, adolescents are striving towards autonomous co-dependency in the world, rather than complete aloneness.

How does psychological wellbeing change in early adolescence?

As a group, 10- to 14-year-old children are prone to typical patterns of thought and behaviour (Eccles & Midgley, 1990). These include:

- increased executive functioning and capacity for abstract thought, including the ability to analyse oneself and others (e.g. Vygotsky, 1931/1998)
- a temporary decline in emotional control and in the ability to recognise other people's emotions (e.g. McGivern, Andersen, Byrd, Mutter & Reilly, 2002)
- more focus on oneself and greater self-consciousness
- enhanced salience and confusion of identity issues (e.g. Erikson, 1968)
- concern over sexuality and dating
- the increased importance and sophistication of friendships.

As a result of these changes, the interactions between the five points of wellbeing take on age-specific qualities, some of which I have already discussed, such as friendships becoming more important for identity development and autonomy. There are further interactions of puberty, wellbeing and school transition, which I explore in Chapter 10 in the section on early maturing children.

From a social perspective, these early adolescent characteristics are the platform on which adolescent subcultures are built, as same-aged children dealing with similar challenges come together to figure out what makes for appropriate and successful behaviour. The subcultures that develop are practice grounds for being a part of an adult society; however, they can promote very different values, goals and norms, as children work through issues that are salient for them at their stage of development (Coleman, 1974). Adolescent subcultures influence wellbeing by setting indigenous standards for identity (e.g. belonging to cliques, taking on a social stereotype to express individuality i.e. Goth, punk, jock) feelings of self-worth (e.g. deriving self-esteem from sexual conquest), perceived competence (e.g. prioritising athleticism or knowledge of popular music) and autonomy (e.g. staying out late with friends becomes a marker of maturity). As you can see from this description, many of these concerns are social; therefore, interventions that promote positive relationships are bound to have a far-reaching effect on children's wellbeing, as I explore more in Chapter 11.

How does psychological wellbeing alter at school transition?

At this point I turn from discussing universal aspects of wellbeing to the personal ways in which these are constructed. Here I focus on how children develop their wellbeing in interaction with their environment. This process is referred to by psychologists as person-environment fit (e.g. Buss, 1987; Hunt, 1975). Put simply, person-environment fit is an equation, where P (person) + E (environment) = F (fit: the effect on wellbeing). This follows an older equation from Kurt Lewin who perceived behaviour as a function of the person's interaction with their environment (Lewin, 1936). In understanding how this process works, we can gain insight into why individual children display particular attitudes or behaviours at school. In response, we can design more appropriate interventions and alter our approach to teaching these children, even the tricky customers.

Focusing for a moment on the environment, we can remember some critical differences that children encounter between primary and secondary schools. There is the change to subject specialist teachers, a larger year group, an older student body, more complex and larger buildings and grounds, and the eventual shift to more complex lesson content and increased academic pressure. These changes exert an environment-down influence over children's development, creating a bridge that children must cross between old and new experiences.

However, there is also a person-up influence over the environment, caused by children's identities, and needs for competence, autonomy and relatedness. Before changing schools, children play a key role in shaping the general outlook on transition held by their year group when they discuss their hopes and fears. After they move, children's unique differences are woven into the social fabric of that group. Individual children can affect the way that classrooms are managed and the teacher's choice of learning objectives, both by exerting individual and group influence. The way in which children treat classroom and whole school resources also impacts physical space, which goes on to have social repercussions. Children's influence over their environments can be unconscious, unplanned, habitual or purposefully managed (Buss, 1987).

The fit (F) in the PEF equation refers to whether children's wellbeing is supported by PE interactions. Put simply, we might ask: Is there a good fit between children and their schools? Specific questions include: Is there a good match between the new curriculum and children's developing career identities? Do children have the emotional support from peers and teachers that they need to avoid depression and anxiety? And; Does the new peer group encourage children to treat each other fairly, or does it facilitate social stigma through stereotyping? The answers to these questions are rooted in the qualities of individual children and school environments, and I discuss more how we can evaluate these in Chapter 12.

When misfits occur between children and their schools, negative outcomes can ensue. For example, children who are dissatisfied with their schooling can slow their participation in lessons and develop negative attitudes towards learning. Those who misfit with the peer group can become socially isolated. These problems can manifest in psychological symptoms of depression, anxiety and aggression. However, misfits can sometimes unintentionally create positive outcomes (Barber, Carlson, Eccles et al., 1987) by creating a better fit in another area of the child's life. For example, a child who is ostracised by peers may focus more on his studies, which then leads to improved grades and an eventual higher starting salary.

It would also be a mistake to think that all fits are 100 per cent positive. In our study of musical identity at school transition, we observed that many children waited until after Christmas to begin musical instrument lessons, as these were oversubscribed (Symonds et al., 2011). In response, one boy Peter became more involved with sport, which gave him an alternative source of self-esteem based on his accomplishments (a self-directed fit). However, because Peter was so engaged in sport by the end of the year, he no longer wanted to learn to play a musical instrument, even when this opportunity became available. Peter rationalised this by declaring himself as 'non-musical'. Therefore, although he achieved a fit through sport, his efforts had the adverse effect of diminishing his musical identity.

A particularly potent idea is that, across a group of children, we can see typical fits and misfits that arise from interactions between the early adolescent characteristics described in the preceding section, and the typical differences between feeder and transfer schools. This *stage–environment fit* theory (Eccles & Midgley, 1989) helps educators anticipate how early adolescents' psychological wellbeing develops at school transition. An example is the interaction between children's increased focus on the self, and the change to unfamiliar classrooms. There, children engage in more social comparison (Feldlaufer, Midgley & Eccles, 1988) and can feel more negative about themselves if they are placed in an achievement group that dulls their competence in comparison to others (Marsh, 1987). Stage–environment fit theory also suggests that there are misfits between some children's need for autonomy and the lack of opportunities for this in secondary schools, between children's need to establish a personal identity and the anonymity of a larger peer group, and between children's need for adult mentoring and the switch to more impersonal relationships with subject specialist teachers. Ultimately, stage–environment fit theory may explain why there is an international trend for children to be less positive about their schooling, after they transition (Gray, Galton, McLaughlin, Clarke & Symonds, 2011). Readers can find out more about stage-environment fit theory in Chapter 9.

How children strive to maintain person-environment fit

In order to illustrate how children create fit, I refer to one of my enjoyments: the television series *Star Trek*. There are many incidences in this drama where Federation officers (the protagonists) must adapt to unfamiliar conditions. The following interchange between First Officer Worf and Chief Science Officer Jadzia Dax in the modern series *Deep Space Nine* concerns Worf's dissatisfaction with moving from living on the starship USS *Enterprise* to living on an anchored space station. Rather than live on the station, Worf decides to move his quarters to a docked starship, which creates familiar conditions to life on *Enterprise*. However, this elicits tension between Worf and his colleagues, as everyone else lives on the space station.

> 'You know, Worf, living on the *Defiant* isn't going to change anything. You're still going to have to get used to life on the station.' (Jadzia)
>
> 'I am not sure I agree.' (Worf)
>
> 'Sooner or later you are going to have to adapt.' (Jadzia)
>
> 'Perhaps in the end it will be all of you who will have to adapt to me.' (Worf)

Star Trek Deep Space Nine, season 4, episode 15, 41:45–42:05)

This example illustrates how children can achieve fit (and protect their immediate psychological wellbeing) by changing either themselves or the environment. When changing themselves, children may strive harder in class to manage a more academic curriculum or learn how to be responsible for their own equipment. However, they can also exhibit 'student pull' (Hunt, 1975) in order to fit the environment to their needs. For example, children might pass notes in class to sidestep the rule of silent work, or disrupt the teacher in an attempt to avoid working. More productively, some children might join student councils in order to change school conditions.

No matter whether it is the environment or person that is changing, children's ability to create fit can be hampered by personal and external conditions. Below I describe three restrictions on fit.

1. First, children may be *less willing* to change themselves, depending on their aptitudes and beliefs. Some may hold 'fixed mindsets' where they believe their personal qualities are innate, therefore impermeable to change, rather than having a 'transformative mindset' where they believe their qualities are dependent on effort (Dweck, 2006). Children who do not wish to, or imagine they can change themselves at transition, can engage in passive or

active resistance. For example, a child might ignore her new teachers' expectations and continue to do what pleases her. Or, she may argue against these demands in an attempt to change them. If the environment is unbendable, psychological unwillingness can create a rift between children and their new schools.

2. Some children may be *less able* to change or invoke change because of their physiology. For example, some special needs children may have more difficulty assimilating new environmental information and as a consequence of their special need lack the finesse or social skills necessary to change their environment. Children who have a less sensitive stress response system may also be less responsive to the need to change, than those who are more easily affected by environmental triggers. These 'dandelion' type children, in comparison to more sensitive 'orchid' children (Ellis & Boyce, 2008) may continue to behave in ways similar to before transition, despite encountering many differences in their environment that provoke change for others.

3. Finally, environments can prevent children from attaining fit, when they generate insurmountable challenges (such as pressuring children outside of their comfort zone) or are overly restrictive. For example, highly structured classroom environments with a set lesson content, seating plan and timing can stop children from finding ways to learn in a manner that best suits them (Hunt, 1975).

Resiliency: a story of fit between child and circumstance

How well a child adapts after transition is also down to the fine-tuning between their emotional, personal and social resources (such as having good self-esteem, being able to socialise and having sporting ability) and their experience of challenge in the new environment. Their response to challenge, and whether this protects their wellbeing, is explained by psychiatrist Sir Michael Rutter as their 'resiliency'. In Rutter's perspective, 'resistance to stress is relative, not absolute; the bases of the resistance are both environmental and constitutional; and the degree of resistance is not a fixed quality – rather, it varies over time and according to circumstance' (Rutter, 1985, p. 599). This notion of resiliency has been used to explain why in unfavourable life circumstances some people develop mental illness, while others seem to be immune.

At school transition, children can overcome challenging situations when they have the tools necessary for coping with a specific stressor. For example, dealing with academic pressure at secondary school is easier for children who come from homes where academic work is prioritised (e.g. Chen & Gregory, 2009). Those who are more outgoing and who transfer with old friends have an easier time of making new friends, especially if they are an ethnic majority in their school (e.g. Weller & Bruegel, 2006). Some tools have more universal applicability than others, such as self-esteem, which gives children more courage to tackle transition challenges and helps them bounce back if things do not work out perfectly after they move. There are some good suggestions for improving children's self-esteem in Howe and Richards (2011). Readers who are interested in resiliency can find more detail on this in Chapter 5, as I explore this notion in relation to parental support.

Case studies of change in wellbeing

In the final part of this chapter, I draw together what we have learned about psychological wellbeing and person-environment fit by illustrating how two children adapted in very different ways after changing schools.

Matthew

Matthew,[1] by all accounts, had a successful transfer to Thorpe Secondary School. His mother was a primary school teacher and he aspired to be a teacher one day. From the very beginning, Matthew's background and career goals promised a good match with his new school's academic focus. His first encounters with teachers and students were positive. In term one he reflected that 'the first day I got here I was really pleased ... I had a really nice form tutor and I had quite a nice form ... after about the first week once we'd had every single lesson possible, I was really pleased with it.' However, Matthew was concerned that he would lose his primary school identity of being a high achiever in the more anonymous environment of secondary school.

Accordingly, he wanted special attention from his secondary school teachers: 'I like to feel that the teachers actually know I'm there and that they seem interested in me ... you don't feel like you're just a normal person you feel like actually the teachers are personally interested in you and I just like to feel like that' (term one). But the move to a higher ability teaching set meant that Matthew was one of many high achievers, rather than being the star of the show. However, rather than feel worse about himself, by the end of the year Matthew had stopped mentioning his need to feel special and instead was pleased to be in a group of friends who were branded as 'boffins' (studious) by their classmates. Here we can see that Matthew used person-environment fit processes by changing how he constructed his self-esteem in order to stabilise his perception that he was more competent than the majority of his peers.

Charlie

Charlie was placed in the same class as Matthew at Thorpe because of his high Key Stage 2 SAT scores. However, he reported a completely different transition experience. Charlie grew up in a single parent household with little support for his academic talents. He had been bullied at primary school and had no friends in his year group, and was nervous about transferring without friends into a new peer group where he might be victimised. Accordingly, Charlie's reflections on transition centred on the social world. In his first term at Thorpe, he was constantly on the lookout for signs of social threat: 'When you come for your induction day everyone was like massively tall and you're just like "I'm going to get trampled on." Everyone has their collars tucked in and the first time I came, I had my collar tucked out and so everyone started laughing at me. You can get picked on by the older people and they all have their threats like they are gonna chuck your head down the toilet.' By term two, Charlie evaluated his transition success, not on his work progress, but on whether he was safe in his wider peer group: 'It was my birthday in May and that's when I thought I'd really settled in, because I was like the youngest in my class and so everyone picked on me for being 11. But now I'm 12, everyone is kind of treating me a bit more older than I am.'

Interestingly, my observations of Charlie indicated that he had made a tight-knit group of friends by the end of the first term. However, his attitude towards school still reflected his bad experiences at primary school, despite his social life having turned a new page. By the end of the year, Charlie concluded that 'I don't like school; you get bullied too much.' We can see here that Charlie did not try to fit into his environment, nor change the environment to suit himself, and in many ways was ignorant of his social development. Possibly, Charlie held a fixed mindset about being a victim, which he could not shake even when circumstances changed. Over the course of the year, Charlie's attitude towards school became more negative, and he turned his interests towards leaving school to join the Army as soon as soon as he reached 16 years of age.

Conclusions

In summary, when children transition to secondary school they encounter many changes that can influence their psychological wellbeing. In order to stay mentally healthy, children often strive to create a fit between their psychology and the changes they experience. They can do this by changing the school environment or by transforming themselves. However, children can experience barriers to self-development, caused by their mindsets, their cognitive abilities and a lack of flexibility in their environment. All of this makes for a wide variety of fits and misfits that influence wellbeing. Although each fit is a personal matter, there are also some trends in fit that teachers can anticipate when we consider how early adolescent characteristics typically interact with the change to a transfer school. There are also qualities that teachers can strive to help develop in children – such as self-esteem and being able to self-enhance even in difficult circumstances – that might improve children's resilience to the challenges of school transition.

Note

1 The names of people and schools have been anonymised.

References

Barber, B., Carlson, E., Eccles, J., et al. (1987). When school doesn't fit: Why adolescents and junior high sometimes seem at odds. *Research News, 38*(3–4), 2–4.

Buss, D. (1987). Selection, evocation, and manipulation. *Journal of Personality and Social Psychology, 53*(6), 1214–1221.

Chen, W.-B., & Gregory, A. (2009). Parental involvement as a protective factor during the transition to high school. *Journal of Educational Research, 103*(1), 53–62.

Coleman, J. C. (1974). *Relationships in adolescence*. London and Boston: Routledge & Kegan Paul.

Côté, J. E., & Levine, C. G. (2002). *Identity formation, agency and culture: A social psychological perspective*. Mahwah, NJ: Lawrence Erlbaum.

Deakin Crick, R., Jelfs, H., Symonds, J., Ren, K., Patton, A., & Grushka, K. (2010). *Learning futures evaluation report*. Bristol: University of Bristol/Paul Hamlyn Foundation.

Deci, E. L., & Ryan, R. M. (1985). *Intrinsic motivation and self-determination in human behaviour*. New York: Plenum Press.

Department for Children Schools and Families (DfES) (2008). *Childhood wellbeing: Qualitative research study*. Research Report DCSF-RW031. London: Counterpoint Research. Available at: www.education.gov.uk/publications/standard/publicationDetail/Page1/DCSF-RW031

Dweck, C. (2006). *Mindset, the new psychology of success*. New York: Random House.

Eccles, J., & Midgley, C. (1989). Stage/environment fit: Developmentally appropriate classrooms for young adolescents. In R. E. Ames & C. Ames (eds), *Research on motivation and education: goals and cognitions* (Vol. 3). New York: Academic Press.

Eccles, J., & Midgley, C. (1990). Changes in academic motivation and self-perception during early adolescence. In R. Montemayor (ed.), *Early adolescence as a time of transition*. Beverly Hills: CA: Sage.

Ellis, B. J., & Boyce, W. T. (2008). Biological sensitivity to context. *Current Directions in Psychological Science, 17*, 183–187.

Erikson, E. (1968). *Identity, youth and crisis*. New York: Norton.

Feldlaufer, H., Midgley, C., & Eccles, J. S. (1988). Student, teacher, and observer perceptions of the classroom before and after the transition to junior high school. *Journal of Early Adolescence, 8*(2), 133–156.

Gray, J., Galton, M., McLaughlin, C., Clarke, B., & Symonds, J. (2011). *The supportive school: Wellbeing and the young adolescent*. Newcastle upon Tyne: Cambridge Scholars Publishing.

Harter, S. (1983). Developmental perspectives on the self-system. In P. H. Mussen (ed.), *Carmichael's manual of child psychology*. New York: Wiley.

Higgins, E. T. (1987). Self-discrepancy: A theory relating self and affect. *Psychological Review, 94*(3), 319–340.

Howe, A., & Richards, V. (eds) (2011). *Bridging the transition from primary to secondary school*. Abingdon and New York: Routledge.

Hunt, D. E. (1975). Person environment interaction: a challenge found wanting before it was tried. *Review of Educational Research, 45*(2), 209–230.

James, W. (1890/1950). *The principles of psychology.* New York: Dover.

Lewin, K. (1936). *Principles of topological psychology.* New York: McGraw-Hill.

Mac Iver, D., Klingel, D. M., & Reuman, D. A. (1986). Students' decision-making congruence in mathematics classrooms: A person-environment fit analysis. Paper presented at the American Educational Research Association, 14–20 April, San Francisco, CA.

Markus, H., & Nurius, P. (1986). Possible selves. *American Psychologist, 41*(9), 954–969.

Markus, H., & Wurf, E. (1987). The dynamic self-concept: A social psychological perspective. *Annual Review of Psychology, 38,* 299–337.

Marsh, H. W. (1987). The big-fish-little-pond effect on academic self-concept. *Journal of Educational Psychology, 79,* 280–295.

McGivern, R. F., Andersen, J., Byrd, D., Mutter, K. L., & Reilly, J. (2002). Cognitive efficiency on a match to sample task decreases at the onset of puberty in children. *Brain and Cognition, 50*(1), 73–89.

McLellan, R., Galton, M., Steward, S., & Page, C. (2012). *The impact of creative initiatives on wellbeing: A literature review.* Creativity, Culture and Education Series. Manchester: Arts Council England.

Midgley, C., & Feldlaufer, H. (1987). Students' and teachers' decision-making fit before and after the transition to junior high school. *Journal of Early Adolescence, 7*(2), 225–241.

Purkey, W. (1988). *An overview of self-concept theory for counselors.* Ann Arbor, MI: ERIC Clearinghouse on Counseling and Personnel Services.

Rosenberg, M., Schooler, C., & Schoenbach, C. (1989). Self-esteem and adolescent problems: modeling reciprocal effects. *Americal Sociological Review, 54*(6), 1004–1018.

Rutter, M. (1985). Resilience in the face of adversity. Protective factors and resistance to psychiatric disorder. *British Journal of Psychiatry, 147*(6), 598–611.

Ryan, R. M., & Deci, E. L. (2000). Self-determination theory and the facilitation of intrinsic motivation, social development, and well-being. *American Psychologist, 55*(1), 68–78.

Seligman, M. E. P. (2011). *Flourish, a visionary new understanding of happiness and well-being.* New York: Free Press.

Symonds, J. E., Long, M., & Hargreaves, J. (2011). *Changing Key: Adolescents' views on their musical development across the primary to secondary school transition.* London: Paul Hamlyn Foundation. Available at: www.phf.org.uk/page.asp?id=1591

UNICEF (2007). *Child poverty in perspective: An overview of child well-being in rich countries.* In R. W. Reiber (ed.), *The collected works of L. S. Vygotsky* (Vol. 5, pp. 29–82). New York: Plenum/Florence: United Nations Children's Fund.

Vygotsky, L. S. (1931/1998). Development of thinking and formation of concepts in the adolescent.

Wallington, S. A. (1973). Consequences of transgression: Self-punishment and depression. *Journal of Personality and Social Psychology, 28*(1), 1–7.

Weller, S., & Bruegel, I. (2006). *Locality, school and social capital.* Families and Social Capital series. Swindon: ESRC.

Part II

What happens to children

Chapter 3

Stress and anxiety

Chapter overview

Children often suffer from stress and anxiety at school transition. In this chapter, I explain how stress and anxiety occur in the body, and discuss the stressors that children encounter when changing schools. I identify which types of children are most at risk for these feelings, by discussing gender, puberty and biological sensitivity to stress. Then, I summarise how anxiety about changing schools and anxiety disorders typically develop in transition-aged children.

A major concern for teachers and parents is that children will become stressed and anxious about changing schools. Having a stress reaction to school transition is normative and may manifest as a positive emotion, for many children report feeling eager anticipation (Rudduck, 1996) as they look forward to new resources and social opportunities after transition. However, studies also find that children have negative symptoms of stress at transition. For example, in a Canadian national sample of children, those changing schools had more incidences of headaches, stomach-aches, backaches, irritability, dizziness and difficulty getting to sleep than those who remained at the same school at age 12 or 13 years (Lipps, 2005). Children experience many types of negative emotion in the lead-up to transition including fear (Cox, Kennedy, Bishop & Porteners, 2005; Shachar, Suss & Sharan, 2002), worry (Howard & Johnson, 2000), nervousness (Howard & Johnson, 2000) and sadness (Cox et al., 2005). When looking at a picture of a boy and girl standing at their new school gates, 88 per cent of girls and 71 per cent of boys from a group of 600 children predicted that those children felt negative emotion about changing schools (Hargreaves & Wall, 2002), indicating that children expect to feel worried and nervous about school transition.

Stress

So why do children have negative emotions about changing schools? The American National Institute of Mental Health defines stress as 'the brain's response to any demand' (NIMH, n.d., p.1). When humans and other animals encounter challenges in their environment, they react by releasing hormones that enable them to cope with these challenges. For example, the hormone cortisol mobilises our energy stores (Romeo, 2010) and creates our 'fight or flight' response to threat. The secretion of cortisol and other stress response hormones is controlled by a biological system in the brain known as the hypothalamic–pituitary–adrenal (HPA) axis. This system helps to generate emotional responses to stress, including fear and anxiety. People can also experience positive responses to stress, including the urge to overcome challenges, although these are more rarely researched than negative stress responses.

Stressors can be small, such as accidentally breaking an egg, or large, such as an earthquake or death in the family. They can occur in close proximity to a person, like being shouted at, or be more distal, as in the threat of global warming or the strain of an economic crisis. Stressors can be real, as those described above, or imagined – for example, when a child is scared by the possibility of being bullied after transition. Almost anything can count as a stressor, depending on how a person perceives and reacts to it.

This is a sad truth, but one of the most commonly cited sources of negative stress in children's lives is school (Harden, Rees, Shepherd, Brunton, Oliver & Oakley, 2001). Most notably, children can be stressed by their relationships with teachers and peers. Peers act as a source of stress when children are bullied, fall out with friends and feel pressured by social hierarchies and norms. Teachers can stress children by being overly strict, threatening, pushy, confusing and holding unrealistic expectations for that child. Children who are punished by teachers can experience further stress at home when these activities are communicated to parents. Work is another source of stress at school, especially when children feel they have too much work, cannot keep up, and push or are pushed too hard.

School transition can be stressful in two main ways. First, many children are concerned before they move, about what will happen when they change schools. As detailed in Chapter 4, children often worry about changes in their friendships, adapting to multiple teachers, harder work, getting lost and their personal ability to cope. Second, the new environment of transfer schools can magnify existing opportunities for school-related stress, by presenting challenge. For example, children encounter new bullies, have problems making friends, struggle to adapt to multiple teachers and take issue with a loss of emotional support from teachers, which I document in Chapter 6. Children are also faced with more difficult work and higher academic expectations in some schools. This can be stressful for less able children, who worry about not being able to cope. High achievers can also be stressed by their fear of failing to perform to their usual high standard. Among children who are highly stressed at transition, the most common stressors are feeling overwhelmed by work, not having enough time to play, being generally anxious about everything, feeling like a failure and being confused by the new school (Karagiannopoulou, 1999).

So, how might experiencing a stressful event, such as school transition, affect children's wellbeing? Hagell, Sandberg and MacDonald (2012) have put forward a set of potential pathways between stressors in adolescence and mental health. Here I shall word these in the context of school transition.

1. Worrying about school transition can incur a *physiological response*, such as lowered and elevated hormone levels, which can encourage, for example, depressed mood, anxiety or productive energy.
2. Children can manage their school transition stress using various *psychological processes*. These can be good or bad for mental health. Take, for example, a girl who worries about being disorganised in her new school. She may repeatedly fret about this (a process called 'rumination') with her friends, leaving everyone feeling frightened. Alternatively she may feel energised by her concerns to become more organised, which adds to her self-esteem as her efforts pay off after transition.
3. *Family processes* can connect school transition stress with mental health. For example, children with a history of abuse are less resilient to stressors, and may find it harder to cope with the demands of school transition. Families can increase children's resilience by instilling healthy psychological habits, and by supporting children's self-esteem and coping efforts, as discussed in Chapter 5.
4. Experiencing *multiple stressors*, i.e. both school transition and a stressful event such as puberty, early dating or divorce, can have a cumulative negative effect on children's mental health (Simmons, Burgeson, Carlton-Ford & Blyth, 1987). The underlying logic here is that too many stressors occurring at the same time deplete children's coping resources, and keep the stress-response system in a permanent state of arousal.

Which children are more vulnerable to stress at transition?

Puberty begins on average at age 11.5 years (Coleman & Coleman, 2002). After pubertal onset, children have higher baseline levels of stress hormones and blood pressure than younger children, and their stress responses are more pronounced (Stroud, Foster, Papandonatos, Handwerger, Granger, Kivlighan et al., 2009). To make things more complicated, although they have increased sensitivity to stress, adolescent children have less control over their stress reactions. When shown pictures of fearful faces, adolescents have greater activity in the emotional centre of their brain (the amygdala) but less activity in the brain region that regulates their response to that emotion (the prefrontal cortex) than adults (Hare, Tottenham, Galvan, Voss, Glover & Casey, 2008). This makes pubertal children susceptible to feeling stressed at transition and having difficulty coping emotionally with the changes.

There are also gender differences in children's physiological stress responses, with girls being more sensitive and reactive than boys. This is thought to link to the hormone cortisol, which is produced in greater amounts in girls than boys in response to stressors (Gunnar, Wewerka, Frenn, Long & Griggs, 2009). Higher cortisol levels for girls are found to associate with general and social anxiety in adolescence, whereas there is no association for boys (Schiefelbein & Susman, 2006). In other words, girls are predisposed to having more severe fight or flight responses to stressors – a process which is accompanied by anxiety. This phenomenon can manifest in psychological stress responses. Take, for example, a recent survey by the American Psychological Association on gender and stress (APA, n.d.). In this study, more women experienced 'a great deal of stress' (28 per cent of those surveyed) than men (20 per cent). Also, more women than men reported emotional and physical signs of stress, including having a headache, feeling tearful and experiencing digestive problems.

On top of gender and pubertal differences, certain children may be more stressed than others because of their experiences of stress at home. There is growing evidence that the stress–response system develops in tune with its surrounding even before birth. It has recently been discovered that the HPA axis of guinea pig and monkey foetuses are reprogrammed according to maternal stress during pregnancy, and that prenatal anxiety associates with cortisol levels in children 10 years later (Glover, O'Connor & O'Donnell, 2010). If a child experiences adversity early in their life course, their HPA axis is thought to be more sensitive to environmental stress (Boyce & Ellis, 2005), ensuring that children are biologically prepared to cope with living in a highly stressful environment. These children are nicknamed 'orchids', because, like the orchid, they have increased sensitivity to all types of conditions, including those of nurture and neglect. In comparison, 'dandelion children', experiencing low levels of early life stress, are more immune to changes in their environment. As a result, dandelion children are thicker skinned and thrive in all types of conditions. Consequentially, dandelion children may experience less stress at transition than orchid children, although orchid children may be better able to identify stressors and adapt to these as necessary.

Children's personal outlook on stressors also makes for individual differences in their stress responses. Psychologists Melanie Zimmer-Gembeck and Ellen Skinner (2008) point out, in their review of adolescent stress and coping, that children who view events as threats often engage in escapism, withdrawal and support seeking. However, those who perceive events as challenges tend to confront the event by learning more about it, and by problem solving. Similarly, children differ in their stress responses depending on whether they believe they can control stressful events. Events that are perceived to be controllable in some way can encourage a child's persistence, exertion and problem solving, while those that are beyond the child's control (for example, being taken to the doctor) may be met with more withdrawal, distraction and negative emotion.

Children's memories of stressful events also determine how they react to stressors at transition. Humans relate new scenarios to old ones, making predictions about how they will cope based on how they coped before. Sometimes these evaluations can be subconscious, drawing on a child's previous emotional reaction – for example, fear or anger. Other times, children can be very aware of how they link a current stressful event to a past one. When Matthew changed schools, he said that 'You're always nervous when you start a new school and I was pretty nervous.' There, Matthew expected to be anxious when changing schools, because he remembered his past anxiety. However, he went on to say, '… although I've had quite a bit of experience at it because I'd moved school three times before I came [here]'. In this statement, Matthew shows evidence of proactive coping by using his experience to offset his current transition anxiety. So, although it is important to know about children's previous transitions when we make plans to help them, we should also be aware that children may utilise these memories differently depending on their bent for optimism or pessimism.

Finally, another critical factor that determines whether children will become more stressed at transition is the amount of social and emotional support they receive from friends, families and teachers. The move to a new and larger peer group can be daunting without good friends to protect you against the threats of being bullied, socially isolated and gaining a bad reputation. Therefore, it is unsurprising that friendships are at the top of children's lists of what matters at transition (Gray, Galton, McLaughlin, Clarke & Symonds, 2011). Children also report more emotional problems when they encounter lower levels of support from teachers (e.g. Barber & Olsen, 2004) and parents (Duchesne, Ratelle, Poitras & Drouin, 2009) across the move. Basically, it is important to facilitate social support for all children, in order to protect their wellbeing at transition.

Anxiety

There are two types of anxiety that crop up in studies of school transition. The first is children's transition anxiety, which can be defined as their worries about changing schools. The second is children's tendency to have symptoms of an anxiety disorder, such as separation anxiety. In the following section, I review what happens to both types of anxiety when children change schools.

Transition anxiety

A common method of studying transition anxiety is to ask children to rate statements about their worries on a numeric scale of agreement/disagreement. For example, a child may respond that they somewhat agree (rated as 3 out of 5) with the statement 'I am scared of being bullied by older children' (Youngman & Lunzer, 1977). Then, researchers average the ratings to give a score for each child, which are used to calculate average ratings for groups of children. Within large groups of children, there are clusters who have increasing or decreasing transition anxiety across the move (Youngman & Lunzer, 1977). However, the broader pattern is that transition anxiety declines when children transfer from typical primary to secondary schools (e.g. Galton & Wilcocks, 1983).

Although there is much to be stressed about before and immediately after transition, children may feel less anxious once they settle into school. In a survey of nearly 600 children in six local authorities in England, researchers found that, by the end of the first term, 73 per cent were happy at their new school and only 3 per cent still felt worried or nervous (Evangelou, Taggart, Sylva, Melhuish, Sammons & Siraj-Blatchford, 2008). A smaller study of Scottish children found that 41 per cent felt well settled immediately after transition, and that this percentage increased to two-thirds of children by the end of the first month (Graham & Hill, 2003). Similar to the English study, only 2 per cent of children had persistent concerns in the first term. This bodes well for primary and elementary school teachers, who can use this evidence to reassure children that they should settle in quickly to their new schools.

A basic tenet is that children feel stressed and anxious when they perceive threat in their environment. Accordingly, the decline in children's transition anxiety may come when they are confident about the features of schooling they were initially afraid of. Returning to the case study of Matthew in Chapter 2, he was initially concerned about the academic quality of his new school, after being a high achiever at primary school. After transition, he reflected that 'once we'd had every single lesson possible, I was really pleased with it,' demonstrating how his early experiences offset his transition fears. Other children have also stopped worrying about getting lost, making friends and meeting new teachers in the first term (Cotterell, 1982; ILEA, 1986), which all makes for a quick surface adjustment to the more notable features of transition.

A final point about transition anxiety is that children are less anxious when the environmental differences between schools are small. We can see these effects operating across studies. For example, children attending ordinary state-run primary schools were more anxious if they transferred to a progressive 'open-plan' school than if they moved to a traditional comprehensive school (Simon & Ward, 1982). Also, children moving to larger schools were more anxious than those transferring between two similarly sized schools (Cotterell, 1992). In Galton and Wilcocks (1983), children who expected to change to a school with similar teaching styles and organisation became anxious when instead they encountered stricter teachers and more demanding work. This suggests that, by making the first years of a new school more similar to the feeder school model, educators can reduce children's transition anxiety, although this must be done carefully, to ensure that there is enough change and challenge to stimulate children. More on these types of 'blocking' interventions can be found in Chapter 11.

Anxiety disorders

Researchers have also observed that children's anxiety disorders develop as they move schools in early adolescence. The American Psychiatric Association identifies seven main types of anxiety disorders: generalised anxiety disorder, separation anxiety, social phobia, simple phobia, panic disorder, post-traumatic stress disorder and obsessive compulsive disorder (APA, 2004). In an interview for the US National Institute of Mental Health (2010), psychologist Joe Sherill noted that children have the most problems with generalised anxiety disorder, social phobia and separation anxiety. These disorders are very relevant to school transition. Generalised anxiety disorder is defined as excessive worry about a number of events or activities for more days than not, for a period of at least six months (APA, 2004). As discussed, children worry about many aspects of their new schools before and immediately after transition, and this may be exacerbated by being more anxious in the first place. Transition might also affect children with social phobia, who may fear transferring to a much larger peer group and meeting multiple teachers. Children with separation anxiety might also be particularly stressed at transition, by separation from their old classroom teacher and close friends, and by the lack of opportunities for their parents to be involved in school.

Studies find that, on average, children report the most symptoms of generalised anxiety disorder at around age 10 to 12 years, just before changing schools and across the school transition period (Hale, Raajmakers, Murius, van Hoof & Meeus, 2008; Van Oort, Greaves-Lord, Verhulst, Ormel & Huizink, 2009). These symptoms are then found to decline rapidly and level off, before increasing at around age 15 or 16 (Van Oort et al., 2009). Similarly, a study of three different groups of children identified that generalised anxiety increased for children transferring into the last year of elementary school, and decreased for children transferring into secondary school and for those already there (Lohaus, Elben, Ball & Klein-Hessling, 2004). Together, these studies indicate that transition-aged children are at increased risk for generalised anxiety disorder, but that their symptoms may decrease after changing schools.

The developmental pattern is similar for separation anxiety symptoms, where levels rapidly decrease as children change from childhood into early adolescence (Hale et al., 2008; Van Oort et al., 2009). The good news for parents and teachers is that children with the highest levels of separation anxiety at 10 to 12 years are most likely to have the steepest decreases in symptoms of the disorder as they grow older. This is especially true for early adolescent boys (Hale et al., 2008). These decreases in separation anxiety may be connected to children's desire to become more autonomous in adolescence, in order to prepare for transition to adulthood (Van Oort et al., 2009).

However, there is inconclusive data on children's social phobia. Symptoms of this disorder are found to be stable across the ages of 10 to 18 years (Hale et al., 2008), decrease across the ages of 10 to 18 years (Van Oort et al., 2009) and rise immediately after transition into high school at age 13 years (Benner & Graham, 2009). These differences may stem from how those researchers measured and analysed social phobia. However, they might also tie to the social environments that children were exposed to, as children transferring to a large urban, multi-cultural high school in the US had increased social phobia (Benner & Graham, 2009) while those in the Dutch school system had stable or declining social phobia(i.e. Hale et al., 2008; Van Oort et al., 2009). Despite these differences, the studies agreed that girls had greater symptoms of social phobia than boys, possibly because girls have a more sensitive HPA axis than boys as discussed.

Conclusions

There are many factors that predispose children to stress at transition. These include being pubertal, being female, experiencing childhood adversity, lacking social support, having had a bad prior transition and viewing change as a threat rather than a challenge. Also, children with existing anxiety disorders may be more vulnerable to the differences in school environment. Teachers can use these characteristics to think about which children in their care might be more anxious than others, and to plan for transition interventions to help them. The raft of transition anxiety surveys might also be a good starting point for measuring children's anxiety in your school system, diagnosing vulnerable children, anticipating more anxious cohorts and evaluating transition interventions. More information on these types of evaluations can be found in Chapter 12.

References

American Psychological Association (n.d.). Stress and gender. Retrieved 9 July 2012 from www.apa.org/news/press/releases/stress/gender-stress.pdf

American Psychiatric Association (2004). *Diagnostic and Statistical Manual of Mental Disorders* (4th ed.) Washington, DC: APA.

Barber, B. K., & Olsen, J. A. (2004). Assessing the transitions to middle and high school. *Journal of Adolescent Research, 19*(1), 3–30.

Benner, A. D., & Graham, S. (2009). The transition to high school as a developmental process among multiethnic urban youth. *Child Development, 80*(2), 356–376.

Boyce, W. T., & Ellis, B. J. (2005). Biological sensitivity to context: An evolutionary developmental theory of the origins and function of stress reactivity. *Development and Psychopathology, 17*, 271–301.

Coleman, L., & Coleman, J. (2002). The measurement of puberty: A review. *Journal of Adolescence, 25*, 535–550.

Cotterell, J. L. (1982). Student experiences following entry into secondary school. *Educational Research, 24*(4), 297–302.

Cotterell, J. L. (1992). School size as a factor in adolescents' adjustment to the transition to secondary school. *Journal of Early Adolescence, 12*(1), 28–45.

Cox, S., Kennedy, S., Bishop, F., & Porteners, S. (2005). *A study of students' transition from primary to secondary schooling: A work in progress.* Wellington, New Zealand: Ministry of Education.

Duchesne, S., Ratelle, C. F., Poitras, S. C., & Drouin, E. (2009). Early adolescent attachment to parents, emotional problems, and teacher-academic worries about the middle school transition. *Journal of Early Adolescence, 29*(5), 743–766.

Evangelou, M., Taggart, B., Sylva, K., Melhuish, E., Sammons, P., & Siraj-Blatchford, I. (2008). *What makes a successful transition from primary to secondary school?* London: DCSF.

Galton, M., & Wilcocks, J. (1983). *Moving from the Primary Classroom* (ed. University of Leicester). London: Routledge & Kegan Paul.

Glover, V., O'Connor, T. G., & O'Donnell, K. (2010). Prenatal stress and the programming of the HPA axis. *Neuroscience and Biobehavioral Reviews, 35*(1), 17–22.

Graham, C., & Hill, M. (2003). *Negotiating the transition to secondary school. Spotlight 89.* Edinburgh: The SCRE Centre.

Gray, J., Galton, M., McLaughlin, C., Clarke, B., & Symonds, J. (2011). *The supportive school: Wellbeing and the young adolescent.* Newcastle upon Tyne: Cambridge Scholars Publishing.

Gunnar, M. R., Wewerka, S., Frenn, K., Long, J. D., & Griggs, C. (2009). Developmental changes in hypothalamus–pituitary–adrenal activity over the transition to adolescence: Normative changes and associations with puberty. *Development and Psychopathology, 21*(1), 69–85.

Hagell, A., Sandberg, S., & MacDonald, R. (2012). Stress and mental health in adolescence: interrelationship and time trends. In A. Hagell (ed.), *Changing adolescence: Social trends and mental health* (pp. 27–46). Bristol: Policy Press.

Hale III, W. W., Raajmakers, Q., Murius, P., van Hoof, A., & Meeus, W. (2008). Developmental trajectories of adolescent anxiety disorder symptoms: A 5-year prospective community study. *Child and Adolescent Psychiatry, 47*(5), 557–565.

Harden, A., Rees, R., Shepherd, J., Brunton, G., Oliver, S., & Oakley, A. (2001). *Young people and mental health: A systematic review of research on barriers and facilitators.* London: EPPI-Centre, Social Science Research Unit, Institute of Education, University of London.

Hare, T. A., Tottenham, N., Galvan, A., Voss, H. U., Glover, G. H., & Casey, B. J. (2008). Biological substrates of emotional reactivity and regulation in adolescence during an emotional go-nogo task. *Biological Psychiatry, 63*(10), 927–934.

Hargreaves, L., & Wall, D. (2002). 'Getting used to each other' cross-phase liaison and induction. In L. Hargreaves & M. Galton (eds), *Transfer from the primary classroom: 20 years on* (pp. 28–53). London: RoutledgeFalmer.

Howard, S., & Johnson, B. (2000). *Programs for students in transition from primary to high school.* Sydney, NSW: NSW Department of Community Services/NSW Department of Education and Training.

ILEA (1986). *ILEA Transfer Project.* London: Inner London Education Authority.

Karagiannopoulou, E. (1999). Stress on transfer from primary to secondary school: The contributions of A-trait, life events and family functioning. *Psychology of Education Review, 23*(2), 27–32.

Lipps, G. (2005). *Making the transition: The impact of moving from elementary to secondary school on adolescents' academic achievement and psychological adjustment.* Family and Labour Studies Division, Analytical Studies (FaLSDAS) Branch, Statistics Canada. No. 28.

Lohaus, A., Elben, C. E., Ball, J., & Klein-Hessling, J. (2004). School transition from elementary to secondary school: Changes in psychological adjustment. *Educational Psychology 24*(2), 161–173.

National Institute of Mental Health (n.d.). Adult stress – Frequently asked questions. Retrieved 9 July 2012 from www.nimh.nih.gov/health/publications/stress/stress_factsheet

National Institute of Mental Health (2010). Joe Sherill on anxiety disorders in children. Retrieved 9 July 2012 from www.nimh.nih.gov/news/media/audio/joel-sherill-on-anxiety-disorders-in-children.shtml

Romeo, R. D. (2010). Adolescence: A central event in shaping stress reactivity. *Developmental Psychobiology, 52*(3), 244–253.

Rudduck, J. (1996). Going to 'the big school': The turbulence of transition. In J. Rudduck, R. Chaplain & G. Wallace (eds.), *School improvement: What can pupils tell us?* (ed. University of Leicester, Ch. 2, pp. 19–28). London: David Fulton.

Schiefelbein, V. L., & Susman, E. J. (2006). Cortisol levels and longitudinal cortisol change as predictors of anxiety in adolescents. *Journal of Early Adolescence, 26*, 397–413.

Shachar, H., Suss, G., & Sharan, S. (2002). Students' concerns about the transition from elementary to junior high school: A comparison of two cities. *Research Papers in Education, 17*(1), 79–95.

Simon, A., & Ward, L. O. (1982). Anxiety, self-concept, attitude to school and transition to the comprehensive school. *Counsellor, 3*(5), 33–39.

Simmons, R. G., Burgeson, R., Carlton-Ford, S., & Blyth, D. A. (1987). The impact of cumulative change in early adolescence. *Child Development, 58*(5), 1220–1234.

Stroud, L. R., Foster, E., Papandonatos, G. D., Handwerger, K., Granger, D. A., Kivlighan, K. T., et al. (2009). Stress response and the adolescent transition: Performance versus peer rejection stressors. *Development and Psychopathology, 21*(1), 47–68.

Van Oort, F. V. A., Greaves-Lord, K., Verhulst, F. C., Ormel, J., & Huizink, A. C. (2009). The developmental course of anxiety symptoms during adolescence: The TRAILS study. *Journal of Child Psychology and Psychiatry, 50*(10), 1209–1217.

Youngman, L., & Lunzer, E. (1977). *Adjustment to Secondary Schooling* (ed. University of Nottingham). Nottingham: School of Education, University of Nottingham.

Zimmer-Gembeck, M. J., & Skinner, E. A. (2008). Adolescents coping with stress: Development and diversity. *Prevention Researcher, 15*(1), 3–7.

Chapter 4

Hopes, fears and myths

Chapter overview

Across countries and eras, children have similar hopes and fears about transition. They also recount characteristic tales of violence, humiliation, dangerous teachers and work pressure occurring in their new schools. Many of these hopes, fears and myths relate to children's concerns and desires about growing up and the new social order. As such, they offer insight into adolescent worlds where meaning is constructed and acted on by children. These hopes, fears and myths form the largest body of research on how children fare before transition, and can be used by teachers to pre-empt their students' concerns and to begin conversations about how to destroy negative assumptions about transition that have circulated for generations.

Introduction

Children can be excellent data gatherers. When it comes to finding out about secondary school, they absorb information like a sponge, picking up much of it from official sources such as teachers, induction days and cross-tier activities like musical performances. Parents, siblings and peers also offer information about transition, both as advice and indirectly as role models. Children can infer a great deal about transition from the media, and from their neighbourhood communities, for example, by watching older children board a school bus. However, to date there has been no integrated investigation on how children receive, process and act on information about transition. Typically, studies ask children what they think about the most before transition, or focus on the stories children tell each other about the move.

School size

Most often, transfer schools are much larger and better resourced. Bigger is often scarier, and between 10 and 20 per cent of children across studies worry moving to a larger school (e.g. Brown & Armstrong, 1986; Robinson & Fielding, 2007).

School size creates many issues for children, including navigating bigger buildings and grounds and a more complex layout. That is why children often fear getting lost in their new school (e.g. Caulfield, Hill & Shelton, 2005; Lucey & Reay, 2000). This might be more of an issue for 10- to 12-year-olds who transfer, because they are smaller and less experienced. Children also worry about their ability to move around school (Hargreaves & Wall, 2002) and adapt to new buildings (Rudduck, Chaplain & Wallace, 1996).

However, children also have positive views about the change in built environment. Larger and better-equipped areas for playing sport are often at the top of children's list of hopes (Symonds, 2009), given that pre-transition schools have limited capacity for these resources. Children also look forward to moving around rooms (Rudduck et al., 1996), rather than sitting in a single classroom for most of the day. In Symonds (2009), Stacey recounted her relief at being able to move regularly: 'I felt more pressure at primary school … mostly because after a lesson I just need to do something. I can't just sit in a chair and just stay there. I have to get up and just move around. Here after the lesson you can get up, walk to your next lesson. It's like free space.'

School timetables

Commonly, children move from a 5 x 5 schedule (five days of five 60-minute lessons) to a 5 x 8 schedule (five days of eight 40-minute lessons) after transition (Symonds & Hagell, 2011). The challenge of understanding new timetables in both practical and written form can frighten some children (Hallinan & Hallinan, 1992; Spelman, 1979) and add to their transition stress. In Symonds (2009), Sam explained that 'in Year 6 I was more stressful because I didn't know what [the new school] was going to be like and in the summer holidays it was even worse because when I got my timetable it was like what are these lessons because they were only in three letters.' These problems with adapting to new timetables are inspiring some feeder schools to let children practise being on a transfer school schedule, and to use transfer planners/diaries before transition (see Chapter 11 for more details).

Learning

Traditionally, secondary schools provide children with a more intensive learning experience. Multiple subject specialists take the place of the familiar classroom teacher, and teach content from the Key Stage 3 curriculum rather than Key Stage 2. Children observe an increase in the complexity of lesson content, especially for enrichment subjects that may have been a minor skill for their Year 6 classroom teachers in comparison to core subjects such as English and mathematics. In Symonds, Long and Hargreaves (2011), Amy outlined her hopes for secondary school music. She thought it would 'be a lot better because they have more things and they'll go higher, not just teach us little tunes on an instrument' (p. 19).

Children base their predictions that they will learn more at secondary school on a range of information. In the above quote, Amy expected to learn more because she expected higher standards from her teachers. In Symonds (2009), Billy assumed that transfer schoolwork would be more complex simply because he would have more teachers than at primary school: 'Why did you think you could learn more?' (Jenny); 'Because there was loads of teachers. There were thirty or more teachers' (Billy). Billy also assumed that he would learn more in PE because the provision for PE was enhanced: '[The] facilities around there are brilliant and you're at PE three times a week and you can do all the normal PE' (Billy). Children also desire to be more challenged by learning (Suffolk County Council, 2001; Zeedyk et al., 2003), learn specific subjects in depth (Robinson & Fielding, 2007), experience new subjects (Brown & Armstrong, 1986; Graham & Hill, 2003), achieve more, gain confidence, and prepare for an adult career (Symonds et al., 2011) after transition.

Like Billy, many children enjoy practical subjects more than sedentary ones such as English and mathematics (Symonds, 2009; Symonds & Hargreaves, 2014). Accordingly, studies document that around two-thirds of children hope for more practical learning in the transfer school. Children's hopes in this area include better sports and drama facilities (Brown & Armstrong, 1986; Cox et al., 2005; Galton, Comber & Pell, 2002; Rudduck et al., 1996; Scottish Executive, 2007), more practical subjects (Graham & Hill, 2003; Scottish Executive, 2007) and more extracurricular activities (Chedzoy & Burden, 2005; Zeedyk et al., 2003).

Children's hopes for learning are often balanced by their fears. Many children worry about encountering more difficult work (e.g. Brown & Armstrong 1986; Zeedyk et al., 2003), increased academic pressure (e.g. Berndt & Mekos, 1995; Shachar, Suss & Sharan, 2002) and adjusting to new subjects (Delamont & Galton, 1986; Evangelou, Taggard, Sylva, et al., 2008). The large number of work related worries may stem from children's desire to protect their self-esteem, as explained by Martin Covington's self-worth theory (1985). In a nutshell, children who base their self-esteem on their achievements may worry about losing self-esteem if they are unable to cope with work demands. Children also fear having more homework after transition (Brown & Armstrong, 1986; Galton et al., 2002), perhaps because they want to protect their free time with friends after school, which becomes increasingly important to them at this age (Symonds, 2009).

Teachers

Few children mention teachers in their lists of hopes and fears. Those who do look forward to meeting new ones (e.g. Galton et al.; 2002, Zeedyk et al., 2003) and to having a larger variety of teachers (Rudduck et al., 1996). However, children also fear that their new teachers will be stricter (e.g. Caulfield et al., 2005; Hargreaves & Wall, 2002) and that they will be confused by multiple teaching styles (Robinson & Fielding, 2007). Some children don't want to have more than one teacher (Pratt & George, 2005) and are worried that they will miss their classroom teacher from primary school (City of Birmingham Education Department, 1975).

Here, children's worries about teachers fall into one of two camps. First, children are concerned about how teachers will affect their psychological well-being. These concerns are well placed, given the significant body of research that associates increased teacher strictness with a loss of engagement, and decreased teacher emotional support with declines in mental health, as I explore in Chapter 6. Second, children's concerns about teachers appear to bleed into their worries about work. Will they be able to perform if they are confused by multiple teaching styles? This concern may also tie to children's insecurities about adaptability and coping, which are detailed in the section below on personal maturity.

Peers

The most prevalent hope across studies is children's wish to make new friends after transition (e.g. Hargreaves & Wall, 2002; Lucey & Reay, 2000; Scottish Executive, 2007; Weller, 2007). A key reason why children want friends at transition is for protection and support. Boys can have problems within the new macho male social order that quickly develops, while girls worry about being physically unattractive and unpopular amongst their new peers (Symonds, Galton & Hargreaves, 2014). Having more friends makes children feel less vulnerable in the large and unfamiliar peer group where these pressures brew. Accordingly, children often worry about not having enough friends (Brown & Armstrong, 1986; Hargreaves & Wall, 2002) and fear entering a larger peer group (Pratt & George, 2005), where they don't know anyone (Shachar et al., 2002). Also, they hope to move with friends from their pre-transition school (Pratt & George, 2005) and worry about losing old friends after transition (e.g. Bryan, 1980; Delamont & Galton, 1986; Pratt & George, 2005). This poses a risk for children who transfer alone, who are more anxious and less excited about the move than those transferring with friends from primary school (Weller, 2007).

Having new friends also enhances the development of children's identities. In pre-transition schools, there is often only one class of children per year group. This means that children have a small supply of friendship candidates, which is further restricted by their tendency to befriend their own gender. When they transition, the larger peer group provides children with a bigger pool of potential friends with similar interests and temperament to themselves. This is an important issue during early adolescence, as friendships are an arena in which children test out and develop their personal identities, sexual strategies and interests. Accordingly, many children hope for an increased supply of well-matched friends post-transition (Galton et al., 2002; Lucey & Reay, 2000; Weller, 2007). They also look forward to parting from unhappy friendships

(Lucey & Reay, 2000; Weller, 2007) and to changing the structure of their friendship groups, if those structures are causing them emotional and social problems (Pratt & George, 2005).

In a similar pattern to friendships, transition provides children with a chance to avoid old enemies (Lucey & Reay, 2000) but also to make new ones. Studies document that children worry about being bullied by same aged peers and by older children (e.g. Hallinan & Hallinan, 1992; Suffolk County Council, 2001), with around 30 per cent of children across studies worrying about being bullied (e.g. Chedzoy & Burden, 2005; Hargreaves & Wall, 2002; Zeedyk et al., 2003). Luckily, studies show that these fears quickly abate, as a much smaller percentage of children are actually bullied in transfer schools (Gray, Galton, McLaughlin, Clarke & Symonds, 2011).

Personal maturity

Being trampled on by older children (Symonds, 2009), feeling small (Brown & Armstrong 1986) and insecure as the youngest year group (e.g. Pratt & George, 2005) are common worries for a minority of children. These fears are not without reason, as Matthew observed in Symonds (2009): 'He [my friend] was walking along the corridor and some girl came up to him and said, "Oh, hi you're so cute, you're so sweet and little and everything." And he got a bit annoyed about that.' Children also worry that their lack of personal maturity will prevent them from being organised in their new schools (Hallinan & Hallinan, 1992; Rudduck, 1996), especially when they will be in charge of their own equipment for the first time.

Children's worries about whether they are ready for secondary school manifest as a general concern, with 16 per cent of around 500 children in inner London schools feeling unprepared for the transition (Evangelou et al., 2008). In Symonds (2009), Samantha recalled sharing this fear with her grandmother: 'My nan was telling me, "Oh Sam, you should now be old enough to know that you're going to secondary school for a reason," cause one night I was really upset about it. So then she told me, "If you want to fly, go with the flow, if you want to sink, stay as you are," and so now I'm trying to learn how to fly. It sounds really silly, but to me it's a thing, a question that keeps me going.' On the flip side of the coin, between 8 and 23 per cent of children have reported looking forward to being more mature after transfer across studies (e.g. Bryan, 1980; Cox et al., 2005; Rudduck et al., 1996) and to gaining more independence in their new schools (Berndt & Mekos, 1995).

Transition myths

Children's fears about transition can be caused by hearing frightening stories about what happens after changing schools. Some of these stories have been in circulation for decades and crop up across countries, and you might even remember some from your childhood. These stories, referred to by researchers as rumours, urban legends and transition myths, are communicated by friends, siblings, older peers (Delamont, 1991) and possibly even by adults, to transferring children. Sara Delamont at Cardiff University is an expert in this area, having first worked on transition myths in the 1976–8 ORACLE study led by Maurice Galton. Across her studies, Delamont (1989, 1991) has grouped the myths reported by children and retrospectively by adults into wider themes/ stories. The four most recurrent of these are:

1.   the lavatory story
2.   the violent gang theme
3.   the fierce/weird/sexually harassing teacher theme
4.   the humiliating experience theme.

Other studies that document transition myths are Measor and Woods (1984) and Symonds (2009). In these studies, children refer to myths about work that is emotionally and/or physically tougher at secondary school. Therefore here I add a fifth category of 'harder work/activity' to the myths. Together these five themes encompass over 95 per cent of all myths reported in Delamont (1991) and summarise all the myths reported in Measor and Woods (1984) and Symonds (2009).

The lavatory story

The lavatory story is the most recurrent school transition myth. It has been around for decades in the UK and has been repeated as far as the US and Australia (Delamont & Galton, 1986). Sometimes referred to as 'the royal flush', this myth warns new students that older students may attack them in school bathrooms by holding their heads down the toilet and pulling the flush. In his final year of middle school in 1979, Darrell told researchers that 'There's rumours … that they flush yer 'ead down the toilet on yer birthday' (Measor & Woods, 1984, p. 20). Similarly, in 2007, Charlie recounted in his first year of secondary school that 'You can get picked on by the older people and they all have their threats like they are gonna chuck your head down the toilet' (Symonds, 2009, p. 145). This myth is an amazing example of how one scary story can act like a virus, infecting thousands of school children across time.

The violent gang theme

In Measor and Woods (1984), Philip retold the story of the 'punch gloves': 'I've heard that there's these boys, and if you have a fight, they wear punch gloves with spikes, and they hit you and leave punch holes in your face' (p. 21). Gang-related myths are also captured by Delamont and Galton (1986) in children's worries about their first day at secondary school. Dawn had heard that on the first day 'You got kicked in' (p. 21) and Bart was worried because 'they said you got beat up a lot' (p. 21). Although the punch gloves might never have existed, studies do document gangs of schoolboy thugs in Year 7 and above. In Symonds (2009) and Benyon (1985), aggressive boys from different feeder schools quickly clustered together to form a group of Year 7 bullies. In Measor and Woods (1984), there were several reports of violent acts by older children towards Year 7 children, including a Year 11 boy signing his name on the foreheads of two Year 7 boys in the toilets. These observations indicate that the violent gang myth may have strong bearing on reality in some schools.

The fierce/weird/sexually harassing teacher theme

It is not only older children who terrify; new teachers are also scary. Teachers in transfer schools often have less opportunity to form close relationships with students, which may augment children's fears that their new teachers will be impersonal, unsavoury, strict and demanding. For example, in Delamont and Galton (1986), Year 7 students were told by Year 9 and 11 children that teachers would force them to clean out the school toilets if they flooded. Children have also been warned about 'scary' homosexual teachers, such as the 'lesbian nymphomaniac' hockey teacher in Delamont (1991, p. 242), and 'queer' Mr Reeder in Measor and Woods (1984, p. 23). These stories about homosexual teachers confuse being gay with being sexually rampant or threatening, thus illustrating this age group's lack of knowledge on homosexuality. It is likely that these stories attract so much attention because early adolescent children are becoming fascinated with sexuality, yet it is still a strange and unfamiliar world to them.

The humiliating experience theme

The fourth group of myths involves being humiliated at the new school. The girls' underwear story (Delamont, 1989) has been around for years in the UK and was even circulated at my all-girls school in New Zealand. This story warns of being forced to walk over mirrors, or having one's knickers inspected, to ensure that they are the correct colour. A similar story cautions children they will be forced to be naked in showers after PE: 'Before I went to Radhurst School for Girls I was told by a girl already attending the school that one of the PE teachers made you have a shower after PE, and those people who forgot their towel were given one paper towel to dry themselves with and if they were not dry they had to run naked round the gym to dry off' (Delamont, 1991, p. 245). These humiliating experiences are most often conveyed by girls and warn about being the object of sexual attention (Delamont, 1996).

The harder work/activity theme

The final theme includes myths about tougher work and activities at transfer schools. In Measor and Woods (1984), Bruce was concerned about having to run to a neighbouring village: 'Some kids told me, in PE you run to Brookfield and back – it's nearly five miles!' (p. 21). Similarly in ORACLE, children worried about the prospect of running around the playing fields and local park before lessons (Delamont, 1989). A well repeated myth in this category involves laboratory rats (Delamont, 1989; Measor & Woods, 1984). In Measor and Woods (1984), girls recounted the myth in disgust, 'One thing I don't want to do is cut up a rat. I don't think that's nice 'cos sometimes they do it alive so that you can see the heartbeat' (p. 25), while boys relished the prospect: 'Most of all, I'm looking forward to cutting up rats, or pigs' hearts' (p. 24). For both genders, dissecting a live animal requires greater emotional control than they might previously have been expected to exert in class. Similarly, the 8 km (5 mile) run necessitated children to have greater physical strength. Expecting their transfer school to be more physically and emotionally demanding fits with the change in maturity status that children anticipate when changing schools.

What purpose do the myths serve?

Anthropologists offer various explanations for why myths and urban legends exist. In his essay 'Myth in primitive psychology', Bronislaw Malinowski (1884–1942) explains that 'Myth fulfills in primitive culture an indispensable function: it expresses, enhances, and codifies belief; it safeguards and enforces morality; it vouches for the efficiency of ritual and contains practical rules for the guidance of man' (Malinowski, 1926/1948, p. 79). Following this logic, Measor and Woods concluded that school transition myths act primarily 'as a cultural blueprint, a social charter, for future behaviour, which contains both hints on norms and rules to observe, and clues to what kind of identity will be most appropriate in the new circumstances' (1984, p. 19).

Taking this perspective, we can assume that each transition myth conveys an underlying message about the school culture that children will be inducted into. Like myths circulated by tribal societies, transition myths use symbols to convey their messages. Delamont (1989) points out how these symbols are often binary discriminations between newcomer/old hand, weak/strong, clean/dirty, safety/danger and aggressor/victim. For example, all the myths in the five categories mentioned above warn children about danger versus safety, and about victim/aggressor states. We can interpret these messages by referring to the key components of the myths as symbols. The toilet in the lavatory myth symbolises dirt and repulsion, which becomes transferred to the child whose head is inside it. We might infer that this is how the older child sees the younger child: as dirt. By forcing the younger child to submit to this lowly status, the older child conveys that they are the stronger actor in a social system where physical violence is a dominant trait.

Another interesting feature of the myths is the gender differences in who is doing the telling. The lavatory and violent gang myths are most often told by boys (Delamont, 1991; Measor & Woods, 1984), whereas humiliating experience myths are more often told by girls (Delamont, 1996). Stories about harder work/activities and teachers tend to be told by both genders. There may be developmental reasons for this. As discussed in Chapter 7, adolescent boys construct and are subject to a male macho culture where aggressive gangs and older children are powerful actors. This would explain their fascination with myths that deal with violence and toughness. In comparison, early adolescent girls can become overly concerned with physical appearances and attractiveness at transition (Symonds et al., 2014) and accordingly may be afraid of exposing their newly pubertal bodies.

How are the myths perpetuated?

It is apparent that some myths have been around for decades. So how does this long-term circulation work? Andrew Noymer at the University of California, Irvine, has used mathematical models and the analogy of disease to explain how urban legends persist over time (Noymer, 2001). An exciting aspect of Noymer's models is that they need an age-graded component to work. This makes them perfectly suited for explaining why school transition myths have lasted for generations. First, Noymer explains that a myth has an initial outbreak, like a disease. Second, the myth begins to die out because some people are sceptical of it or are immune to the myth. However, the myth is retained within a small per cent of the population where a cycle of transmission exists between listeners and storytellers. The listeners have to be at a critical age, where they lack the experience to differentiate the myth from reality. Storytellers are those who have 'aged out' of the listening phase, but who have an agenda in retelling the myths. As Measor and Woods (1984) put it, the retelling of myths is a 'celebration of their [children's] successful negotiation of the transfer. They have survived, literally, "to tell the tale"' (Measor & Woods, 1984, p. 26). Therefore, school transition is a perfect candidate for keeping myths alive, as the graduation from listener to storyteller becomes a rite of passage when changing schools.

Conclusions

Children's expectations about school transition clearly reflect their developmental state. In early adolescence, many children report that friends and peers become central to their lives, and accordingly friendships rank highest in children's worries and hopes about school transition. Another milestone in early adolescence is experiencing rapid physical and mental change. Worries and hopes about tougher, more complex school experiences signal that children associate school transition with growing older but also with a risk of personal failure due to their perceived immaturity. The hopes and fears reported across studies internationally, spanning the 1960s to present day point to a well-defined set of key concerns that educators can target when talking to children about the move.

In comparison, transition myths illustrate how children construct the world of early adolescence in the school context (Pugsley, Coffey & Delamont, 1996). The topics of interest are invented by children, for children, and as such convey a wealth of information about school subcultures and which aspects of schooling children find important. Delamont (1991) calls the messages in transfer myths 'both enduring and depressingly conformist' (p. 257), as these recount a world where 'men are men, women are women, all the standards are double, and all the behavioural norms caricatured extremes' (pp. 256–257). More about why gender stereotypes prevail after school transition can be found in Chapter 7 and in Symonds et al. (2014).

These expectations and myths can serve the purpose of preparing children for their new schools, when children react by programming themselves to cope in the new environment. This preparation can manifest in positive adjustment – for example, when children strive harder to be organised or practise social skills necessary for making friends. However, children's reactions can also spiral into anxiety and stress, should they become convinced that transfer schools are dangerous. As explored in Chapter 3, some children may succumb more to anxiety than others. From my experience of talking with groups of children about transition, it is very soothing for some to get their fears out in the open, and to find out that other people feel the same way. What is more, many of us can tell children that their heads will stay dry on their birthdays, because really this is just a myth.

References

Benyon, J. (1985). *Initial encounters in the secondary school: Sussing, typing and coding.* Lewes: Falmer Press.

Berndt, T. J., & Mekos, D. (1995). Adolescents' perceptions of the stressful and desirable aspects of the transition to junior high school. *Journal of Research on Adolescence, 10,* 141–158.

Brown, J., & Armstrong, M. (1986). Transfer from primary to secondary: The child's perspective. In M. Youngman (ed.), *Mid-schooling transfer: Problems and proposals* (pp. 29–46). Windsor: NFER-Nelson.

Bryan, K. A. (1980). Pupil perceptions of transfer between middle and high schools. In A. Hargreaves & L. Tickle (eds), *Middle schools, origins, ideology, and practice* (pp. 229–246). London: Harper and Row.

Caulfield, C., Hill, M., & Shelton, A. (2005). *The transition to secondary school: the experiences of black and minority ethnic young people.* Glasgow: Glasgow Anti Racist Alliance.

Chedzoy, S. M., & Burden, R. L. (2005). Making the move: Assessing student attitudes to primary–secondary transfer. *Research in Education, 74*, 22–35.

City of Birmingham Education Department. (1975). *Continuity in education: Junior to secondary.* Birmingham: Birmingham Education Development Centre.

Covington, M. V. (1985). The self-worth theory of achievement motivation: Findings and implications. *Elementary School Journal, 85*(1), 5–20.

Cox, S., Kennedy, S., Bishop, F., & Porteners, S. (2005). *A study of students' transition from primary to secondary schooling: a work in progress.* Wellington, New Zealand: Ministry of Education.

Delamont, S. (1989). The nun in the toilet: Urban legends and educational research. *Qualitative Studies in Education, 2*(3), 191–202.

Delamont, S. (1991). The HIT LIST and other horror stories: Sex roles and school transfer. *Sociological Review, 39*(2), 238–259.

Delamont, S. (1996). Daps, dykes and five mile hikes: Physical education in pupils' folklore. *Sport, Education and Society, 1*(2), 133–146.

Delamont, S., & Galton, M. (1986). *Inside the secondary classroom.* London: Routledge & Kegan Paul.

Evangelou, M., Taggart, B., Sylva, K., Melhuish, E., Sammons, P., & Siraj-Blatchford, I. (2008). *What makes a successful transition from primary to secondary school?* London: Department of Education.

Galton, M., Comber, C., & Pell, T. (2002). The consequences of transfer for pupils: Attitudes and attainment. In L. Hargreaves & M. Galton (eds), *Transfer from the primary classroom, 20 years on* (pp. 131–158). London and New York: RoutledgeFalmer.

Graham, C., & Hill, M. (2003). *Negotiating the transition to secondary school. Spotlight 89.* Edinburgh: The SCRE Centre.

Gray, J., Galton, M., McLaughlin, C., Clarke, B., & Symonds, J. (2011). *The supportive school: Wellbeing and the young adolescent.* Newcastle upon Tyne: Cambridge Scholars Publishing.

Hallinan, P., & Hallinan, P. (1992). Seven into eight will go: Transition from primary to secondary school. *Australian Educational and Developmental Psychologist, 9*(2), 30–38.

Hargreaves, L., & Wall, D. (2002). 'Getting used to each other' cross-phase liaison and induction. In L. Hargreaves & M. Galton (eds), *Transfer from the primary classroom: 20 years on* (pp. 28–53). London: RoutledgeFalmer.

Lucey, H., & Reay, D. (2000). Identities in transition: Anxiety and excitement in the move to secondary school. *Oxford Review of Education, 26*(2), 191–205.

Malinowski, B. (1948). Myth in primitive psychology. In B. Malinowski and R. Redfield (eds.), *Magic, science and religion and other essays* (pp. 72–119). London: Free Press.

Measor, L., & Woods, P. (1984). *Changing schools.* Milton Keynes: Open University Press.

Noymer, A. (2001). The transmission and persistence of 'urban legends': Sociological application of age-structured epidemic models. *Journal of Mathematical Sociology, 25*(3), 299–323.

Pratt, S., & George, R. (2005). Transferring friendship: Girls' and boys' friendships in the transition from primary to secondary school. *Children and Society, 19*(1), 16–26.

Pugsley, L., Coffey, A., & Delamont, S. (1996). I don't eat peas anyway! Classroom stories and the social construction of childhood. In I. Butler & I. Shaw (eds), *A case of neglect? Children's experiences and the sociology of childhood.* Aldershot: Avebury.

Robinson, C., & Fielding, M. (2007). *Children and their primary schools: Pupils' voices* (Primary Review Research Briefing 5/3). Cambridge: University of Cambridge/ Esmee Fairbairn Foundation.

Rudduck, J., Chaplain, R., & Wallace, G. (eds) (1996). *School improvement: What can pupils tell us?* London: David Fulton.

Scottish Executive (2007). *Transitions evaluation. Insight 36.* Edinburgh: Scottish Executive Education Department.

Shachar, H., Suss, G., & Sharan, S. (2002). Students' concerns about the transition from elementary to junior high school: A comparison of two cities. *Research Papers in Education, 17*(1), 79–95.

Spelman, B. J. (1979). *Pupil adaptation to secondary school.* Belfast: Northern Ireland Council for Educational Research.

Suffolk County Council. (2001). Transfer review. Retrieved 26 April 2012 from www.school-portal.co.uk/GroupHomepage.asp?GroupID=783552

Symonds, J. (2009). Constructing stage-environment fit: Early adolescents' psychological development and their attitudes to school in English middle and secondary school environments. Doctoral thesis, Faculty of Education, University of Cambridge. Available at: www.dspace.cam.ac.uk/handle/1810/223866

Symonds, J. E., Galton, M., & Hargreaves, L. (2014). Emerging gender differences in times of multiple transitions. In I. Schoon & J. Eccles (eds), *Gender differences in aspirations and attainment* (pp. 101–122) . London: Cambridge University Press.

Symonds, J., & Hagell, A. (2011). Adolescents and the organisation of their school time: Changes over recent decades in England. *Educational Review, 63*(3), 291–312.

Symonds, J., & Hargreaves, L. (2014). Emotional and motivational engagement at school transition: A qualitative stage-environment fit study. *The Journal of Early Adolescence, OnLineFirst* (Nov 3, 2014).

Symonds, J., Long, M., & Hargreaves, J. (2011). *Changing Key: Adolescents' views on their musical development across the primary to secondary school transition.* London: Paul Hamlyn Foundation. Available at: www.phf.org.uk/page.asp?id=1591

Weller, S. (2007). Sticking with your mates?' Children's friendship trajectories during the transition from primary to secondary school. *Children and Society, 21*, 339–351.

Zeedyk, M. S., Gallagher, J., Henderson, M., Hope, G., Husband, B., & Lindsay, K. (2003). Negotiating the transition from primary to secondary school: perceptions of pupils, parents and teachers. *School Psychology International, 24*, 67–79.

Chapter 5

Parents

Chapter overview

Parents can help children at transition by intervening when problems arise, and by nurturing the skills children need to cope with the challenges. This chapter sets out the many ways that parents do this, using a framework developed from resiliency theory (Rutter, 1985, 1987). It illustrates how a mixed bag of parental support influenced Samantha's adjustment in a case study. Then, the chapter concludes with a discussion on home–school partnerships and their benefits for parents, children and schools.

Introduction

Children's wellbeing is improved when their parents offer them emotional and social support (Malecki & Demaray, 2003). At transition, the effects of this support come via two main pathways: children's history of everyday interactions with parents at home, and through the direct involvement of parents in the challenges that children face at transition. Children's relationships with parents are not necessarily interrupted at school transition, unlike those with peers and teachers. Because of this, parents are an important source of continuity for children's self-esteem and identity at transition (Gniewosz, Eccles & Noack, 2011), which helps children make sense of the changes they experience.

Using an idea from US psychologist Glen Elder (1998), I perceive parent–child relationships as a long-term process of 'linked lives', where activity in the short term influences what happens later on, for both people. For example, if a child is worried about walking to their new school, sound parental advice might improve their ability to avoid the dangers of traffic, and prevent a future accident. In turn, by accepting their parent's advice, the child may alleviate the parent's immediate fears, which later encourages the parent to give them more responsibility. Elder also reminds us that people's interactions are influenced by their personal histories, psychological characteristics and the environment surrounding them. Put simply, any conversation between parents and children is the tip of an experiential iceberg. These notions are important for helping us understand how support and its time-lagged outcomes are dependent on the history of the parent–child relationship. This chapter begins by examining this background context, and its influence on children's adaptation at transition.

Everyday parental support and adjustment at transition

From psychiatry comes the concept of protective and risk factors (Rutter, 1985, 1987). These are the aspects of people's lives that help or hinder their resiliency to mental illness. The theory was first adapted to school transition by educational researchers Jindal-Snape and Miller (2008). These authors described how children are protected at transition when their everyday experiences with their parents encourage resilience, and when their parents are emotionally supportive and have harmonious relationships with their children and partners. Conversely, children are more at risk for maladjustment at transition if their parents have issues with anger, mental illness, criminality and substance abuse, if there are family disruptions and if parents do not give children stable guidance. These factors ticking away in the background of children's lives have a substantial influence on children's development, predisposing them to cope well or poorly when they change schools.

As discussed in Chapter 2, self-esteem is a person's 'core confidence' that they use to stand up to the world. In this respect, it is the foundation of resiliency (Rutter, 1987). Children's self-esteem develops early on in interaction with their parents, who help to improve it when they assure children they are worthy of love and respect. An example of how this links to adaptation at transition comes from a US study where children who were allowed to partake in family decision making had higher self-esteem than others, after changing schools (Lord, Eccles & McCarthy, 1994). Also, by providing a family background that is consistently loving, parents can increase the stability of children's self-esteem, which helps children remain confident in the face of multiple transition challenges.

Children are more at risk of maladaptation at transition if they are in poor mental health. They may inherit specific alleles from their parents, which makes them more susceptible to depression and anxiety disorders. Furthermore, children are more at risk of developing mental illness if there is increased risk in their home environment, due to their parents being mentally unwell (e.g. Collishaw, Maughan, Goodman & Pickles, 2004). Children also learn how to cope with stressors by observing their parents' behaviour, and when their parents engage in negative forms of coping – for example, dismissal, avoidance and aggression – this can put children at risk for using these coping styles too. Finally, if parents are feeling low and are unwilling to offer emotional support to their children, their children are in turn more likely to be depressed after school transition (Newman, Newman, Griffen, O'Connor & Spas, 2007).

Children's social adjustment at transition is also influenced by their family background. A Glaswegian study examined this in the context of ethnic minority children. By interviewing parents and children, Caulfield, Hill and Shelton (2005) found that ethnic minorities were disadvantaged from making friends at their new schools because their parents' social circles did not include ethnic majority parents or children. Also, due to cultural differences in their upbringing, ethnic minority children were less likely to see their friends every day after school, and accordingly their school friends knew little about their home lives. In London, children of professional fathers were more likely to move to a school outside of their catchment area and therefore transfer alone (Weller, 2007), which is another way that family background can indirectly influence children's social adjustment.

Finally, children's academic adjustment after transition is tied to what happens at home. A powerful force is the overall 'match' between home and school cultures (Chen & Gregory, 2009; Frey, Ruchkin, Martin, Schwab & Mary, 2009). For example, parents' occupations, educational level and time spent reading books predicted children's achievement at transition (de Graaf, 1988), possibly through various means, including the intergenerational transmission of educational aspirations (Chen & Gregory, 2009; Turner, 2007) and by shaping their children's interests in intellectual and cultural activities. Children have received more help from their parents in developing their intellectual competency if their parents were more academic (Baker & Stevenson, 1986), and have had higher grades after transition if their parents encouraged them to master tasks independently (Gutman, 2006), so indicating that parental pedagogical style also matters.

Targeted support and children's adjustment at transition

Parents can also influence children's adjustment by offering direct, targeted support to help children overcome transition challenges. They tend to do this in four ways, outlined in Rutter's (1987) model of alleviating risk, which was first applied to school transition research by Jindal-Snape and Miller (2008), with particular risk factors in mind such as adjusting to new peers and teachers and harder work. Below I use this model to explain how parents help children at transition by removing risks, diminishing risks, directly scaffolding children's resiliency (which helps children overcome risks) and by putting children in contexts that help their resiliency grow.

Removing risk

Perhaps the only way to completely remove risk at transition is through careful selection of a transfer school. Theoretically, school choice is possible for everyone, given that families can move to a new catchment area or can use social networks to obtain a school place. However, these actions require substantial financial and social capital. Accordingly, Weller and Bruegel (2006) found that parents who sought out non-catchment-area schools were more often white, middle class and socially mobile, or were highly motivated middle-class immigrants living in deprived areas. School choice can influence children's adjustment by changing the likelihood of whether they will encounter antisocial peers and poor-quality teaching, criteria which were predominant in selection efforts by mothers in Ireland (O'Brien, 2005). I would also recommend that parents select schools based on whether there is a good system for managing transition, as transition interventions and organisation have a significant impact on children's adjustment (see Chapter 11). However, as discussed, if parents send children to schools outside of their catchment area they can increase their child's risk of being socially isolated or bullied (Weller, 2007). Parents can offset this risk if they send their children to schools with a minimum of one sibling or friend (Weller & Bruegel, 2006).

Diminishing risk

Of course, not all risk factors are removable. Some are tied to the act of transition (e.g. moving into a completely new environment) and to the features of transfer schools (e.g. a loss of teacher support, integrating into a new peer group). Rather than remove these risks, parents can intervene to diminish their impact. Some risks are predictable, such as schools disciplining children without the correct equipment and uniform. There, parents can alleviate risk if they correctly outfit their child. Another common risk is the existence of a mismatch between the school timetable and homework requirements, and parents' home schedules (O'Brien, 2005; and in the case study of Samantha in this chapter). Other risks are harder to identify, as these arise throughout the transition process as part of children's personal experience, for example, victimisation. Here, parents need to *monitor* their children to spot potential risks, *evaluate* whether the risk needs their attention, and then *intervene* if they decide that it does (Falbo, Lein & Amador, 2001).

Parents have better luck intervening at transition if they have some professional background in this area, such as social work, psychology or teaching (O'Brien, 2005). It is also easier for parents to monitor, evaluate and intervene with risk when there is a good connection between home and school. However, parents find that they have less access to information about their children in transfer schools, as typical secondary school cultures inhibit parental involvement (Osborn, McNess & Pollard, 2006). Invested parents may wish to increase the information flow by volunteering at school, for example, by staffing school clubs and fundraising. Parents who have made these efforts developed closer relationships with teachers in transfer schools, and consequentially had more information relayed to them about their children (Falbo et al., 2001).

Supporting resiliency

As discussed, an important component of children's resiliency is self-esteem (Rutter, 1985). Critically, children's confidence in themselves can affect how they appraise and react to risks at transition. There are many ways in which parents (and teachers) can set out to encourage children's self-esteem growth. These include demonstrating how much they value and trust children, recognising children's achievements, building on children's existing strengths and praising children's efforts and abilities (in Galton, Gray, Rudduck, Berry, Demetriou, Edwards, et al., 2003). Parents can also build self-esteem at school transition by giving children opportunities to gain competency and responsibility. For example, because of transition parents have encouraged their children to do chores for the first time (sometimes in return for pocket money), have allowed them to travel unsupervised with friends to neighbouring towns and have made their children's bedtimes later to reflect their increased maturity (Symonds, 2009). In turn, children perceived that they were becoming more adult, which gave them more confidence to cope with transition.

Another way that parents can support resiliency is by alleviating children's anxiety, as children cope better with risk factors if they are less nervous about them. However, parents can find this difficult if they are also concerned about the move. In a study of Scottish children (Zeedyk, Gallagher, Henderson, Hope, Husband & Lindsay, 2003), children and parents worried to a similar degree about bullying, getting lost, peer relations and coping with schoolwork at transition. In contrast, a North American study found that parents worried more about academic planning, teachers, homework and older students, while children worried more about getting lost, peer pressure and new subjects (Smith, Akos, Lim, & Wiley, 2008). Both studies indicate that parents need to carefully avoid increasing their children's anxieties by sharing their fears and by ruminating (needlessly prolonged discussion) about their children's anxieties with them, for, as Zeedyk et al. (2003) point out, 'It seems reasonable to assume that a causal relation may exist between the two; if a parent becomes aware of a child's concerns, they may well come to share them, and vice versa' (p. 73).

Resiliency includes knowing how to cope with challenges. When children encounter threat at transition, their reactions can be emotional, cognitive and behavioural. A child may want to make new friends but feels shy (emotional), develops a strategy to deal with their shyness (cognitive) and acts out that strategy by approaching quieter children (behavioural). When parents become aware of specific transition challenges, they can intervene at any level of this process by giving advice and examples of how to react. In Ireland, mothers helped their children cope emotionally with school entrance examinations, and scaffolded their cognition and behaviour with advice on how to avoid sexual attack and traffic hazards on the way to school (O'Brien, 2005). Although children may not take this type of advice at first, having a logical structure to fall back to can make a big difference if the situation arises.

Another issue of concern for parents is how well their children will cope with an increased workload and academic focus at the transfer school. Parents can intervene with this risk by building their children's 'academic resiliency' in several ways. First, they can encourage children to have positive attitudes towards school and schoolwork. Second, they can increase their children's academic motivation by co-constructing goals with their children, offering rewards and making their children aware of the realities of failure (Symonds, 2009). Third, they can facilitate children's academic competency by tutoring them at home (O'Brien, 2005). And, fourth, they can help children develop academic organisational skills that will ultimately assist their achievement, such as tutoring them on how to use diaries and planners (Falbo et al., 2001).

Facilitating activities that support resiliency

Finally, parents can also help children develop resiliency by carefully choosing which activities their children engage in after school. 'Constructive' out-of-school activities (Hagell, Peck, Zarrett, Giménez-Nadal & Symonds, 2012) often involve a degree of adult control, such as sports training, performing arts, church groups and other types of interest associations. These activities provide children with structured pathways to self-improvement, whereas in comparison there is less structure when children spend time completely alone or with friends during unsupervised play. Constructive activities can offer children opportunities for social bonding and skills development, particularly if they involve team efforts and prolonged or intensive training. When children take advantage of these opportunities and do well in them, their self-esteem, mental health, personal, emotional and social skills can be enhanced, which in turn supports their resiliency to many common transition challenges.

A case study is of children's social relationships. It is well established that children are especially concerned about finding new friends after transition (see, for example, Galton, 2010), while parents worry about new friends being a bad influence. Here, parents who intervene have a positive effect on children's friendships and social values (e.g. Frey et al., 2009; Laird & Marrero, 2011). By enrolling their children in constructive activities, parents increase children's chances of meeting peers with particular sporting or academic talents and similar family backgrounds. If those children attend the same transfer school, they bond together in prosocial friendship groups that are more likely to share the schools' academic and behavioural values (Falbo et al., 2001), thereby increasing children's chances of doing well at school (e.g. Measor & Woods, 1984).

Case study of parental influence: Samantha

When parents' and children's lives become linked at school transition, they engage in a type of synchronised life planning. Elder (1998) argues that this life planning can set long-term pathways of advantage or disadvantage in motion.

Below I briefly explore Samantha's experience of parental support as she moved from primary to secondary school in the east of England (Symonds, 2009), and the links between this mixed bag of support and her end of year academic adjustment. Samantha (Sam) was chosen to participate in my study of transition and school engagement, because her attitude to school was so poor.

Both of Sam's parents had finished high school, and her mother was a qualified social worker. They lived together with Sam's 4-year-old brother, Justin. Her father worked in the early morning as a delivery man, while her mother worked afternoons and evenings at local schools. The restrictions caused by her parents' schedules made weekday family life rather hectic: '[Mum] gets home at about 8, and Justin is already in bed by then, so he doesn't get to see Mum in the evening. And in the morning it's just like a rush: get up, get changed, go to school. If you miss the bus, well, you miss the bus and then it's manic.'

Despite this busy timetable, Sam felt that her mother was always there to offer emotional support and advice. Possibly, this was related to her professional capacity as a child–care worker. This support was consistent, as Sam recounted in stories about the lead-up to transition and the transfer year. At primary school, Sam's mother advised her on how to handle arguments between friends who were stressed about moving schools. 'In the end my mum's, like, "If people are going to be nasty to you, then just leave it to them." Because there's no point in going after it ... because in the end you're all going to be away from each other.' Later, at secondary school, Sam's mother gave her advice and support about her first boyfriend: 'When I had my first boyfriend and he wouldn't leave me alone ... my mum was all, like, helping me and everything' (term three). This tendency for Sam's mother to be emotionally available made her the most important thing in the world to Sam: 'The thing out of everything I really need is my mum' (Sam); 'Why?' (Jenny); 'Because, like, when I'm in problems, she'll help me because she's been there, she's done that, you know.' This emotional closeness remained across the transition year, despite Sam's growing social independence. 'I'm growing up now, so she knows that I'm getting different minds for different things; like going out with my friends and going to the farm and going to see things. But we still do get together sometimes and sit by the sofa and watch one of those soppy old movies and be all lovey-dovey and everything.'

Despite receiving emotional support, Sam noted that neither of her parents had any direct involvement in her social or academic problems at school. For example, although she gave advice on the issue, Sam's mother did not intervene in the last year of primary school when she found out that Sam was being bullied. This resulted in Sam sorting out the problem for herself: 'And I got quite tired of it, so I eventually went up to them and said, "Can you stop picking on me? I don't want you to bully me because ... it's making my life miserable, and my mum's." Because (at home) I would go, "Oh, mum this, oh, mum that," and she'd start crying and everything.'

Sam's parents' shift work also impacted how she dealt with the challenge of increased homework. Because her mother worked until 8.00 p.m., Sam was often responsible for putting her younger brother to bed: 'Quite frankly, my dad does not do looking after children well.' Once Justin was asleep, and Sam had spent some time with her mother, she often watched television or played Nintendo in her room until 9.00 or 10.00 p.m. Because Sam's parents did not help her with completing or scheduling her homework, this led to some poor decision making by Sam on when to get it done: 'Last night I knew I was going to get badly told off [by teachers] if I didn't do my homework. I stayed up until like eleven, and finished it. Then I had to wake up at six again, which makes it more stressful.' This lack of academic support at home may have compounded problems that Sam was already having with her achievement at school: 'Because I'm quite a low level, and ... I'm dyslexic as well.'

Other areas of Sam's life also evidenced a lack of structure. She reported being allowed to stay up until midnight on the weekend nights, something which was unusual amongst her peers, who normally went to bed between 8.00 p.m. and 10.00 p.m. (Symonds, 2009). She noticed that, towards the end of the transition year, her father gave her more freedom at home and with her friends, whereas before he had set some limits on her behaviour: 'He just takes things differently. Like when I say, "Can I go out to play?" he'll say, "Well, yes you can – go on then, off you go." Where usually I'd have to like reason him, saying, "Oh, OK, I'll be back at dark."' Also, Sam's parents did not enrol her in any constructive activities outside of school. Instead, when Sam had free time, she would usually 'play out with my friends and do activities like going to the park and going to the shop.'

Possibly because she received considerable freedom at home, Sam found school organisation to be oppressive and unbearable. Throughout the year, she complained of not being allowed to talk with friends in class, and disliked having to wear school uniform. Sam's mother had mentioned home schooling to her and consequently Sam developed the idea that she would prefer to be educated at home, at her own pace. This would allow her more time to develop her identity: 'I don't really want to be here ... What's the point in coming here when you can maybe do it at home and have free time to be you?' Sam also wanted to avoid the new, faster-paced timetable of secondary school, which had effects that were compounded by her rushed home schedule: 'I would like to actually relax, and not worry about, "Oh, God, I've forget that, or oh goodness, I've got this," or something like that.' Sam also saw her school timetable and her parents' work schedules as a problem for family cohesion: 'I know that adults have to be at work all the time, so you don't really get to have a chance to see them. Only on weekends, which is only two days.'

Sam had an overall negative attitude towards school that did not improve after transition. Her parents contributed to each of her negative opinions about school in active and passive ways, for example, by not helping her with her homework, by setting few boundaries at home and by expecting her to be adult in her decision making and by looking after her little brother. These latter two aspects of Sam's home life were at odds with her school's culture, as at school she was expected to conform to rules and was treated as a minor. However, a major positive in Sam's life was her mother's emotional support, which may have offset risk in Sam's emotional adjustment at transition.

Conclusions

The types of support outlined in this chapter only scratch the surface of this immense topic. But, even with a restricted view, this chapter has demonstrated that parents are extremely important to children's wellbeing at transition. Indeed, the home lives that parents provide set the scene for how well children cope with the move. And, parents can have a positive impact on children's adjustment when they intervene with school transition challenges. However, as discussed, there is often less opportunity for schools and parents to communicate after transfer; therefore some of these risk factors may be unknown to parents, and parental support may be invisible to schools. That is why researchers recommend creating more home–school partnerships at transition, so that schools can capitalise on 'parent power' and parents can learn more about their children's needs at transition (Osborn et al., 2006). This two-way information flow can be encouraged by involving parents in transition interventions that involve regular question and answer sessions, or surveys of parental opinion (Smith, 1991). More about these methods can be found in Chapter 11.

References

Baker, D. P., & Stevenson, D. L. (1986). Mothers' strategies for children's school achievement: Managing the transition to high school. *Sociology of Education, 59*(3), 156–166.

Caulfield, C., Hill, M., & Shelton, A. (2005). *The transition to secondary school: The experiences of black and minority ethnic young people.* Glasgow: Glasgow Anti Racist Alliance.

Chen, W.-B., & Gregory, A. (2009). Parental involvement as a protective factor during the transition to high school. *Journal of Educational Research, 103*(1), 53–62.

Collishaw, S., Maughan, B., Goodman, R., & Pickles, A. (2004). Time trends in adolescent mental health. *Journal of Child Psychology and Psychiatry, 45*(8), 1350–1362.

de Graaf, P. M. (1988). Parents' financial and cultural resources, grades and transition to secondary school in the Federal Republic of Germany. *European Sociological Review, 4*(3), 209–221.

Elder, G. H. J. (1998). The life course as developmental theory. *Child Development, 69*(1), 1–12.

Falbo, T., Lein, L., & Amador, N. A. (2001). Parental involvement during the transition to high school. *Journal of Adolescent Research, 16*(5), 511–529.

Frey, A., Ruchkin, V., Martin, A., Schwab, S., & Mary. (2009). Adolescents in transition: School and family characteristics in the development of violent behaviors entering high school. *Child Psychiatry and Human Development, 40*(1), 1–13.

Galton, M. (2010). Moving to secondary school: What do pupils say about the experience? In D. Jindal-Snape (ed.), *Educational transitions: Moving stories from around the world* (pp. 107–124). New York and Abingdon: Routledge.

Galton, M., Gray, J., Rudduck, J., Berry, M., Demetriou, H., Edwards, J., et al. (2003). *Transfer and transitions in the middle years of schooling (7–14): Continuities and discontinuities in learning*. London: DfES.

Gniewosz, B., Eccles, J., & Noack, P. (2011). Secondary school transition and the use of different sources of information for the construction of the academic self-concept. *Social Development, 21*(3), 537–557.

Gutman, L. M. (2006). How student and parent goal orientations and classroom goal structures influence the math achievement of African Americans during the high school transition. *Contemporary Educational Psychology, 31*(1), 44–63.

Hagell, A., Peck, S., Zarrett, N., Giménez-Nadal, J. I., & Symonds, J. (2012). Trends in adolescent time use in the United Kingdom. In A. Hagell (ed.), *Changing adolescence: Social trends and mental health* (pp. 27–46). Bristol: Policy Press.

Jindal-Snape, D., & Miller, D. J. (2008). A challenge of living? Understanding the psycho-social processes of the child during primary–secondary transition through resilience and self-esteem theories. *Education Psychology Review, 20*(3), 217–236.

Laird, R. D., & Marrero, M. D. (2011). Mothers' knowledge of early adolescents' activities following the middle school transition and pubertal maturation. *Journal of Early Adolescence, 31*(2), 209–233.

Lord, S. E., Eccles, J. S., & McCarthy, K. A. (1994). Surviving the junior high school transition: Family processes and self-perceptions as protective and risk factors. *Journal of Early Adolescence, 14*(2), 162–199.

Malecki, C. K., & Demaray, M. K. (2003). What type of support do they need? Investigating student adjustment as related to emotional, informational, appraisal and instrumental support. *School Psychology Quarterly, 18*(3), 231–252.

Measor, L., & Woods, P. (1984). *Changing schools*. Milton Keynes: Open University Press.

Newman, B. M., Newman, P. R., Griffen, S., O'Connor, K., & Spas, J. (2007). The relationship of social support to depressive symptoms during the transition to high school. *Adolescence, 42*(167), 441–459.

O'Brien, M. (2005). Mothers as educational workers: Mothers' emotional work at their children's transfer to second-level education. *Irish Educational Studies, 24*(2), 223–242.

Osborn, M., McNess, E., & Pollard, A. (2006). Identity and transfer: A new focus for home–school knowledge exchange. *Educational Review, 58*(4), 415–433.

Rutter, M. (1985). Resilience in the face of adversity. Protective factors and resistance to psychiatric disorder. *British Journal of Psychiatry, 147*(6), 598–611.

Rutter, M. (1987). Psychological resilience and protective mechanisms. *American Journal of Orthopsychiatry, 57*(3), 316–331.

Smith, J., Akos, P., Lim, S. & Wiley, S. (2008). Student and stakeholder perceptions of the transition to high school. *High School Journal. 91*(3), 32–42.

Smith, K. A. (1991). Easing the transition between elementary and middle school. *Schools in the Middle, 1*(3), 29–31.

Symonds, J. E. (2009). Constructing stage-environment fit: Early adolescents' psychological development and their attitudes to school in English middle and secondary school environments. Doctoral thesis, Faculty of Education, University of Cambridge. Available at: www.dspace.cam.ac.uk/handle/1810/223866

Turner, S. L. (2007). Preparing inner-city adolescents to transition into high school. *Professional School Counseling, 10*(3), 245–252.

Weller, S. (2007). Sticking with your mates?' Children's friendship trajectories during the transition from primary to secondary school. *Children and Society, 21*, 339–351.

Weller, S., & Bruegel, I. (2006). *Locality, school and social capital: Findings report.* Families and Social Capital ESRC Group, London: South Bank University.

Zeedyk, M. S., Gallagher, J., Henderson, M., Hope, G., Husband, B., & Lindsay, K. (2003). Negotiating the transition from primary to secondary school: Perceptions of pupils, parents and teachers. *School Psychology International, 24*, 67–79.

Chapter 6

Teachers

Chapter overview

Before they change schools, children are mainly taught by one teacher. The departure from this familiar face to a world where each subject is taught by a specialist is one of the most striking features of transition. Children often regard this move positively, by expecting their new teachers to have greater subject knowledge and to treat them more like adults. They also anticipate difficulties adjusting to multiple teaching styles and fear their new teachers will be stricter. This chapter compares the characteristics of subject specialist teachers and their relationships with first year students to those of their feeder colleagues, and links many of these differences to the development of children's emotional health, motivation and achievement at transition.

Encountering subject specialists

If you are a primary or elementary school student, one of the biggest challenges you will face at transition is a complete break in teaching arrangements. Currently you might have the same teacher for most of your subjects. Only a handful of practical subjects, including music and physical education, are taught by someone else. However, after transition you will be taught each subject by a teacher who has advanced expertise in that area. In our project on musical identity and school transition (Symonds, Long & Hargreaves, 2011), Izzie explained how she, like other children, was excited about the prospect of being taught music by a subject specialist. She expected 'harder stuff but better stuff ... they'll teach you like older and teach you in adult's notes'. In this project we followed Izzie and 24 of her peers as they transferred from six primary schools to three secondary schools in different parts of England. In four of the six primary schools, children reported mainly playing instruments in lessons rather than learning music theory. For children in these schools, the move to subject specialist classrooms was a big leap forwards: 'In our last school we were just learning to play the instrument. In this [school] we're like learning the notes and how long they last for ... So it feels like it's like a big jump but kind of exciting as well' (Trevor, secondary school, term one).

The children's first impressions of their new teachers were that they were passionate about teaching music. Amy illustrated this in her description of the 'little things' her music teacher did: 'We have this little thing where sometimes on the register if we're early we have to, he will sing something to you like saying, good morning but in a singing voice. And you'd have to sing it back to him like saying, I'm here or and if someone weren't here he's like, not here. So it's more musical. So we like we enjoy it more.' This passion could rub off on children who were inspired by their teacher's enthusiasm and the more complex learning demands. As Roach explained, 'I think it's better what we do now, we have a teacher that [pause] only a teacher for music' (Roach); 'And have you noticed why that makes a difference?' (Marion); 'Because they specialise in music and they explain a lot more' (Roach). Another boy, Trevor, said similarly, 'I think I like the college way better, because it explains in more detail about the notes and then you can go on to bigger steps. So if you learn more about the notes you can play better if you were given a sheet of music to play.'

Becoming more musically skilled at secondary school was one of the many positive changes reported by children in Changing Key. After they transferred, many children became more confident about their own abilities, more engaged in music and some even aspired to become professional musicians. Bobby managed to roll all of these issues into one statement: 'Well, I think I am changing more musical because our music lessons, I don't like the one what we had in [primary school] with this like clapping. But we get to learn real songs … here, not stuff like Greensleeves or something' (Bobby); 'And how does that make you feel?' (Marion); 'Well it makes me feel a bit like I want a career in music' (Bobby).

Having to start from scratch

Although many children were impressed by learning more music theory at secondary school, those who already knew the basics viewed this differently. They noted that transfer school teachers covered mainly what they had learned before transition in the first term, before combining theory and learning instruments in term two. It was only in term three that teachers encouraged all children to spread their wings and engage in creative music making activities. Here, the transfer school teachers were 'starting from scratch', which is a deliberate technique employed across subjects and schools (Hargreaves & Galton, 2002; Suffolk County Council, 1996) that has persisted for decades in England (Galton & Wilcocks, 1983).

A key reason that teachers focus on basic material in the first term is to enable all children to learn from a level playing field. This evens out disparities in subject knowledge that can arise from a lack of subject coverage at some feeder schools. Certainly, starting from scratch may be a good gamble for teachers of enrichment subjects such as art and music, as these are often squeezed out of the feeder school curriculum to make room for end of year examinations that assess core subjects of English, mathematics and science. Also enrichment subjects are often the lesser jewels in the crowns of feeder school classroom teachers. However, starting from scratch is rather unnecessary for core subjects such as English and mathematics, which have already been rigorously delivered at feeder schools in preparation for the examinations. Observations of teachers show little difference in how core subjects are taught and equipped between feeder and transfer schools (Galton & Pell, 2002). Even in the 1980s, Benyon remarked that 'the traditional numeracy and literacy curriculum largely persists and calls into question the secondary school folklore about the failure of the junior sector to concentrate on 'basics'' (1985, p. 157).

So why do some core subject teachers persist in starting from scratch? Hargreaves and Galton (2002) explain that these teachers may want to gather a first-hand picture of children's abilities, as the achievement data given to secondary school teachers can be a product of extensive coaching. Also by starting from scratch, all teachers become better aware of their new cohort's strengths and weaknesses, without the risk of confusing children by pushing them too far. Furthermore, starting from scratch may be a gentle way to jostle children from the slumber of a long summer holiday, and ease them into new teaching styles and subject content. However, despite its apparent benefits, starting from scratch can have a negative effect on children who are more experienced in that subject matter and/or who desire a significant shift in lesson content and teaching styles after transition. In Changing Key, children who had already learned an instrument outside of school felt disadvantaged by the slow start to the year, and could be frustrated and bored in lessons. To this regard, the decision to start from scratch should not be made lightly. Certainly, there should be provision for more advanced learners in the first term, for example by allowing them to tutor less experienced classmates which can build their self-esteem (Symonds et al., 2011).

Core subject teaching

Almost 40 years ago, Maurice Galton and colleagues asked the question 'what happens to students when they move to new teachers?' (Galton & Wilcocks, 1983, p. 25). Specifically, Galton was interested in how the differences between the curriculum and teaching of pre- and transfer schools affected children's learning. His curiosity manifest in the first Observational and Classroom Learning Evaluation study (ORACLE), which tracked children across transition to either middle or primary school, during the years of 1976 and 1978 in Leicestershire, UK. Two decades later, Galton repeated the ORACLE study in similar schools with Linda Hargreaves and colleagues (Hargreaves & Galton, 2002). The more recent student allows us to compare teaching styles in feeder and transfer schools. There, trained observers watched teachers over the course of a lesson, and checked off the teachers' main activities from a list at 30-second intervals. Below I present the sum of these observations for teachers in English, mathematics and science lessons across transition.[1]

Teacher attention

In core subjects, teachers directed their attention to the whole class, small groups of children and individual children at similar frequencies across transition (Figure 6.1). In both school types, teachers spent most of their time teaching the whole class (feeder school = 46 per cent of the time, transfer school = 52 per cent) rather than individual students. However they did teach individual children for a significant minority of their time (feeder school = 39 per cent, transfer school = 38 per cent). Despite the benefits of scaffolding children's social interaction in learning collaborations, teachers spent the least amount of their time teaching small groups of children (feeder school = 15 per cent, transfer school = 10 per cent). Although their attention was reasonably similar in both school types, there was a slight trend for teachers to engage more in group work and less in whole class teaching in feeder schools.

Teacher talk

Galton and colleagues observed that teachers mainly did two things when they talked to their audiences: made statements and asked questions (Figure 6.2). When teachers were silent, they most often listened to children read and report back on their work, marked or demonstrated. Like teacher attention across transition, the types of teacher talk that children were exposed to differed very little as they changed schools. Across transition, teachers spent nearly equal amounts of time making statements (feeder = 61 per cent, transfer school = 57 per cent), asking questions (feeder school = 22 per cent, transfer school = 19 per cent) and being silent and listening (feeder school = 17 per cent, transfer

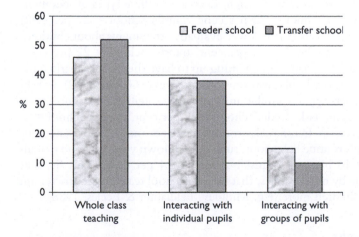

Figure 6.1 Teacher attention

Source: Data sourced from Galton, Hargreaves, Comber, Wall and Pell (1999) and from Galton and Pell (2002). All percentages are rounded to the nearest whole number.

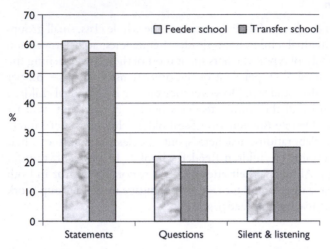

Figure 6.2 Teacher talk

Source: Data sourced from Galton, Hargreaves, Comber, Wall and Pell (1999) and from Galton and Pell (2002). All percentages are rounded to the nearest whole number.

school = 25 per cent). In general, children spent most of their time listening to teachers rather than working silently or being engaged in active discussion.

Teacher statements

When they were making statements, teachers mostly introduced facts, ideas and problems (Figure 6.3). There was a slight decrease in these types of statements after transition (feeder school = 33 per cent, transfer school = 27 per cent). After transition, teachers also made fewer evaluative statements about children's work or effort (feeder school = 26 per cent, transfer school = 22 per cent), possibly because children had stopped lining up to have their books marked like they had done in feeder school classrooms (Hargreaves & Galton, 2002). In both school types, teachers spent a similar amount of time telling children what to do regarding a learning task (feeder school = 25 per cent, transfer school = 27 per cent); however, in transfer classrooms, teachers made more statements directing children's routine behaviour, such as 'put down your pens and pencils' (feeder school = 16 per cent, transfer school = 24 per cent). This fits with observations made by other studies, that transfer school teachers are stricter and want to control children more (e.g. Midgley, Feldlaufer & Eccles, 1988).

Teacher questions

In both school types, teachers mainly asked children about the lesson content or routine matters such as organising books (Figure 6.4). When they were

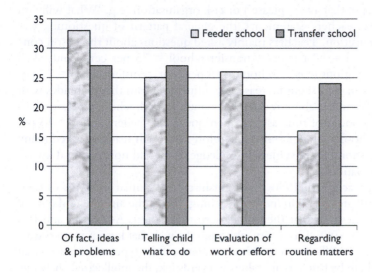

Figure 6.3 Teacher statements

Source: Data sourced from Galton, Hargreaves, Comber, Wall and Pell (1999) and from Galton and Pell (2002). All percentages are rounded to the nearest whole number.

asking about lesson content, teachers either sought factual answers (e.g. 'What is the capital of Italy?'), asked closed questions which required one correct answer to a problem (e.g. 'What is 10 plus 18?') or used open questions that provoked children's imaginations (e.g. 'Why do you think that Joan opened the box?'). For routine questions, teachers focused either on classroom etiquette

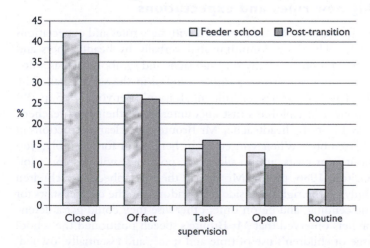

Figure 6.4 Teacher questions

Source: Data sourced from Galton, Hargreaves, Comber, Wall and Pell (1999) and from Galton and Pell (2002). All percentages are rounded to the nearest whole number.

(e.g.. 'Can you put that away, please') or task organisation (e.g. 'What will you do next?'). Like teachers' statements, the general pattern of questioning was similar across transition. Teachers mainly asked questions about the lesson content (feeder school = 82 per cent, transfer school = 73 per cent) and asked fewer routine questions (feeder school = 18 per cent, transfer school = 27 per cent). Here we can see a slight increase in routine questions that coincides with the increase in statements about routine behaviour. In both school types, teachers spent the least amount of time asking open questions (feeder school = 13 per cent, transfer school = 10 per cent). Therefore, although teachers asked many challenging questions about subject knowledge, these did not usually draw on children's imaginations.

In summary, teachers in 1990s Leicestershire were similar in terms of their whole class, small group and individual teaching, and in the amount and type of statements and questions that they used, across transition. As Galton and Pell explained (2002, p. 108), '[i]n reality, although the way that lessons were organised may have made different demands on students, if the types of questions that were asked of them by teachers are taken as a yardstick, the intellectual challenge remained somewhat similar'. However, outside of this yardstick, there may have been subtle differences in teacher talk across transition that were not picked up by this observation method, existing, for example, in the sequence of discussions with children and in the complexity of individual question types. This suggests that further study on teacher talk and school transition is necessary, in order to provide a finer-grained map of pedagogical differences between feeder and transfer schools.

Encountering new rules and expectations

After changing schools, children are presented with new rules and expectations for their behaviour. These are communicated verbally by headteachers and other teaching staff and non-verbally through signs and symbols such as a no-bullying policy on a noticeboard or a 'quiet' symbol in the school hall. The introduction of behaviour policies, or 'rule inculcation' (Benyon, 1985, p. 39) is a central component of children's first encounters with their new teachers. In the first ORACLE study, headteacher Mr Bronte gave clear instructions in the first Year 7 assembly: 'When you come in here again for assembly, you will come without your coats, and in silence … politeness will get you a lot' (Delamont & Galton, 1986, p. 48). Mr Bronte then described how children should walk calmly on the righthand side of corridors, use the correct stairs for ascending and descending, and be on time; otherwise they could get a detention. The researchers observed that Mr Bronte's speech positioned the school as being in charge of children's use of time and space, and essentially 'owned' their behaviour while they were under its roof.

Although there may be one set of 'whole school' rules, teachers can have their own rules that apply to their individual classrooms. As stated by a teacher in the first ORACLE study, 'my rules, for my room, for my area!' (Delamont & Galton, 1986, p. 47). For children, this can be initially confusing and take time to get used to. As Jacob described it to me, 'because all the teachers were saying different stuff to me, and were contradicting each other, they were saying one thing and when I was doing that, another teacher told me not to do it, and it was really weird because I didn't know what to do'.

During the first few days and weeks, teachers emphasise their rules more than normal, for example, by using repetition: 'will you please put your pens and pencils down now' followed by 'pens and pencils down' (Measor & Woods, 1984). Teachers of practical subjects such as design technology and physical education have the most new rules to convey, as their subjects can put children in physical danger. For example, science teachers have outlined a series of rules on wearing safety goggles, handling heat and not touching/tasting chemicals in their first conversations with children (Delamont & Galton, 1986). Teachers have also instructed new children about the sequence of learning activities, for example, lining up quietly outside of their classroom (Measor & Woods, 1984) or sitting at their desks and reading silently before the teacher arrives. In Benyon (1985), Miss Floral taught children to expect an 'opening "static" phase, "action" phase, "production" phase, and … "showing" phase' (p. 44) in each drama lesson, and in doing so marked a difference to the 'sit in silence' etiquette of many of her colleagues.

To enforce their rules and expectations, teachers have used stereotyped arguments that centre on children's responsibility for their own behaviour (Benyon, 1985; Measor & Woods, 1984; Symonds, 2009). The urge to grow up is a powerful motivator for children, and teachers have taken advantage of this by promising children that if they obey rules they will be more mature. In Benyon's study of an all-boys' comprehensive, teachers equated words such as 'sensible' and 'responsible' with 'growing up' and argued that children needed to leave behind the 'irresponsible antics' of their junior schools (Benyon, 1985, p. 43). As Mr Union said, 'Now listen, lad, you're not in the junior school now. Kindly ask me before you go walking around the room like a zombie. Shake the straws out of your head and start growing up right now!' (p. 156).

Teachers also use the argument of 'glittering prizes' (Benyon, 1985, p. 44) to make children conform – for example, encouraging children to work hard at school to achieve future career goals, social status and cognitive rewards. Although some children of yesteryear placed little value on education given their desire to become unskilled labourers (Willis, 1977), in the modern era the glittering prizes argument is felt keenly by many children who view school as critical to their future career success (Galton, Hargreaves, & Pell, 2003). As Stacey explained to me, in transfer school 'you have to work harder, and try and get better marks and it's not messing about time any more … Because you've moving up schools, and after you need to get a good job, and you need to get the grades to be able to get into whatever college you need to get into to be able to get that job.'

To this regard, the ambitions of teachers (to have children conform to school rules) and children (to grow up successfully) can be merged. This brings interesting possibilities for the development of children's psychological wellbeing, but not all of these are pleasant. For example, if a boy believes that he needs a good education for future career success, but cannot behave well in class, how might this influence his educational attitudes and mental health? Also, what happens to children who disagree with the principles behind school rules, such as that all children should obey their teachers? Some schools and teachers seek to address these issues by putting children in charge of classroom etiquette. This allows children to set rules they inherently believe and agree on, and allows teachers to harness children's ability to enforce rules through peer pressure. It can also improve teacher–student relationships when children feel their views are respected.

Being labelled by teachers

Like most humans, teachers ascribe an identity and social position to people whom they have just met, based on what they know about the world. In transfer schools, teachers have stereotyped new children based on their apparent ability, work effort, physical appearance and behaviour, and also with regards to their older siblings, family backgrounds, and by comparing them to the previous year's cohort (Benyon, 1985). By labelling children using stereotypes, teachers make it easier for themselves to manage new classes whom they hardly know, for this 'relays new children as more predictable' (Benyon, 1985, p. 143).

Children who have unusual physical characteristics such as bright-red hair (Hargreaves & Galton, 2002) or who encourage attention through their behaviour are especially vulnerable to being labelled by teachers. These children are more quickly marked out for labelling, while more conservative children are labelled later. Mr Megaphone described this happening in an all-boys school: 'you get to know the villains first, the angels next, and then the rest of them' (Benyon, 1985, p. 141). In the same school, groups of teachers used labels to discuss new children in the staffroom, which pushed the staff towards a shared opinion on particular students. This 'staffroom broadcasting' (Benyon, 1985, p. 152) quickly determined which new children teachers should be on the lookout for.

Labelling children can have adverse short- and longer-term effects. For example, in Symonds (2009), teachers were observed to have firmed up their impressions of some children by term two, which affected their delivery of time and emotional resources: 'They can be nice to the nice students, but they're horrible to the nasty students they don't really like and they won't tend to help as much' (Charlie). By stereotyping children, teachers encourage children to hold 'self-fulfilling prophecies' where children use their teachers' expectations to construct their image of themselves. At transition, low achievers are most susceptible to believing in the stereotypes teachers hold for them, especially if these labels are positive (Madon, Jussim & Eccles, 1997). In this manner, self-fulfilling prophecies can affect children's psychological wellbeing and work effort, and for these reasons teachers should be wary of stereotyping new children, even if it gives them some initial comfort in the first term.

Increases in teacher strictness

Although many children expect to be more responsible and independent when they change schools, the actual amount of freedom and trust they receive from teachers can be a different kettle of fish. This can boil down to the different perspectives of feeder and transfer school teachers on adolescence. In the US, psychologists Midlgey, Feldlaufer and Eccles (1988) followed a group of children across transition and found that their 64 junior high school maths teachers rated them as less trustworthy and in more need of control than their 107 elementary school maths teachers did. The researchers rationalised that this was more likely to reflect a difference in teachers' attitudes, rather than for a cohort of children to have changed their behaviour in such a short period. Also in England, children have observed their transfer school teachers to be stricter, perhaps because some are following the folk wisdom of 'don't smile until Christmas' (i.e. the end of the first term). This outlook promises teachers that if they 'start off hard and ease up later' (Benyon, 1985, p. 45), then children will be more motivated to conform to their expectations. However, this initial strictness is not always a ruse, as transfer school teachers can also play things the other way around. In Symonds (2009), Samantha described how her teacher began the year by being nice, but then dropped her friendly face just before term two: '[Now] she just wants to do things her way. And if you don't like it, then tough. You're here to learn, you're not here to mess about' (Samantha). Although no transition studies focus exclusively on teacher strictness, this type of research could provide valuable details as to why children's psychological wellbeing often declines when they lose emotional support from teachers across transition, as I discuss below.

Declines in emotional support

In many studies, children have noted that their transfer school teachers are less friendly and caring than their feeder school teachers (Feldlaufer, Midgley & Eccles, 1988; Ferguson & Fraser, 1998; Jennings & Hargreaves, 1981; Seidman, LaRue, Lawrence, Mitchell & Feinman, 1994). This is no surprise when considering that transfer school teachers only have a short amount of time to spend with children each day, and have no prior knowledge of them, whereas their feeder school colleagues can build a close relationship with children, whom they teach for most of the day. Although transfer teachers get to know their students better with time, children have felt less and less supported by their teachers across the first transfer year in Norway (Bru, Stornes, Munthe & Thuen, 2010) and across two years after transition in the US (Skinner, Marchland, Furrer & Kindermann, 2008).

Children receive emotional support from teachers through two main avenues: individual teacher and student relationships, and the relationship conveyed by the staff as a body towards all students (Gray, Galton, McLaughlin, Clarke & Symonds, 2011). In Symonds (2009), children were keenly aware of how they felt about individual teachers, and soon began to describe all of their teachers using these feelings as stereotypes. As Kevin remarked, 'nobody particularly really likes them, like is friendly with them. They are just adults that we know, and um, well basically all we do is we just walk into the lesson, they talk to us, we do the work and then we walk out.' Likewise, Samantha advised that 'they're just there to do their job, they're not there to be like your best friend'. Even Matthew, who was well behaved and aspired to become a teacher, felt that his relationships with teachers were poor: 'Generally I do quite want to be liked by teachers. In some cases that's impossible' (Matthew). Having several supply/substitute teachers during the year simply worsened the effect: 'Our teacher's been gone since December so we've got a replacement' (Ruby); 'We had the one with the short hair' (Samantha); 'We called her witch' (Ruby); 'Yeah we've had three … all horrible' (Samantha). Despite feeling detached from their teachers, the children wanted to have better relationships with them. When I asked 'What do you need at school to feel happy?', Ruby replied, 'more friendly teachers, who give us a chance to talk and be kind to us', while Charlie advised that teachers needed to 'interact more and be more friendly'.

Importantly, the quality of children's relationships with teachers associates with their psychological wellbeing. In Canadian high schools, children who perceived a loss of teacher emotional support after transition had worsening depressive symptoms and poorer self-esteem (De Wit, Karioja, Rye & Shain, 2011). There are similar findings from Utah, where children's perceptions of teacher support were the strongest predictor of how their self-esteem and depression developed after transition, in comparison to their attitudes towards school, perceptions of school rules, experiences of teacher monitoring, and the amount of freedom they received in class (Barber & Olsen, 2004). In other areas of the US, changes in teachers' emotional support have been associated with the development of children's attitudes towards learning (Skinner et al., 2008) and motivation to learn mathematics (Midgley, Feldlaufer & Eccles, 1989) at transition. In the east of England, relationships with teachers have more strongly predicted children's enjoyment of school than their relationship with peers, experiences of freedom in learning and mental health, after they changed schools (Symonds, 2010). As I discuss in Chapter 9, the development of poor-quality relationships with teachers after transition strongly predicts children's later school attendance and levels of misbehaviour (Smith, 2006). Together, these findings suggest a developmental pathway between teacher support, children's attitudes and their eventual participation in school. Accordingly, declining emotional support from teachers after transition is no laughing matter.

Conclusions

Although children look forward to the positive changes that come with subject specialist teaching, they generally perceive a continued loss of emotional support and an increase in teacher strictness in their new schools. Perhaps because neither children nor teachers have time to get to know each other well after transition, they are in danger of stereotyping each other. This seems to have different results: for teachers, it helps make unfamiliar children more predictable, while for children it positions teachers as an 'out group'. Not knowing children also requires teachers to present them with new rules and expectations. Despite the variety of rules presented, each conveys a similar message: that it is time to focus on academic learning and that inattentive behaviour will not be tolerated. Together with a loss of closeness with teachers, these changes may give children the impression they should be more adult in their new schools. However, children's expectations for independence are often at odds with the described increase in teacher strictness in the new schools. Combined with the similarity in how core subjects are taught across transition, children's hopes for more independent and challenging learning may be dashed early on, which may cause some children to be very disappointed with what they hoped would be a transformative learning experience (Galton & Pell, 2002).

Note

1 In order to compare feeder and transfer data for English, mathematics and science teaching only, I have re-analysed the feeder school data from Galton, Hargreaves, Comber, Wall and Pell (1999) and compared this to transfer data from Galton, Comber and Pell (2002). Although there is feeder school data presented in Galton, Comber and Pell (2002), this is the sum of observations of teachers in English, mathematics, science, history, geography and art.

References

Barber, B. K., & Olsen, J. A. (2004). Assessing the transitions to middle and high school. *Journal of Adolescent Research, 19*(1), 3–30.

Benyon, J. (1985). *Initial encounters in the secondary school: Sussing, typing and coding.* Lewes: Falmer Press.

Bru, E., Stornes, T., Munthe, E., & Thuen, E. (2010). Students' perceptions of teacher support across the transition from primary to secondary school. *Scandinavian Journal of Educational Research, 54*(6), 519–533.

De Wit, D. J., Karioja, K., Rye, B. J., & Shain, M. (2011). Perceptions of declining classmate and teacher support following the transition to high school: Potential correlates of increasing student mental health difficulties. *Psychology in the Schools, 48*(6), 556–572.

Delamont, S., & Galton, M. (1986). *Inside the secondary classroom.* London: Routledge & Kegan Paul.

Feldlaufer, H., Midgley, C., & Eccles, J. S. (1988). Student, teacher, and observer perceptions of the classroom before and after the transition to junior high school. *Journal of Early Adolescence, 8*(2), 133–156.

Ferguson, P. D., & Fraser, B. J. (1998). Student gender, school size and changing perceptions of science learning environments during the transition from primary to secondary school. *Research in Science Education, 28*(4), 387–397.

Galton, M., Hargreaves, L., & Pell, T. (2003). Progress in the middle years of schooling: continuities and discontinuities at transfer. *Education 3–13, 31*(2), 9–19.

Galton, M., & Pell, T. (2002). Teaching in the transfer schools. In L. Hargreaves & M. Galton (eds), *Transfer from the primary classroom, 20 years on* (ed. University of Cambridge, pp. 97–130). London and New York: RoutledgeFalmer.

Galton, M., & Wilcocks, J. (1983). *Moving from the primary classroom* (ed. University of Leicester). London: Routledge & Kegan Paul.

Galton, M., Hargreaves, L., Comber, C., Wall, D., & Pell, A. (1999). *Inside the primary classroom: 20 years on.* London and New York: Routledge.

Gray, J., Galton, M., McLaughlin, C., Clarke, B., & Symonds, J. (2011). *The supportive school: Wellbeing and the young adolescent.* Newcastle upon Tyne: Cambridge Scholars Publishing.

Hargreaves, L., & Galton, M. (2002). *Transfer from the primary classroom: 20 years on.* London: RoutledgeFalmer.

Jennings, K., & Hargreaves, D. J. (1981). Children's attitudes to secondary school transfer. *Educational Studies, 7*(1), 35–39.

Measor, L., & Woods, P. (1984). *Changing schools.* Milton Keynes: Open University Press.

Midgley, C., Feldlaufer, H., & Eccles, J. S. (1988). The transition to junior high school: Beliefs of pre- and transfer school teachers. *Journal of Youth and Adolescence, 17*(6), 543–562.

Midgley, C., Feldlaufer, H., & Eccles, J. S. (1989). Change in teacher efficacy and student self- and task-related beliefs in mathematics during the transition to junior high school. *Journal of Educational Psychology, 81*(2), 247–258.

Seidman, E., LaRue, A., Lawrence, A. J., Mitchell, C., & Feinman, J. (1994). The impact of school transitions in early adolescence on the self-system and perceived social context of poor urban youth. *Child Development, 65*(2), 507–522.

Skinner, E., Marchland, G., Furrer, C., & Kindermann, T. (2008). Engagement and disaffection in the classroom: Part of a larger motivational dynamic? *Journal of Educational Psychology, 100*(4), 765–781.

Smith, D. J. (2006). *School experience and delinquency at ages 13 to 16.* Edinburgh: Centre for Law and Society/University of Edinburgh.

Suffolk Local Authority (1996). *A report on an investigation into what happens when pupils transfer into their next school at the ages of 9, 11 and 13.* Ipswich: Suffolk Education Department. Available at: www.school-portal.co.uk/GroupHomepage.asp?GroupID=783552

Symonds, J. E. (2009). Constructing stage-environment fit: Early adolescents' psychological development and their attitudes to school in English middle and secondary school environments. Doctoral thesis, Faculty of Education, University of Cambridge, UK. Available at: www.dspace.cam.ac.uk/handle/1810/223866

Symonds, J. (2010). *Are middle schools better for early adolescent development than transition into secondary school? A study of two school environments.* National Middle Schools Forum. Available at: www.middleschools.org.uk/research.php

Symonds, J., Long, M., & Hargreaves, J. (2011). *Changing Key: Adolescents' views on their musical development across the primary to secondary school transition.* London: The Paul Hamlyn Foundation. Available at: www.phf.org.uk/page.asp?id=1591

Willis, P. (1977). *Learning to labour: How working class kids get working class jobs.* New York: Columbia University Press.

Chapter 7

Peers

Chapter overview

This chapter reveals what happens to children's relationships with peers as they change schools. It amalgamates research on how friends are made and lost, sexual and romantic relationships, older children, friends outside of school and bullying; and discusses how children's perceptions of the quality of these relationships associate with their psychological wellbeing. The chapter concludes with ideas on how to improve wellbeing by targeting peer relationships in transition interventions.

Introduction

Peer relationships are children's primary concern at school transition (Berndt & Mekos, 1995; Galton, 2010; Pratt & George, 2005). Around this period, friendships take on unique importance, as children entering adolescence strive to develop their identities in interaction with their friends, away from adult influence (see Chapter 8 for more details). Accordingly friends become as important as parents for offering social support and advice (Bokhorst, Sumter & Westenberg, 2010; Malecki & Demaray, 2003). At transition, entering a new peer group is a major challenge for children who can best be understood and supported by others in that setting. For this reason, friends become the most important source of emotional support for children across transition, over teachers and parents (Kurita & Janzen 1990).

Children encounter at least three distinct changes in peers and peer relationships as they transfer schools. First, children change from being the eldest students in feeder schools to the youngest students after transition. There, some children make friends with older children. Second, the year group is larger, as it comprises cohorts of children from several feeder schools. This presents children with increased social networking possibilities amongst peers with more diverse personal characteristics. It also enables children with shared ethnic or socioeconomic characteristics to cluster together, as there are more of them in total, although their proportion in relation to other children is often similar to that at primary school (Burgess, Johnston, Key, Propper & Wilson, 2007). Third, new classroom groups are created, which can disrupt children's habit of working with specific friends, despite schools' attempts to place children with at least one close friend after transition. Often within the first year, children are streamed by ability, which marks a change from their previously mixed ability classrooms. This influences children's friendships and self-perceptions (in ways I shall discuss later) by increasing the homogeneity of their classmates.

How are peer relationships studied at transition?

When we think about children's school peers, many permeations of children come to mind. First there is the *roll group* made up of all the children in the school. This can be broken down into *year groups*, such as Years 6 and 7 in the UK and Grades 5 and 6 in the US. Year groups are particularly important because they are the primary base for children's social interaction in school. Next we have *classroom groups* and groups of children in extracurricular activities. Often within classrooms exist smaller *cooperation groups* where children work together. These four types of groups are mainly constructed by adults, except in the case where children can choose who they work with.

Another way to break down children's peer groups is to consider these in terms of friendships. Starting at the broadest level, friendships can include *loose groups* of children who network together through shared friends, *cliques* of large or small proportion who interact mainly with each other, and *dyads*, i.e. pairs of friends (Kiuru, Nurmi, Aunola & Salmela-Aro, 2009). In adolescence, children's dyads are often 'best friend' pairs. Despite this title, on average adolescents have up to five best friends (Berndt, 1999), which can cause problems when children are surveyed about who their best friend is.

Researchers have studied peer relationships at transition in several ways. Some ask children about their peer-related *hopes and fears* before transition, with a small number following up on children's actual experiences. Their findings are discussed in Chapter 4. Others focus on the *patterns of friendships* at transition, by mapping who children are friends with across the move. Fewer studies exist on *friendship characteristics* at transition, i.e. the similarities and differences between friends. Research has been done on how children select friends who match them on certain characteristics, and on whether friends become more similar to each other across time. Together, these processes are called 'homophily'. Next, a raft of mainly quantitative research examines *friendship quality*, which refers to many aspects of what makes a positive relationship between friends, and *peer acceptance*, e.g. whether children are popular within their year group. Finally, researchers compare children's friendships to aspects of their psychology such as mental health and motivation, in order to understand the *influence of peer relationships* on children's wellbeing.

Changes in peer relationships at transition

Patterns of friendships

Imagine that you are asked to compile a list of your friends at work. Your colleagues are asked to do the same thing. A researcher then compares your lists in order to find matching pairs of friends and friendship groups (which may be a little unsettling considering that nominations are not always mutual!). This technique is called 'sociometry' and researchers use it to explore how friendships stay the same or alter across transition. A key sociometric topic is how many friends children have before and after changing schools. Canadian and US research found that children had fewer mutual friendships after transition than before, but that these increased across the year as children got to know new peers (Hardy, Bukowski, & Sippola, 2002; Cantin & Boivin, 2004; Newman Kingery & Erdley, 2007). In England, up to 70 percent of children reported making new friends after transition (Chedzoy & Burden, 2005) and with around 60 per cent having more friends than they did at primary school (ILEA, 1986). These studies suggest that internationally, school transition at age 11–12 years presents an opportunity for children to expand their friendship networks.

Other research considers which children are most likely to break or retain friendship ties across transition. In a study of children living in London, the Midlands and the Southeast, Susie Weller (2007) found that children with professional/managerial fathers were most at risk of transferring alone to a new school, and were less likely to have relatives there. Most of these children transferred to selective academic schools, although a few transferred to ordinary state schools. Friendship ties were most often broken in an affluent London suburb with high competition for secondary school placements, and were most often kept in a white working-class area of a large Midlands city. Weller's (2007) study is interesting, as it provides a fresh perspective on economic advantage at transition. Where usually this acts as a protective factor by increasing children's chances of parental support and involvement, it can also be a risk factor for transferring alone without friendship support.

Friendship matching

'Now that I've come to secondary school, it's a much bigger school: you find that there are more people with a similar personality to you, and who find the same things funny and who you can actually really get on with.' As Matthew's statement demonstrates, after transition, children strive to find friends in their new peer group who are similar in beliefs, values, temperaments and backgrounds to themselves. By doing so, they create a support network that strengthens their existing aptitudes and interests. These new groups of friends often resemble each other in terms of academic achievement, school satisfaction and school engagement (Kiuru et al., 2009), career aspirations, social class and IQ (Nash, 1973). However, to date no studies have examined the extent to which friends become more like each other as a result of transition, despite this socialisation process being common across the middle years of schooling (Ryan, 2001).

Children use many techniques to find friends similar to themselves after transition. Old friends come in handy as buffers while children meet new people (Weller & Bruegel, 2006) and are sometimes discarded when children strive to progress socially and rid themselves of old, maladaptive ties (Lucey & Reay, 2000). New friends are introduced through 'snowballing' (Weller, 2007) as children get to know more people. However, some children take a step back from making friends immediately, as they prefer to evaluate their peers from a distance before deciding on who best suits them (Symonds, 2009). Others quickly evaluate their peers on highly visible characteristics such as physical attractiveness or clothing, and this can result in groups of children with similar social goals such as sexual attractiveness and social 'toughness' (Kinney, 1993; Symonds, Galton & Hargreaves, 2014). Children's luck in meeting people similar to themselves is also influenced by the wider groups chosen for them by adults, such as who is in their year or classroom group. When adults group children together based on academic ability or subject interest (as in extracurricular activities), this offers children a more homogenous group of peers to choose from, essentially making the task of friendship matching easier to do.

Gangs and cliques

'Year 7s are much more into gangs now. I don't mean gangs as in going around beating people up, but as in more largish groups of people. And then, if you're not in the gang, you are considered to be a bit of an outsider' (James).

In feeder schools, children tend to socialise in large, loose knit groups, or in smaller groups of best friends (Kvalsund, 2000; Symonds, 2009). However, after transition, children tend to form large groups of friends similar in nature and appearance to themselves. Their main activity at lunchtime is standing around and talking in these groups, whereas beforehand more children played sport and games at lunch time (Kvalsund, 2000; Symonds, 2009). Although this change can be influenced by having less sports equipment and a shorter lunch period in transfer (Symonds, 2009), it is also a product of children's desire to grow up, for by talking in cliques they emulate the behaviour of older children. Accordingly, activities that resemble 'play' take on a negative social stigma, and children avoid these in order to protect their social status. Talking becomes the new focal point of group activity, and children report an increase in discussing their career interests, social interactions and dating in post-transition schools (Symonds, 2009).

Children tend to label gangs and cliques according to their most visible distinguishing characteristics. In the US, Kinney (1993) spent a year investigating how children overcame social stereotypes as they moved from middle to high school. He found that the peer group in middle school was divided by children into nerds and trendies. The nerds were able to shake off their label in high school, where more distinct social groups developed within a larger group of peers. In my study of a secondary school in the east of England, Charlie and Jacob took me on a tour of the playground and pointed out groups of thugs (aggressive boys who were disinterested in education), chavs (sporty-looking boys with very short hair) and emos (a modern version of the 1980s Gothic stereotype), essentially showing how labels can be locally derived. In this school, children in the larger, mixed sex groups were characterised by other children as dating more, belonging to lower-ability streams and having more interest in competitive sport.

Children use labels such as 'chavs' and 'nerds' to indicate a group's position in a social tracking system (Kinney, 1993) known as a peer hierarchy. As Charlie put it, 'In year 7 it's basically a rank of people. You've seen it, haven't you? Outside in the playground, where the basketball court is.' Children use markers to determine a group's position in the social order that are based on whatever that year group decides is most important for popularity. At school transition, these markers advocate traditional masculine and feminine values including toughness for males and attractiveness for females. Unfortunately, academic ability is often equated with weakness (Whitehead, 2003), and teaching with being a feminine profession (Erikson, 1968); therefore, many boys try to appear less academic to gain social status (Measor & Woods, 1984). Because of this, groups of lower-ability children who are rougher and tougher often become the most dominant group in the transfer year. As Matthew put it, 'tougher people ... are considered a bit more highly than other groups. Some groups just sort of stay back, out of the scenery ... and just sort of hang about in discreet little places. Those groups stand right in the middle of the playground or school hall and chat and are completely oblivious to whatever else is happening around them.'

Gender differences in friendship groups

In mixed gender feeder schools, groups of male friends spend most of their lunchtime playing soccer or 'tennis football' (Delamont & Galton, 1986; Symonds, 2009). After transition, they continue to play sport at lunch or talk in cliques when there are few facilities for sport (Symonds, 2009). On both sides of transition, non-sporty boys split off into smaller special interest groups, who share a love of activities such as computer gaming, martial arts or fantasy role playing (Symonds, 2009). After transition, boys who fit neither criteria can find a temporary social niche by annoying other children on the playground or by continuing childlike behaviours from primary school, such as teasing girls or playing tag. These boys are often viewed as immature by sporty groups (Nash, 1973; Symonds, 2009), as Angus described in Nash (1973, p. 114): 'I wouldn't go around with him. He plays tig and baggy – throwing haversacks around – that's daft. Just wee ones do that.' At the bottom rung of the social order are boys without friends, who are either rejected by others or who choose not to socialise. Amongst these are overly aggressive boys, who lack the social skills necessary for acceptance in groups of thugs, despite their physical toughness.

Girls' groups are also defined by their shared interests. In Symonds (2009), there were several best friend dyads. Yasmin and Deirdre enjoyed sport, Ayesha and Joanna liked cooking, whilst Chloe and Stacey disliked school and were more interested in shopping and dating. In comparison to boys, girls tend to bond more over issues such as attractiveness, appearance and interest in dating (Kinney, 1993), and conversation is used to develop complex social relationships. Girls remark that they are more analytical after transition (Symonds, 2009), as conveyed by Ayesha: 'We're talking about more adult things than we used to in Year 6. Not what's on the telly or anything, but about school and everyone. These in-depth discussions can often lead to girls 'falling out' (i.e. disagreeing) with each other – a term that secondary school children have used with remarkable consistency across a 40-year period: 'Me and Jenny have fallen out with Janet, you know' (Measor & Woods, 1984, p. 89); 'It's because when you're younger you don't really fall out. Because you don't know what it is' (Joanna, in Symonds, 2009, p. 161).

Bullies and victims

In many schools, children's reports of bullying others or being victimised have increased after transition (Blyth, Simmons & Bush, 1978; Pelligrini & Long, 2002). There, boys have threatened each other with physical aggression, while girls have taunted each other verbally. Also, some male-to-female bullying has been documented (Pellegrini, 2001). In the US, bullying has increased at the start of each new year in middle school, then declined in a wave-like pattern, with the biggest surge coming straight after children entered a new school (Pelligrini, 2001). Generally, children who start out bullying others keep doing it across transition (Schafer, Korn, Brodbeck, Wolke & Schulz, 2005).

There are many suggestions as to why children (especially boys) bully more after transition. From a resiliency perspective, aggressive boys might be extra-sensitive to transition stressors, as their aggression might reflect a host of risk factors operating in their family backgrounds, such as abusive or uninvolved parents, that encourage their aggression and predispose them to having few positive coping skills. Aggressive boys might also suffer from low self-esteem and seek to protect this in an unfamiliar school by being dominant over others. Changes in the peer group can also exacerbate bullying, as boys strive to make a name for themselves and establish their position in the macho social order (Pellegrini, 2002). The switch to subject specialist teaching could also have an effect, as teachers who are less familiar with children may be less able to spot or deal with bullying as it occurs. Unfortunately, in some schools, children and teachers' attitudes towards bullying also become more relaxed after transition, as they agree with stereotypes that bullying is a normal part of adolescence (Lester, Cross, Shaw & Dooley, 2012; Pellegrini, 2002).

However, in other schools, bullying and aggression have decreased after transition (Berndt & Mekos, 1995; Lipps, 2005; Schafer et al., 2005). Possibly this relates to the overall quality of the peer group, or to old bully–victim patterns being broken by the move to a new school. In Symonds (2009), Ruby, Sam and Matthew were pleased not to be bullied any more, after transition. They said this was because they had made new, more supportive friends, because the bullies were in another class and because they were in a peer group where there was social stigma against people teasing others (this was seen as childish).

Although some children do escape the cycle of bullying at transition, their adjustment can still be affected by their prior victimisation experiences. Feeder school victims have been more anxious about transition (West, Sweeting & Young, 2008) and afraid of the new peer group at feeder school (Symonds, 2009). Being bullied on entry to transfer schools has inhibited children from making new friends and has damaged their self-esteem (Evangelou, Taggart, Sylva, Melhuish, Sammons & Sirai-Blatchford, 2008). And, these stresses have had a negative impact on children's learning, emotional bonding with school and adjustment to new routines in the first year (Lester et al., 2012). Sadly, children who are bullied after transition are also more likely to experience peer rejection throughout their time at transfer school (Schafer et al., 2005). These negative consequences are echoed in the large numbers of children (around 30 per cent) who are concerned about being bullied after transition, while they are still at primary school (Chedzoy & Burden, 2005; Evangelou et al., 2008).

Dating

'What's acceptable for you and your friends in a relationship?' (Jenny); 'Second base' (Chloe); 'So, what's that?' (Jenny); 'Well um some people kiss; some people snog and some people don't talk. But I don't think anyone has had sex' (Chloe). As Chloe described, children engage in a wide range of dating behaviours at transition. Because there are no exclusive studies of dating and transition, I turn mainly to Symonds (2009), where children were questioned about their pubertal development and sexuality, to Measor and Woods (1984), who paid close attention to gender at transition and to quantitative studies that included dating as a minor variable. Unfortunately, none of the research mentioned how dating (and attitudes towards dating) developed for homosexual, hermaphrodite or transgender children; therefore, I can only discuss dating between biologically classifiable girls and boys.

Children have reported more dating in their peer group after transition (Symonds, 2009), although this may not be a transition effect per se, because it is also true for same-aged children who remain in middle or elementary schools (Simmons & Blyth, 1987; Symonds, 2009). However, there are qualitative changes in children's dating that can be linked to school transition. In Symonds (2009), it was only after transition that sexuality and romantic love became intertwined for many children, whereas children reported little sexual interest or ambition when dating at primary school. Children who transferred were also more inclined to emulate the 'teenage' sexual behaviours of older children and to have more interest in dating a wider range of peers, in comparison to those who remained in middle school.

The dating behaviours of transition-aged children can lack the finesse and commitment of older adolescents, as described by two girls in Symonds (2009). Ruby explained that girls generally lacked courage to make dating proposals, and instead relied on their friends to do it for them. 'It's like if a girl asks a boy out they'll get their friend to do it. Whereas a boy will just come up to you and go, "Will you go out with me?" but a girl will get their friend to do it cause they're too scared.' Samantha described how relationships could be made and broken at the speed of light, something that may be characteristic of early adolescents: 'He asked me out at lunch, and then I dumped him on Thursday night ... Now I've got another one.'

However, not all children are interested in dating at this age. Children who are more academic tend to date less (Measor & Woods, 1984), for, as Matthew put it in Symonds (2009), 'Our teaching group is not really into that sort of thing cause I suppose that we're more interested in the work.' Other children have reported preference for their hobbies over dating, like James who liked reading and role-playing games, and Lauren who spent most of her time riding horses. Children can also dismiss dating in a bid to protect their self-esteem, if they feel nervous about their dating prospects. Possibly this is why Charlie at secondary school felt that dating was worthless and, in his impression, couples at transfer school 'just [stood] ... around there looking like lemons' (Symonds, 2009).

Older children

'When you came for your induction day everyone was like massively tall and you're just like "I'm going to get trampled on"' (Charlie). Like Charlie in Symonds (2009), many children worry about encountering older peers after transition. In Northern Ireland, those who were most worried about older children were also more anxious about changing schools (Spelman, 1979). Charlie was concerned about older children, because he had been bullied by an older boy in his village, indicating how children's past experiences with older peers can affect their outlook at transition.

However, most older children are not a problem, as uncovered in a study of over 2,000 children changing schools in London (ILEA, 1986). Here, only 10 per cent of older secondary school children were viewed as unfriendly, whereas 20 per cent were viewed as friendly or very friendly, and the rest as mixed (ILEA, 1986). Two decades later, in Symonds (2009), Billy and Ruby reported that having older friends boosted their popularity and self-esteem. In the same study, Matthew liked having older children in a mixed-age tutor group, as they helped him with his schoolwork and acted as academic role models. Children in England and Norway have also reported that making friends with older children protected them against being bullied (Kvalsund, 2000; Symonds, 2009). In these ways, and in many others, such as buddy systems and mentoring, older children can enhance children's wellbeing after transition. However, for the most part there is a negative stereotype about older children at secondary school, which may relate to a lack of social integration between year groups – something that educators can seek to address.

Friendships outside of school

A comparison of Year 7 children in middle and secondary school found they spent similar amounts of time playing with friends after school, without an adult present (Symonds, 2009). Across the two schools, 50 per cent of children 'played out' one to four hours a week, and 30 per cent five to ten hours weekly. Also, both groups of children mainly met up with friends in local parks or village centres, and played together until dark, 'when the teenagers come out drunk' (Ruby). These activities did not change after transition for a few secondary school children who mainly socialised with old friends from their local communities: 'We go get some fish and chips, play football, play on game consoles, and play cricket, stuff like that' (Brian).

However, the majority of children who transferred schools experienced changes that transcended the time they spent with friends and their main activities. This was in part due to making new friends within a wider catchment area that included other villages and small towns. In order to see their friends outside of school, some transfer school children used public transportation independently for the first time. This provoked new (and less common) behaviours of going to the movies and shopping in neighbouring towns. Doing these activities without adults present made several of the girls feel more grown-up. However, this had a negative impact on Stacey's attitude towards school, by encouraging her to evaluate her experiences of being out of school, against how she felt during schooltime: 'It's not as fun as you could have when you're outside the school with your friends … Outside of school you can chat all the time. Go to the shops, go shopping and all this. In school you can't go shopping apart from in the cafeteria, which you don't really get shopping, do you?' (Stacey).

Changes in peer support

In studies of peer support at transition, children have been asked to describe how they feel about a specific friendship, e.g. 'We help each other all the time,' and their social interactions with their peer group, e.g. 'Most children in my class like me,' and have reported on the popularity and social acceptance of other children in their peer group. Generally after transition, children have perceived that their individual friendships become more supportive (Fenzel, 2000; Wargo Aikins, Bierman, & Parker, 2005), as does their school year group (Cantin & Boivin, 2004; Crockett, Petersen, Graber, Schuleners & Ebata, 1989; Waters, Lester, Wenden, & Cross, 2012). Similarly, difficulties with peers (Fenzel, 2000; Seidman, LaRue, Lawrence, Mitchell & Feinman, 1994) and feelings of isolation and loneliness (Galton, Hargreaves & Pell, 2003) have declined. This improvement in peer support is gradual, rather than a large shift immediately after transition, as evidenced by studies where perceptions of peer support only changed notably towards the end of the first term (Cotterell, 1982; Gillison, Standage & Skevington, 2008).

Although the evidence points to a general trend for increased peer support, a handful of studies find other patterns. For example, a US study of transition between elementary and junior high school found a decline in close friend support for girls (Martínez, Aricak, Graves, Peters-Myszak & Nellis, 2011), while another US study found that peer acceptance decreased between the third term of elementary school and the second term of middle school (Newman Kingery et al., 2011). Possibly, something in the school or neighbourhood cultures underpinned these inverse patterns, as both studies were of predominantly white, middle–class children living in the same era.

How peer relationships influence wellbeing at transition

As discussed in Chapter 2, children strive to have positive identities. This is facilitated by supportive peers, but can get tricky when children are bullied or perceive losses in friendship and popularity. Luckily as discussed, the majority of studies find that peer support increases after transition and children have more friends than before. In line with this, children's perceptions of how socially competent they are (their *social self-concept*) also generally increase when they change schools (Fenzel, 2000; Seidman et al., 1994). Children's social self-concepts are most vulnerable in the first few weeks after transition (Wigfield, Eccles, Mac Iver Reuman & Midgley, 1991), as during this period children reform their social network and re-evaluate their social skills.

Changing to a new peer group also makes children feel uncertain about their academic self-concept, i.e. their intellectual ability and competency as workers. After they transfer, children tend to judge themselves against others more often (Feldlaufer, Midgley & Eccles, 1988) – a process known as social comparison. Much of this takes place in new classrooms. When children are taught alongside unfamiliar peers, they lose their sense of how capable they are in relation to others. This is a particular issue for children who were previously top of their class in feeder schools, and who are placed in high-ability streams. This reduces the bandwidth of achievement they can compare themselves to: suddenly they are small fish in a big pond rather than a big fish in a small pond (Marsh & Parker, 1984). On a positive note, streaming for all subjects improves the academic self-concepts of lower-ability children (Chmielewski, Dumont & Trautwein, 2013), as their achievements are no longer overshadowed by more academic peers.

There are many ways in which peer relationships influence children's self-esteem at transition, in addition to those described above. Friends offer protection from social isolation and victimisation, which can make children feel worthless. As Matthew said in Symonds (2009), 'having more friends boosts me up in confidence and stuff, so it feels like you're a bit more popular and you feel a bit better about yourself'. Making new friends similar to oneself might also boost children's self-esteem, as these friends act as a mirror that validates children's actions. At transition, children's self-esteem is protected by having a good relationship with at least one friend (Newman Kingery et al., 2011), by maintaining high-quality friendships from before transition (Wargo Aikins et al., 2005) and by having good relationships with classmates (De Wit, Karioja, Rye & Shain, 2011). As described in Chapter 2, self-esteem is a good base for children's resiliency to a host of transition challenges; therefore, interventions that target peer relationships might help resiliency via self-esteem.

Peer support also influences children's mental health at transition. Children have lower depression and anxiety after transition if they have higher levels of pre-transition peer support (De Wit et al., 2012; Hirsch & DuBois, 1992). The first authors hypothesise that experiencing peer support in feeder schools provides children with an 'emotional bank account' of memories to draw on to help them overcome transition challenges (Hirsch & DuBois, 1992). Studies that examine reciprocal pathways between peer support and mental health find that mental health has the stronger influence, although the association goes both ways (Hirsch & DuBois, 1992; Newman Kingery et al., 2011). When set in time, this plays out as children with poorer mental health having more difficulty making friends and being accepted by their peer group after transition (Hirsch & DuBois, 1992).

Conclusions

This chapter demonstrates that peer relationships have far-reaching effects on children's wellbeing at transition. Although it is welcome news that children generally perceive an increase in peer support and in social self-concept after transition, this is not true of all children, nor is it the norm in all schools. Therefore it is important to plan for improving peer support when coordinating transition, and to think about how particular school structures help determine how children and their peers get along.

First, the potential increase in bullying at transition can be targeted with fairly simple measures, such as communicating a zero tolerance of bullying policy in assemblies and classrooms, by giving children clear guidelines on who to turn to, and by having older children work as playground monitors who report the first signs of bullying to an authoritative adult. These interventions may be especially important during the first term, when gangs of thugs develop, and when aggressive boys seek to establish their dominance in the social hierarchy. Ideally schools would also provide extra support for children who were bullied at primary school, and aggression management programmes for any child caught bullying that focus on improving children's perspectives of themselves and others.

Second, the tendency of children to form new social hierarchies based on stereotypes and to spend most of their time talking in cliques could be discouraged by helping children engage in extracurricular activities at lunch time. This would also improve life for smaller groups of friends with special interests. Unfortunately, lunchtime is under one hour in most transfer schools (Blatchford & Baines, 2008); therefore it may be more productive to provide sports equipment and alternative places to go, such as an open-access computer laboratory, rather than structured activities per se. The situation can also be improved by involving children in activities that facilitate tolerance of individual differences and social cohesion. In Chapter 13, I describe how one assistant headteacher achieved this through employing a set of transition interventions designed to prevent peer conflict and stereotyping amongst her cohort of mixed social backgrounds. Regardless of what intervention you deliver, any effort to create positive peer relationships at transition will benefit children's psychological wellbeing, thereby improving everyone's chances of a successful transition.

References

Berndt, T. J., & Mekos, D. (1995). Adolescents' perceptions of the stressful and desirable aspects of the transition to junior high school. *Journal of Research on Adolescence, 10,* 141–158.

Berndt, T. J. (1999). Friends' influence on students' adjustment to school. *Educational Psychologist, 34*(1), 15–28.

Blatchford, P., & Baines, E. (2008). *A follow up national survey of breaktimes in primary and secondary schools.* London: University of London/Institute of Education/The Nuffield Foundation.

Blyth, D. A., Simmons, R. G., & Bush, D. M. (1978). The transition into early adolescence: A longitudinal comparison of youth in two educational contexts. *Sociology of Education, 51,* 149–162.

Bokhorst, C., Sumter, S. R., & Westenberg, P. M. (2010). Social support from parents, friends, classmates, and teachers in children aged 9 to 18 years: Who is perceived as most supportive? *Social Development, 19*(2), 417–426.

Burgess, S., Johnston, R., Key, T., Propper, C., & Wilson, D. (2007). *The formation of school peer groups: students' transition from primary to secondary school in England.* Bristol: Centre for Market and Public Organisation/Bristol Institute of Public Affairs, University of Bristol.

Cantin, S., & Boivin, M. (2004). Change and stability in children's social network and self-perceptions during transition from elementary to junior high school. *International Journal of Behavioral Development, 28*(6), 561–570.

Chedzoy, S. M., & Burden, R. L. (2005). Making the move: Assessing student attitudes to primary–secondary transfer. *Research in Education, 74*, 22–35.

Chmielewski, A. K., Dumont, H., & Trautwein, U. (2013). Tracking effects depend on tracking type: an international comparison of students' mathematics self-concept. *American Educational Research Journal, 50*(5), 925–957.

Cotterell, J. L. (1982). Student experiences following entry into secondary school. *Educational Research, 24*(4), 297–302.

Crockett, L. J., Petersen, A. C., Graber, J. A., Schuleners, J. E., & Ebata, A. (1989). School transitions and adjustment during early adolescence. *Journal of Early Adolescence, 9*, 181–210.

De Wit, D. J., Karioja, K., Rye, B. J., & Shain, M. (2011). Perceptions of declining classmate and teacher support following the transition to high school: Potential correlates of increasing student mental health difficulties. *Psychology in the Schools, 48*(6), 556–572.

Delamont, S., & Galton, M. (1986). *Inside the secondary classroom*. London: Routledge & Kegan Paul.

Erikson, E. (1968). *Identity, youth and crisis*. New York: Norton.

Evangelou, M., Taggart, B., Sylva, K., Melhuish, E., Sammons, P., & Siraj-Blatchford, I. (2008). *What makes a successful transition from primary to secondary school?*. London: Department of Education.

Feldlaufer, H., Midgley, C., & Eccles, J. S. (1988). Student, teacher, and observer perceptions of the classroom before and after the transition to junior high school. *Journal of Early Adolescence, 8*(2), 133–156.

Fenzel, M. L. (2000). Prospective study of changes in global self-worth and strain during the transition to middle school. *Journal of Early Adolescence, 20*, 93–116.

Galton, M. (2010). Moving to secondary school: What do students say about the experience? In D. Jindal-Snape (ed.), *Educational transitions: Moving stories from around the world* (pp. 107–124). New York and Abingdon: Routledge.

Galton, M., Hargreaves, L., & Pell, T. (2003). Progress in the middle years of schooling: Continuities and discontinuities at transfer. *Education 3–13, 31*(2), 9–19.

Gillison, F., Standage, M., & Skevington, S. (2008). Changes in quality of life and psychological need satisfaction following the transition to secondary school. *British Journal of Educational Psychology, 78*, 149–162.

Hardy, C. L., Bukowski, W. M., & Sippola, L. K. (2002). Stability and change in peer relationships during the transition to middle-level school. *Journal of Early Adolescence, 22*(2), 117–142.

Hirsch, B. J., & DuBois, D. L. (1992). The relation of peer social support and psychological symptamotology during the transition to junior high school: A two year longitudinal analysis. *American Journal of Community Psychology, 20*(3), 333–347.

ILEA. (1986). *ILEA transfer project*. London: Inner London Education Authority.

Kinney, D. A. (1993). From nerds to normals: The recovery of identity among adolescents from middle school to high school. *Sociology of Education, 66*(1), 21–40.

Kiuru, N., Nurmi, J. E., Aunola, K., & Salmela-Aro, K. (2009). Peer group homogeneity in adolescents' school adjustment varies according to peer group type and gender. *International Journal of Behavioral Development, 33*(1), 65–76.

Kurita, J. A., & Janzen, H. L. (1996). The role of social support in mediating school transition stress. Paper presented at the biennial meeting of the American Psychological Association, August, Toronto, Ontario.

Kvalsund, R. (2000). The transition from primary to secondary level in smaller and larger rural schools in Norway: Comparing differences in context and social meaning. *International Journal of Educational Research*, *33*(4), 401–424.

Lester, L., Cross, D., Shaw, T., & Dooley, J. (2012). Adolescent bully-victims: Social health and the transition to secondary school. *Cambridge Journal of Education*, *42*(2), 213–233.

Lipps, G. (2005). *Making the transition: The impact of moving from elementary to secondary school on adolescents' academic achievement and psychological adjustment.* Analytical Studies Branch Research Series. Ontario: Statistics Canada, Family and Labour Studies Division.

Lucey, H., & Reay, D. (2000). Identities in transition: Anxiety and excitement in the move to secondary school. *Oxford Review of Education*, *26*(2), 191–205.

Malecki, C. K., & Demaray, M. K. (2003). What type of support do they need? Investigating student adjustment as related to emotional, informational, appraisal and instrumental support. *School Psychology Quarterly*, *18*(3), 231–252.

Marsh, H. W., & Parker, J. W. (1984). Determinants of student self-concept: Is it better to be a relatively large fish in a small pond even if you don't learn to swim as well? *Journal of Personality and Social Psychology*, *47*(1), 213–231.

Martínez, R. S., Aricak, O. T., Graves, M. N., Peters-Myszak, J., & Nellis, L. (2011). Changes in perceived social support and socioemotional adjustment across the junior high school transition. *Journal of Youth and Adolescence*, *40*(5), 519–530.

Measor, L., & Woods, P. (1984). *Changing schools.* Milton Keynes: Open University Press.

Nash, R. (1973). *Classrooms observed, the teacher's perception and the student's performance.* London and Boston: Routledge & Kegan Paul.

Newman Kingery, J., & Erdley, C. A. (2007). Peer experience as predictors of adjustment across the middle school transition. *Education and Treatment of Children*, *30*(2), 73–88.

Newman Kingery, J., Erdley, C. A., & Marshall, K. C. (2011). Peer acceptance and friendship as predictors of early adolescents' adjustment across the middle school transition. *Merrill-Palmer Quarterly*, *57*(3), 215–243.

Pellegrini, A. D. (2001). A longitudinal study of heterosexual relationships, aggression, and sexual harassment during the transition from primary school through middle school. *Journal of Applied Developmental Psychology*, *22*(2), 119–133.

Pellegrini, A. D. (2002). Bullying, victimization, and sexual harassment during the transition to middle school. *Educational Psychologist*, *37*(3), 151–163.

Pellegrini, A. D., & Long, J. D. (2002). A longitudinal study of bullying, dominance, and victimization during the transition from primary school through secondary school. *British Journal of Developmental Psychology*, *20*, 259–280.

Pratt, S., & George, R. (2005). Transferring friendship: Girls' and boys' friendships in the transition from primary to secondary school. *Children and Society*, *19*(1), 16–26.

Ryan, A. M. (2001). The peer group as a context for the development of young adolescent motivation and achievement. *Child Development*, *72*(4), 1135–1150.

Schafer, M., Korn, S., Brodbeck, F., Wolke, D., & Schulz, H. (2005). Bullying roles in changing contexts: The stability of victim and bully roles from primary to secondary school. *International Journal of Behavioural Development*, *29*(4), 323–335.

Seidman, E., LaRue, A., Lawrence, A., J., Mitchell, C., & Feinman, J. (1994). The impact of school transitions in early adolescence on the self-system and perceived social context of poor urban youth. *Child Development*, *65*(2), 507–522.

Simmons, R. G., & Blyth, D. A. (1987). *Moving into adolescence: The impact of pubertal change and school context* (Vol. 2). New Brunswick and London: Transaction Publishers.

Spelman, B. J. (1979). *Pupil adaptation to secondary school.* Belfast: Northern Ireland Council for Educational Research.

Symonds, J. E. (2009). *Constructing stage-environment fit: early adolescents' psychological development and their attitudes to school in English middle and secondary school environments.* Doctoral thesis, Faculty of Education, University of Cambridge, UK. Available at: www.dspace.cam.ac.uk/handle/1810/223866

Symonds, J. E., Galton, M., & Hargreaves, L. (2014). Emerging gender differences in times of multiple transitions. In I. Schoon & J. Eccles (eds), *Gender differences in aspirations and attainment* (pp. 101–122). London: Cambridge University Press.

Wargo Aikins, J., Bierman, K. L., & Parker, J. G. (2005). Navigating the transition to junior high school: The influence of pre-transition friendship and self-system characteristics. *Social Development, 14*(1), 42–59.

Waters, S. K., Lester, L., Wenden, E., & Cross, D. (2012). A theoretically grounded exploration of the social and emotional outcomes of transition to secondary school. *Australian Journal of Guidance and Counselling, 22*(2), 190–205.

Weller, S. (2007). Sticking with your mates?' Children's friendship trajectories during the transition from primary to secondary school. *Children and Society, 21,* 339–351.

Weller, S., & Bruegel, I. (2006). *Locality, school and social capital.* Families and Social Capital ESRC Research Group. London: South Bank University.

West, P., Sweeting, H., & Young, R. (2008). Transition matters: Students' experiences of the primary–secondary school transition in the West of Scotland and consequences for well-being and attainment. *Research Papers in Education, 25*(1), 21–50.

Whitehead, J. M. (2003). Masculinity, motivation and academic success: A paradox. *Teacher Research, 38,* 147–160.

Wigfield, A., Eccles, J. S., Mac Iver, D., Reuman, D. A., & Midgley, C. (1991). Transitions during early adolescence: Changes in children's domain-specific self perceptions and general self-esteem. *Developmental Psychology, 27*(4), 552–565.

Chapter 8

Identity and self-esteem

Chapter overview

When people experience a significant life event such as changing schools, it can have a profound effect on how they feel about themselves and who they think they are. This chapter discusses how transition influences change in children's personal and collective identities, with a focus on children's peer relationships, academic confidence, maturity status and career aspirations. It finds that transition acts as a prism by diffracting children's identities (Noyes, 2006) but also as a lens by bringing elements of identity into sharp relief. As children reconfigure their identities across transition, they enter a period of identity instability, which teachers may wish to intervene with in order to assist children develop into positive, productive individuals.

Introduction

When you are asked to introduce yourself to strangers in a meeting, it can be challenging to form a response. You might struggle to choose which aspects of yourself to describe and how to communicate them. It may be easy to lean on parts of your identity that are relevant to that group, such as your career role, skills and interests. Or perhaps the group expects you to disclose your personal history, as in group therapy. In both cases, you have a wide set of identity information to choose from, which illustrates the complexity and scale of identity as it exists in our minds. These cases also illustrate how we can simultaneously have personal identities (i.e. 'all of my career history, values and goals') and collective identities (i.e. 'the bits of my career identity that strengthen my ties to this social group, and my identity as a group member') (Eccles, 2009). Below I describe more about what identity is and how we construct it in everyday life, so that readers can better understand how children's identity changes at school transition.

Our identity is narrated to us by our ego, the salient and agentic 'voice' of our minds (Côté & Levine, 2002). The ego appraises different aspects of our personal history and experience, for example, how well we swam laps today and whether or not we are a good parent, and compiles them into a fluid, on call identity abstraction. It uses self-related information that is stored in the self-concept, including first order experiences (e.g. 'my stomach hurts') and second order abstractions that it also constructs (e.g. 'I am a good horse rider'). We form our identities mainly from our perceptions of our skills, characteristics and competencies (e.g. 'I can ride a bike', 'I am a social person', 'I am good at mathematics'), and personal values and goals (e.g. 'mathematics is important and I want to teach it') (Eccles, 2009). Readers may remember we can only access part of the self-concept at any one time (Markus & Wurf, 1987); therefore, we change our identities piece by piece as we remember, appraise, organise, store and discuss identity-related information. This activity does not occur in a vacuum, for what is happening around us impacts on how identities are expressed and made (Côté & Levine, 2002).

Children who are in the early adolescent developmental period (age 10 to 14) are going through important physical and social changes that influence their identities. Critically, many of them experience a cognitive shift, which enhances their ability to create thought abstractions (Vygotsky, 1931/1998), i.e. 'my mathematics skills' and to hypothesise using these (Piaget, 1972), i.e. 'I am likely to fail this test, as I have few mathematics skills.' Accordingly, children spend more time thinking about, practising and regulating elements of their identity in early adolescence than in late childhood (Erikson, 1968).

This activity occurs in a social world where people expect children to become more independent and progress towards adult goals such as finding a career. However, children (at least, those well supported by the state and their parents in developed countries) have relatively little knowledge of society, perceiving it as 'a larger unit, vague in its outline and yet immediate in its demands' (Erikson, 1968, p. 128). Instead, their peers provide them with a safe haven for identity construction, where they can practise and develop components of their identity in a forum that offers support, guidance, ideas and challenge and is relatively free of adult control. Although age 10- to 14-year-old children begin to favour the company of peers over adults (Simmons, Blyth & McKinney, 1983), adults still play an important role in identity construction by scaffolding how children make sense of identity-related information and by embodying aspects of the person the child would like to be.

The challenges of developing a more adult identity after childhood are interpreted by Erikson as an 'identity crisis' where children reach 'a necessary turning point, a crucial moment, when development must move one way or another, marshaling resources of growth, recovery and further differentiation' (1968, p. 16). This period of rapid change is spurred on by environmental discontinuity at school transition. Children prepare to become 'transfer students' before they move schools, by forming expectations of their new environment and how they will behave in it. Their impressions of themselves change after transition in response to new information regarding teachers and peers, social feedback and their work efforts and difficulties. Also, children strive to become different people in their new schools, in order to fulfil prior expectations and goals about their new social role. In this sense, transition acts as a prism by diffracting children's identities (Noyes, 2006). But these discontinuities also bring existing facets of children's identity into sharp relief, working like a lens that focuses children on self-development. Accordingly, research finds that children's overall impressions of their physical and mental selves develop intensively across the transition period (Petersen & Crockett, 1985, Seidman, LaRue, Lawrence, Mitchell & Feinman, 1994) and that transition elicits an increase in self-consciousness (Jones & Thornburg, 1985).

In the first part of this chapter, I cover what happens to children's social, maturational, academic and career identities as they change schools. There I investigate children's personal and collective identities, following Eccles' distinctions (2009) illustrated in the first paragraph of the introduction. Then, in the second section I explore how changes in children's feelings about their identity (i.e. their self-esteem) influence their psychological wellbeing at transition. I end the chapter by discussing how teachers can capitalise on the shakeup in children's identities to prevent losses in self-esteem and engagement at transition.

Social identity

Social identity at transition has been studied mainly regarding children's social skills and networks with friends and peers. There is little research on how children perceive themselves as part of a social group that includes parents and teachers. Concerning children's *personal* social identities, researchers have surveyed children about how popular and competent they are at making friends. This leaves many areas untouched, such as whether children's specific social skills – for example, evaluating other people's actions, employing empathy and negotiation – develop when they encounter new peers and teachers. More detailed information arises from studies that interview and observe children regarding their *collective* social identities, i.e. how children portray and evaluate identity in groups. Generally, both types of research find that children's social identities intensify after a brief period of interruption in their new schools.

Social competency beliefs

In the mid-1980s, Susan Harter from the University of Denver, Colorado, designed a series of questions about how socially competent children felt in school (Harter, 1982). She asked children to rate the extent to which they found it hard to make friends, had a lot of friends, were popular with others, did things with a lot of kids and wished people liked them. She called this a measure of children's social self-concept. Researchers who use this and similar measures also use the term 'social competency beliefs'. As children age from 7 or 8 years to 15 or 16 years, they generally become more positive about their social competency (Cole, Maxwell, Martin, Peeke, Seroczynski, Tram, et al., 2001). However, there can be a slight stalling in this growth (Cole et al., 2001), or a temporary dip in social competency (Eccles, Wigfield, Flanagan, Miller, Reuman & Yee, 1989; Zanobini & Usai, 2002) immediately after children change schools at age 10–12 years. In comparison, children's social competency beliefs are generally more similar within individual school years, and within types of schools (e.g. primary, secondary school) than they are across a transition point (Cole et al., 2001; Eccles et al., 1989). In other words, children's social competency is diffracted at school transition, but is well on the road to recovery by the end of their first year in the new school (Eccles et al., 1989).

Collective social identity

Children's collective social identities are the distinctive features of a friendship or group of friends, as observed by children in those groups and/or bystanders. As I explored in Chapter 7, transition aged children often label friendship groups according to their most visible features, i.e. the jocks and the trendies (Kinney, 1993) and the emos, chavs and thugs (Symonds, 2009). As new groups of friends form after transition, these labels or 'group identities' play a significant role in determining children's social standing. Pairs or groups of children who hold fewer markers of social status as defined by the values of their year group (such as less evidence of teenage behaviour) are given a lower social ranking by others, and often by themselves (Symonds, 2009). Through homophily, i.e. the process of friends becoming more like each other, these social stereotypes can intensify after transition, when children seek out groups of friends who are similar to them (e.g. Weller & Bruegel, 2006) and display their membership characteristics to others. Appearances play a large role, and are often used by children to communicate their group's adherence to gender-stereotyped norms (e.g. female attractiveness and male strength) or rejection of those norms (e.g. through alternative dress). For example, in my research on transition to secondary school, Stacy and Chloe communicated their group identity by wearing stripy socks and nail varnish, while Brian thought that his group (the thugs) were higher in social standing than other children because they wore 'cool jackets' (Symonds, 2009).

Other types of shared behaviours, including sport and musical preference, also define groups of friends that form after changing schools. In the Changing Key study of children's musical identities at school transition (Symonds, Long & Hargreaves, 2011), children began listening to different music after transition, as they made friends with new musical tastes. Interestingly, many children expected to conform to whatever music was most popular with their new friends: '[I]n the six weeks before I started here, I decided … I should listen to other kinds of music and what my mates like so I can stand it' (Holly, term one). Accordingly, children reported that their musical preferences mirrored those of their friends after transition: 'My favourite singer now has changed … I started going out with my [new] friends and they're listening to her songs and so I started listening to them' (Lily, term two). There was also pressure from the year group as to what music was popular, which in part could define children's social standing: 'Well, it's quite a big thing in secondary school because if you don't, like, know any new [latest release pop] music, you're a bit weird' (Amy, term two). Children expected that musical preference would continue to be a marker of their group identities after the first transition year, as was the case for Joan, who presumed she would like whatever music her friends liked in Year 8: 'Depends what my friends like where I'm moving to' (Joan, Year 7, term three); 'So it's important to blend in' (Jenny); 'Yeah' (Joan).

Maturity identity

Children aged 11 and 12 are experiencing a unique period in their development. They are moving out of childhood, and into the teenage years, when they are expected to take on more adult responsibilities. When thinking about their psychological and physical maturity:'[t]heir status is marginal and varies, depending upon whether they compare themselves to younger children or older adults' (Higgins & Parsons, 1983, p. 26). As discussed in Chapter 1, school transition acts as a status passage that allows children to progress to a higher level of psychosocial maturity (or perceived maturity!) in a short time period. Children play an active role in this process by interpreting changes in environment, such as becoming a secondary school student and leaving younger children behind, as maturity status markers. Accordingly, children often note changes in their personal and collective maturity identities, after they transfer schools.

Maturity status beliefs

In Symonds (2009), children often used the terms 'growing up' and 'grown-up', and compared themselves to younger and older children when talking about maturity status. As Matthew put it, 'I feel a lot more grown-up. I feel that I'm more half adult rather than just a child … just going to secondary school really you tend to feel a lot older and at primary school you feel like a little child and at secondary school you feel like, sort of a teenage person.' As we can see in Matthew's choice of words, he expects the changes he has experienced in maturity status (i.e. 'I feel') to be common to other children after transition (i.e. 'you feel'). Certainly, children gave similar reasons for why they felt more mature after transition, indicating a shared interpretation of maturity status markers in the environment.

Many children, especially boys, used the visible group difference of feeder versus transfer school student to estimate their maturity status. Matthew expressed relief at no longer having 'thousands of young kids underneath you', while Kevin explained that 'you feel more mature because you feel like you've left everyone else behind'. Looking at the older age group, Billy described how being part of a teenage collective made him feel more mature: '[Cause] it's secondary school and there's more older people, I think that as there's older people, I'm more older as well.' In comparison, more girls attributed changes in teaching and learning to an increase in maturity status. As Ruby explained, '[When] you was in primary school, if you fell over and grazed your knee … they'd come rushing to you like they're your mum. But in here they're just like, "get up and go first aid".' Here Ruby used evidence from one teacher's behaviour to support her increased maturity, whereas Stacy felt more mature because of a whole school focus on school leaving examinations" '[When] it comes to big school it's just like [pause] you've got to work harder, and try and get better marks and it's not messing about time any more.'

Collective maturity identities

Children also described enforcing their maturity beliefs on other children, which had the effect of creating a collective maturity identity for those who had just changed schools. As observed on the playground, children's main lunchtime activity was standing around talking in cliques, rather than playing games from primary school, such as jump rope and tag. Children who persisted with these behaviours were branded as immature by others: '[They're] a bit more weirder than the ones who play sports' (Bobby); 'When you say weird, what do you mean?' (Jenny); 'Childish! Well, I think it's childish' (Bobby). This phenomenon has been documented as far back as the early 1970s, although it probably existed long before then. As quoted already in Chapter 7, Angus said, 'I wouldn't go around with him. He plays tig and baggy – throwing haversacks around – that's daft. Just wee ones do that' (Nash, 1973, p. 114).

Several girls also noted a change in verbal conflict, with the name-calling from primary school either being dropped or changing to a more sophisticated form of disagreement between friends and enemies. Below, Ruby discriminates against children who continued with the name calling from primary school: '[They're] in Y7 now, they shouldn't be acting like they're in reception, they should be acting like they're part of grown-ups and they're becoming younger when they do that.' Boys also noted how their age could act for or against them when it came to being harassed by peers: 'I was the youngest in my class and so everyone picked on me for being 11 still. But now I'm 12 everyone is kind of treating me a bit more older than I am' (Charlie). These examples show how peer pressure can create a collective maturity identity after children change schools.

Academic identity

Perhaps the most well-researched component of children's identities at transition is their sense of how capable they are at individual subjects and schoolwork.

This is called academic or scholastic identity by most studies, and is one way of looking at how traditional school curricula can impact children's self-concepts. However, when thinking about this type of identity, we should remind ourselves that our Western notion of scholastic identity might not ring true for all societies (see Markus & Kitayama, 1991), and indeed may not even exist for individual children, other than in their responses to survey questions. Also, children are observed to have collective academic identities, which are expressed when groups of children communicate their compliance to, or rejection of, work expectations in the classroom. Some children employ this latter behaviour in a bid to increase their popularity, and this can have longer-term detrimental effects on their achievement if they seek to put forward a deviant front.

Academic competency beliefs

Children's ratings of how good they are at individual subjects tend to decline as they progress through the primary and secondary school years (Jacobs, Lanza, Osgood, Eccles & Wigfield, 2002; Wigfield & Eccles, 1994). These declines occur as children become more realistic about their skills (Cole et al., 2001) and less enthusiastic about particular subjects (Wigfield & Eccles, 1994). In comparison, their general sense of how clever they are can increase with age (Cole et al., 2001), possibly as they become more expert at sustaining a positive academic identity in order to maintain a healthy self-concept. For both domain-specific and global ability beliefs, two things generally happen at school transition. First, children rate themselves as less competent immediately after changing schools (Cantin & Boivin, 2004; Cole et al., 2001; Jacobs et al., 2002; Wigfield & Eccles, 1994; Zanobini & Usai, 2002). Second, there is a loss of stability in their judgments across the transition period (Cole et al., 2001; Wigfield & Eccles, 1994). These temporary changes in children's competency beliefs occur as they adjust to specific features of the post-transition school environment that I detail below.

- First, *new teachers* give children less evaluative feedback (Galton & Pell, 2002) and may be less capable of accurately judging children's abilities in the first term before getting to know them well. During this period of instability, rather than rely on teacher feedback or grades to construct their academic competency beliefs, children turn to more stable sources of information, such as parental evaluations, before returning to grades as a method of self-assessment in the third term (Gniewosz, Eccles & Noack, 2011).
- Second, a change of *subjects and extracurricular activities* can alter how children see themselves academically. Here, children develop their academic identities by assessing their emotional reactions and successes or failures in these activities. They also evaluate themselves on the basis of whether or not they were selected for a skills-based extracurricular activity such as

sports teams, orchestra or the school musical (Symonds et al., 2011). Also, children can be encouraged to take up new activities or drop old ones such as playing the piano (Sloboda, 2001) at transition, and in turn they work these new skills or loss of old ones into their academic identities.

- Third, after transition many children are placed in *set ability groups* for the first time, which changes the information they use to compare themselves to others by. A study of 20 countries participating in the Programme for International Student Assessment (PISA) found that children who were in high-ability streams for core subjects felt better about themselves, while those in lower-ability streams felt worse. However, children who were streamed for all their subjects felt more positive if they were in a lower stream compared to being in a higher one (Chmielewski, Dumont & Trautwein, 2013). The authors explained that children who were streamed for core subjects could still compare themselves positively to lower achievers who they encountered in mixed ability subjects such as PE. However those who were streamed for all subjects were more likely to feel like a little fish in a big pond (Marsh & Parker, 1984), as these encounters were rarer.

- Fourth, simply being around *new peers* can influence how children construct their academic competency beliefs. Because they are unfamiliar with many of their classmates, children tend to engage more in social comparison after transition (Feldlaufer, Midgley & Eccles, 1988), as described in Chapter 7. This means they are on the lookout for information about their peers' abilities, and may communicate more about their own abilities (or lack of) in class. This academic posturing influences the development of children's collective academic identities, as I discuss below.

Collective academic identities

In the mid-1980s, Linda Measor and Peter Woods followed children transferring into their first year of high school from a middle school in the English Midlands. Focusing mainly on one class of children, they observed that in the first few weeks after transition children were embarrassed to ask for help and conformed for the most part to the teachers' rules. This created an atmosphere of compliance and little student–teacher interaction, which was recognised by the students as being an initial front. By the end of the first month, a group of boys began to break through this front by drawing graffiti on their belongings and configuring their uniform to a punk style. These boys soon began to challenge the teacher as to who was boss in the classroom, a technique dubbed by Benyon (1985), who observed the same thing happening in the first year of an all-boys' school, as 'sussing'. In these ways, the boys marked themselves out as being deviant, i.e. not complying to the adult school culture. Soon, a small group of girls also established themselves as deviant through passive forms of resistance such as ignoring the teachers' instructions.

At this point, only two academic identity groups were apparent, deviant and compliant. Generally, the latter group were more academically capable. Later in the term, Measor and Woods identified a third group of boys, who created a position for themselves between these two groups. Although they were also academic, the boys chose to hide it by joking around and by being occasionally deviant, in order to gain popularity with the deviant crowd. However, they were also able to effectively manage their relationships with teachers by getting down to work when necessary, thereby maintaining their potential to do well in class. Measor and Woods called them the 'knife-edgers', as they balanced themselves between the deviant and compliant identities of their peers.

Although this study was conducted many years ago, with only one class of children, similar academic identity groups appear in other school settings, e.g. Pollard's 'goodies, gangs and jokers' (Pollard, 1981), and in recent eras (Symonds, 2009). This suggests that whatever pressures are operating on children to mark themselves as deviant, compliant or knife-edger are still in play in UK secondary schools after transition. One explanation is that deviant children seek to gain social status in the new Year 7 group, which is often judged using stereotypical male and female characteristics. As discussed in Chapter 7, being a high achiever can be equated with a lack of masculinity (Whitehead, 2003), as physical strength is not necessary for achievement. Also as pointed out by Erikson, who was an expert on adolescent identity formation, '[the] fact that the majority of teachers ... are women ... can lead to a conflict with the non-intellectual boy's masculine identification, as if knowledge was feminine, action masculine' (1968, p. 125). This may be a particular issue for children who encountered mainly female teachers in elementary school, as they may perpetuate this stereotype in their first year post-transition.

Career identity

Although some children may ponder what adult job they will have from mid-childhood, early adolescence marks a new phase in the development of children's career identities. Unlike in childhood, where children are free to dismiss adult responsibilities, adolescence is a period where they are encouraged to form realistic career aspirations. Many children take readily to this challenge, as it allows them to imagine how their industriousness and unique skills can be recognised and rewarded in a future social role (Erikson, 1968). In early adolescence, children are spurred by their interests to think about what job might best match with their skills and values (Ginzberg, Ginzberg, Axelrad & Herma, 1951). However, they are still testing the waters of career possibilities, as they are not well acquainted with the adult world of work and still have much to figure out about their personal qualities (Erikson, 1968). Because of these limits on their knowledge, early adolescents often make career choices based on information that is immediately available to them, such as the job choices of proximal adults, such as teachers, parents or family friends (Marcia, 1989).

However, many realise that their choices do not need to be acted on until much later (Super, 1953), which gives them leeway to explore different career options or not to explore any options at all.

Some people may be sceptical that age 11- or 12-year-old children have an invested interest in choosing a career. However, a study of 610 Year 7 children from across the UK found that over 85 per cent of these children had a fairly concrete idea of what job they wanted in the future and that 65 per cent had held this ambition for two years or more (Atherton, Cymbir, Roberts, Page & Remedios, 2009). As predicted by the occupational theorists, these children had only patchy knowledge of the occupational and higher education structures. Accordingly, they aspired to a very limited set of higher status jobs or simply wanted to 'go to university' in order to improve their future career success. What all of this tells us is that children transferring schools in early adolescence are 'ripe for the picking' in terms of how different environmental stimuli in their new school can influence their career identities.

Between 2010 and 2011, we conducted an in-depth study of children's musical identity as they moved from primary to secondary school in three areas of England (Symonds et al., 2011). Readers may wish to extrapolate what happened in the context of music to other subjects, as unfortunately we are not aware of studies of identity, transition and other areas of the curriculum. Similar to the findings from Atherton and colleagues (2009), children in Changing Key in their last year of feeder school had a restricted range of musical aspirations, with some wanting to be pop singers, rappers, guitarists, drummers, classical musicians and music teachers. Many were lured by ideas of fame and fortune – 'I want to try and sing while I'm playing the guitar. And go *on Britain's Got Talent* and stuff like that' (Alex) – while others aspired to the careers of local adult role models such as their violin teacher.

The move to secondary school inspired children to develop new or existing musical career goals, when they were provided with increased resources for learning music. These resources included better-quality classroom equipment, more extracurricular musical activities, subject specialist teaching and the opportunity to enrol for instrumental lessons provided at school. Still, many children's ambitions were simplistic and evidenced a lack of knowledge about musical career pathways: 'I want to go into singing more and in the future I want to be like a pop singer or something' (Lily, term one); 'And has changing schools made you feel more certain or less certain about that?' (Interviewer); 'More certain ... Because at primary they don't do lessons and singing, but [here] you can pay to have singing lessons' (Lily). Only a few children developed more sophisticated career goals, as they made more realistic evaluations of their skills and opportunities: 'I wanted to be a singer but it was unlikely ... That was my dream job but I needed something that was more likely to happen so something like a journalist' (Holly, term one).

Although there is not much research in the area of career choice and school transition, other studies have also found that 11- and 12-year-old children lack knowledge about employment and educational pathways as they move schools. Children in the east of England reported aspiring to become school teachers, as they did well at these subjects (Symonds, 2009), whilst Scottish children chose jobs based on what they saw most adults doing in their local communities (Nash, 1973). Unlike research carried out in the 1970s (Measor & Woods, 1984), modern studies find that both girls and boys aspire to have a career after finishing school. However, these career choices can be gender stereotyped, such as girls wanting to become beauticians and boys accountants (Symonds, 2009). What this research tells us is that 11- and 12-year-old children would benefit from receiving more careers information, advice and guidance, as their career aspirations, however tentative these are, motivate their choice of subjects for their end of school examinations (Atherton et al., 2009) and moderate their attitudes towards particular subjects in the first year at transfer school (Measor & Woods, 1984; Symonds, Galton & Hargreaves, 2014).

Self-esteem

As discussed in Chapter 2, self-esteem is our emotional evaluation of the self-concept. To this regard it is also our feelings about identity, such as whether we are a good or worthless person in one or all domains. Studies of self-esteem at transition survey children using one of two measures: the Rosenberg Self-Esteem Scale (Rosenberg, 1965) and the self-worth subscale of Harter's Self-Perception Profile for Children (Harter, 1985). Both measures ask children to give an overall evaluation of themselves by rating a series of statements, for example, 'I am happy the way I am' (Harter) and 'on the whole, I am satisfied with myself' (Rosenberg).

When we compare studies of children's self-esteem at transition, there appears to be no consensus as to whether children's self-esteem improves or gets worse as a function of school transition. Studies that map how average scores for self-esteem develop have found steady patterns of increase (Barber & Olsen, 2004; Fenzel, 2000; Hirsch & Rapkin, 1987; Newman Kingery, Erdley & Marshall, 2011; Nottlemann, 1987; Proctor & Choi, 1994; Simmons et al., 1979) and decrease (Cantin & Boivin, 2004; Eccles, Wigfield, Flanagan, et al., 1989; Seidman et al., 1994; Wigfield & Eccles, 1994) between the pre- and post-transition year. Readers with a healthy scepticism may wonder whether these differences are related to variation in children's characteristics, school environment and the era and country of study. However, there is no clear pattern to indicate why self-esteem increases for some samples and declines for others (Symonds & Galton, 2014).

A different way to look at self-esteem at transition is to consider the range of developmental patterns that might crop up within a single study, rather than considering all children in that study as one average group. Certainly this method is more in tune with people's individuality and has more useful implications for schools. For example, we can do more with the knowledge that

Sam and Susie both felt less confident after transition, while Jane, Jim and Jasmine had no change in how they felt about themselves, than we can with the knowledge that a group of five children had stable self-esteem on average. In studies of over 1,000 children, researchers have found that self-esteem remains stable for the majority of children, but increases or declines (with different 'end' points that can include recovery) for significant minorities across transition (Eccles, Lord, Roeser, Barber & Hernandez Josefowicz, 1997; Seidman & French, 2004). These findings indicate that the lack of consensus amongst studies of children's average self-esteem development may be caused by minority groups of children within those studies tipping the scales in one direction or another (Symonds, Galton & Hargreaves, 2014).

It is not only useful to know that large groups of children have different patterns of self-esteem development after transition; it is also valuable to understand that each pattern has longer-term implications for children's psychological wellbeing and achievement. In Michigan, psychologist Jacquelynne Eccles and her colleagues followed children from Grade 6 in elementary school, across transition to middle school in Grade 7, to the end of high school at Grade 12. They found that, before transition, self-esteem was reasonably similar across children but that after transition it followed one of three patterns: decline (28 per cent of children), increase (44 per cent) or stable (28 per cent). Children whose self-esteem declined between Grades 6 and 7 had greater anxiety about schoolwork, self-consciousness, depressive symptoms, victimisation, substance use, school disengagement and truancy than other groups. By the end of high school, those with declining self-esteem were less likely than others to graduate. In comparison, children whose self-esteem increased were more likely by the end of high school to report alcohol and substance use, especially if they were low achievers. A similar study of children in New York state also found that those whose self-esteem declined after transition had greater depressive symptoms than other children, several years after transition (Seidman & French, 2004). Although these findings may be distressing, they also indicate that we can identify children with declining self-esteem at least by the end of their first year in a new school; therefore we should be able to intervene in order to prevent further decline and associated negative outcomes.

At this point, you might be wondering why self-esteem declines for some children but increases for others. Although the answer to this is rooted in individual children's experiences and psychology, there are common factors that appear to contribute to changes in self-esteem after transition. First, children who perceive a lack of emotional support from new teachers also tend to have declining self-esteem (Barber & Olsen, 2004; De Wit, Karioja, Rye & Shain, 2011). Second, children's self-esteem is likely to decline if they experience hassles with peers (Fenzel, 2000), such as bullying (Evangelou, Taggart, Sylva, Melhuish, Sammons & Siraj-Blatchford, 2008), in their new schools. These relational factors of teacher support and peer conflict are more powerful in predicting self-esteem change than other features of school environment, including school rules, teacher monitoring, freedom in lessons (Barber & Olsen, 2004) and hassles with schoolwork (Fenzel, 2000). Children are also more likely to have declining self-esteem if they simultaneously experience other life transitions while changing schools (such as dating, moving home and puberty) (Simmons, Burgeson, Carlton-Ford & Blyth, 1987) or have changed schools many times in the past (Jones & Thornburg, 1985).

Perhaps the most intriguing feature of self-esteem decline after transition is that it occurs more readily for girls. Classic US school transition research first uncovered this pattern in the mid-1970s by comparing the self-esteem development of girls and boys who either transferred from elementary to middle school at age 11 or 12 or remained in a K–8 system (i.e. primary school). Here, researchers found that more girls who changed schools had declining self-esteem (56 per cent), compared to boys who transferred (35 per cent) and girls (40 per cent) and boys (39 per cent) who didn't transfer schools (Simmons & Blyth, 1987). Similarly, my study of children in the English Midlands found that a greater percentage of girls had declining self-esteem across Year 7 if they had recently transferred schools (39 per cent), compared to boys who had recently transferred (34 per cent), and girls (13 per cent) and boys (31 per cent) in their third year of middle school (Symonds, Hargreaves & Galton, 2014). Other studies have found similar discrepancies between genders, with girls having lower self-esteem in general after transition (Nottelmann, 1987, Wigfield & Eccles, 1994) and steeper declines in self-esteem than boys (Cantin & Boivin, 2004; Symonds et al., 2014; Zoller Booth, Chase Sheehan, & Earley, 2007).

As discussed in Chapter 3, girls are more likely to have negative emotional responses to disruption in their environment, due to biological differences in the HPA axis (aka the stress response system). Also, girls can be more concerned about their physical appearance than boys after transition (Symonds, 2009), which appears to predict their self-esteem more strongly than it does for boys (Lord, Eccles & McCarthy, 1994). In particular, early-maturing girls are vulnerable to self-esteem loss, given that they are more likely to have declining body image than on-time or late developers (Petersen & Crockett, 1985). Accordingly, Simmons and colleagues found that the worst declines in self-esteem across transition occurred for girls who hit puberty earlier than their peers and experienced multiple stressful changes in their environment (Simmons et al., 1979).

Conclusions

School transition provides children with fertile soil for identity development. So far, research has documented significant changes in children's social, academic and career identities and perceptions of their maturity status. Transition also appears to catalyse whether children grow into more positive or negative versions of their past selves in these domains. Through self-enhancement, children struggle to maintain their self-esteem through all of these identity changes at transition. For some children, this may involve constructing identities that are at odds with the purpose of schooling, in order to ascertain social standing with their peers. Generally, children have a harder time maintaining their self-esteem when their teachers are not emotionally supportive and when they encounter conflict with peers. In particular, girls are vulnerable to self-esteem loss, especially if they experience puberty earlier than others in their year group. These changes in identity and self-esteem indicate that school transition is a window of opportunity for educators and psychologists to intervene in facilitating the development of children's psychological wellbeing.

This may involve identifying children who are at risk for negative changes in identity and self-esteem loss, and providing them with targeted support. This chapter gives clues as to who these children might be (i.e. early-maturing girls, boys who present a deviant academic front and children who are bullied). It also outlines how specific features of secondary school environments influence how children develop their identities in different domains. Of particular relevance to academic identities are classroom resources, extracurricular activities, new subjects, different-ability peers and ability streaming. Introduction to new subjects, teachers and peers can also impact their career identities. In comparison, children's social identities are constructed more from interaction with peers at lunchtime, and are tied to the development of social hierarchy within the new peer cohort. Unfortunately, in many schools these hierarchies are based on gender stereotypes such as toughness for boys and attractiveness for girls, perhaps relating to children's desire to grow up quickly after transition, as demonstrated by their perceptions on maturity status. It may be harder to change these school structures and peer cultures than it is to target vulnerable children after transition. However, teachers who are able to intervene in these areas may find a larger payoff, as when children's identities and self-esteem are better supported at transition they have a greater chance of experiencing psychological wellbeing throughout secondary schooling (Eccles et al., 1997).

References

Atherton, G., Cymbir, E., Roberts, K., Page, L., & Remedios, R. (2009). *How young people formulate their views about the future: Exploratory research*. London: Department for Children, Schools and Families, Research Report DCSF-RR152.

Barber, B. K., & Olsen, J. A. (2004). Assessing the transitions to middle and high school. *Journal of Adolescent Research, 19*(1), 3–30.

Benyon, J. (1985). *Initial encounters in the secondary school: Sussing, typing and coding*. Lewes: Falmer Press.

Cantin, S., & Boivin, M. (2004). Change and stability in children's social network and self-perceptions during transition from elementary to junior high school. *International Journal of Behavioral Development, 28*(6), 561–570.

Chmielewski, A. K., Dumont, H., & Trautwein, U. (2013). Tracking effects depend on tracking type: An international comparison of students' mathematics self-concept. *American Educational Research Journal, 50*(5), 925–957.

Cole, D. A., Maxwell, S. E., Martin, J. M., Peeke, L., G., Seroczynski, A. D., Tram, J. M., et al. (2001). The development of multiple domains of child and adolescent self-concept: A cohort sequential longitudinal design. *Child Development, 72*(6), 1723–1746.

Côté, J. E., & Levine, C. G. (2002). *Identity formation, agency and culture: A social psychological perspective*. Malwah, NJ: Lawrence Erlbaum.

De Wit, D. J., Karioja, K., Rye, B. J., & Shain, M. (2011). Perceptions of declining classmate and teacher support following the transition to high school: Potential correlates of increasing student mental health difficulties. *Psychology in the Schools, 48*(6), 556–572.

Eccles, J. (2009). Who am I and what am I going to do with my life? Personal and collective identities as motivators of action. *Educational Psychologist, 44*(2), 78–89.

Eccles, J. S., Lord, S. E., Roeser, R. W., Barber, B. L., & Hernandez Jozefowicz, D. M. (1997). The association of school transitions in early adolescence with developmental trajectories through high school. In J. Schulenberg, J. I. Maggs & K. Hurrelmann (eds), *Health risks and developmental transitions during adolescence* (pp. 283–321). New York: Cambridge University Press.

Eccles, J. S., Wigfield, A., Flanagan, C. A., Miller, C., Reuman, D. A., & Yee, D. (1989). Self-concepts, domain values, and self-esteem: Relations and changes at early adolescence. *Journal of Personality, 57*(2), 283–310.

Erikson, E. (1968). *Identity, youth and crisis*. New York: Norton.

Evangelou, M., Taggart, B., Sylva, K., Melhuish, E., Sammons, P., & Siraj-Blatchford, I. (2008). *What makes a successful transition from primary to secondary school?* London: Department of Education.

Feldlaufer, H., Midgley, C., & Eccles, J. S. (1988). Student, teacher, and observer perceptions of the classroom before and after the transition to junior high school. *Journal of Early Adolescence, 8*(2), 133–156.

Fenzel, M. L. (2000). Prospective study of changes in global self-worth and strain during the transition to middle school. *Journal of Early Adolescence, 20*, 93–116.

Galton, M., & Pell, T. (2002). Teaching in the transfer schools. In L. Hargreaves & M. Galton (eds), *Transfer from the primary classroom, 20 years on* (ed. University of Cambridge, pp. 97–130). London and New York: RoutledgeFalmer.

Ginzberg, E., Ginzberg, S. W., Axelrad, S., & Herma, J. L. (1951). *Occupational Choice: An approach to a general theory*. New York: Columbia University Press.

Gniewosz, B., Eccles, J., & Noack, P. (2011). Secondary school transition and the use of different sources of information for the construction of the academic self-concept. *Social Development, 21*(3), 537–557.

Harter, S. (1982). The perceived competence scale for children. *Child Development, 53*(1), 87–97.

Harter, S. (1985). The Self-Perception Profile for Children. Unpublished manuscript, University of Denver, CO.

Higgins, E. T., & Eccles Parsons, J. (1983). Social cognition and the social life of the child: Stages as subcultures. In E. T. Higgins, D. N. Ruble & W. W. Hartup (eds), *Social cognition and social development* (pp. 15–62). Cambridge: Cambridge University Press.

Hirsch, B. J., & Rapkin, B. D. (1987). The transition to junior high school: A longitudinal study of self-esteem, psychological symptomatology, school life, and social support. *Child Development, 58*, 1235–1243.

Jacobs, J. E., Lanza, S., Osgood, W. D., Eccles, J. S., & Wigfield, A. (2002). Changes in children's self-competence and values: Gender and domain differences across grades one through twelve. *Child Development, 73*(2), 509–527.

Jones, R. M., & Thornburg, H. D. (1985). The experience of school-transfer: Does previous relocation facilitate the transition from elementary- to middle-level educational environments? *Journal of Early Adolescence, 5*(2), 229–237.

Kinney, D. A. (1993). From nerds to normals: The recovery of identity among adolescents from middle school to high school. *Sociology of Education, 66*(1), 21–40.

Lord, S., E., Eccles, J. S., & McCarthy, K. A. (1994). Surviving the junior high school transition: Family processes and self perceptions as protective and risk factors. *Journal of Early Adolescence, 14*(2), 162–199.

Marcia, J. E. (1989). Identity and intervention. *Journal of Adolescence, 12*, 401–410.

Markus, H. R., & Kitayama, S. (1991). Culture and the self: Implications for cognition, emotion, and motivation. *Psychological Review, 98*(2), 224–253.

Markus, H., & Wurf, E. (1987). The dynamic self-concept: A social psychological perspective. *Annual Review of Psychology, 38*, 299–337.

Marsh, H. W., & Parker, J. W. (1984). Determinants of student self-concept: Is it better to be a relatively large fish in a small pond even if you don't learn to swim as well? *Journal of Personality and Social Psychology, 47*(1), 213–231.

Measor, L., & Woods, P. (1984). *Changing schools.* Milton Keynes: Open University Press.

Nash, R. (1973). *Classrooms observed, the teacher's perception and the student's performance.* London and Boston: Routledge & Kegan Paul.

Newman Kingery, J., Erdley, C. A., & Marshall, K. C. (2011). Peer acceptance and friendship as predictors of early adolescents' adjustment across the middle school transition. *Merrill-Palmer Quarterly, 57*(3), 215–243.

Nottelmann, E. D. (1987). Competence and self-esteem during transition from childhood to adolescence. *Developmental Psychology, 23*(3), 441–450.

Noyes, A. (2006). School transfer and the diffraction of learning trajectories. *Research Papers in Education, 21*(1), 43–62.

Petersen, A. C., & Crockett, L. J. (1985). Pubertal timing and grade effects on adjustment. *Journal of Youth and Adolescence, 14*, 191–206.

Piaget, J. (1972). *The principles of genetic epistemology.* London: Routledge & Kegan Paul.

Pollard, A. (1981). *Coping with deviance.* Sheffield: University of Sheffield.

Proctor, T., & Choi, H. S. (1994). Effects of transition from elementary school to junior high school on early adolescents' self-esteem and perceived competence. *Psychology in the Schools, 31*, 319–327.

Rosenberg, M. (1965). *Society and the adolescent self-image.* Princeton, NJ: Princeton University Press.

Seidman, E., & French, S. E. (2004). Developmental trajectories and ecological transitions: A two-step procedure to aid in the choice of prevention and promotion interventions. *Development and Psychopathology, 16*(4), 1141–1159.

Seidman, E., LaRue, A., Lawrence, A., J., Mitchell, C., & Feinman, J. (1994). The impact of school transitions in early adolescence on the self-system and perceived social context of poor urban youth. *Child Development, 65*(2), 507–522.

Simmons, R., G., Blyth, D., A., & McKinney, K. L. (1983). The social and psychological effects of puberty. In J. Brooks-Gunn & A. C. Petersen (eds), *Girls at puberty, biological and psychosocial perspectives* (pp. 229–272). New York & London: Plenum Press.

Simmons, R., G., Blyth, D., A., Van Cleave, E. F., & Bush, D. M. (1979). Entry into early adolescence: The impact of school structure, puberty, and early dating on self-esteem. *American Sociological Review*, *44*, 948–967.

Simmons, Burgeson, Carlton-Ford, & Blyth, D. A. (1987). The impact of cumulative change in early adolescence. *Child Development*, *58*(5), 1220–1234.

Simmons, R., G., & Blyth, D., A. (1987). *Moving into adolescence: The impact of pubertal change and school context* (Vol. 2). New Brunswick and London: Transaction Publishers.

Sloboda, J. (2001). Emotion, functionality, and the everyday experience of music: Where does music education fit? *Music Education Research*, *3*(2), 243–254.

Super, D. (1953). A theory of vocational development. *American Psychologist*, *8*(5), 185–190.

Symonds, J. E. (2009). Constructing stage-environment fit: Early adolescents' psychological development and their attitudes to school in English middle and secondary school environments. Doctoral thesis, Faculty of Education, University of Cambridge. Available at: www.dspace.cam.ac.uk/handle/1810/223866

Symonds, J. E., & Galton, M. (2014). Moving to the next school at age 10–14 years: An international review of psychological development at school transition. *Review of Education*, *2*, 1–27.

Symonds, J. E., Galton, M., & Hargreaves, L. (2014). Emerging gender differences in times of multiple transitions. In I. Schoon & J. Eccles (eds), *Gender differences in aspirations and attainment* (pp. 101–122). London: Cambridge University Press.

Symonds, J. E., Long, M., & Hargreaves, J. (2011). *Changing Key: Adolescents' views on their musical development across the primary to secondary school transition*. London: Paul Hamlyn Foundation. Available at: www.phf.org.uk/page.asp?id=1591

Vygotsky, L. S. (1931/1998). Development of thinking and formation of concepts in the adolescent. In R. W. Reiber (ed.), *The collected works of L. S. Vygotsky* (Vol. 5, pp. 29–82). New York: Plenum.

Weller, S., & Bruegel, I. (2006). *Locality, school and social capital*. Families and Social Capital ESRC Research Group. London: South Bank University.

Whitehead, J. M. (2003). Masculinity, motivation and academic success: A paradox. *Teacher Research*, *38*, 147–160.

Wigfield, A., & Eccles, J., S. (1994). Children's competence beliefs, achievement values, and general self-esteem: change across elementary and middle school. *Journal of Early Adolescence*, *14*(2), 107–138.

Zanobini, M., & Usai, C. (2002). Domain specific self-concept and achievement motivation in the transition from primary to low middle school. *Educational Psychology*, *22*(2), 203–217.

Zoller Booth, M., Chase Sheehan, H., & Earley, M. A. (2007). Middle grades' school models and their impact on early adolescent self-esteem. *Middle Grades Research Journal*, *2*(1), 73–97.

Chapter 9

Motivation, engagement and achievement

Chapter overview

Children's personal achievement is an outcome of their participation in learning and motivation to learn, which are connected to their feelings about school. This chapter covers each area, beginning with an examination of children's intrinsic motivation. Next, children's feelings about school and learning behaviours are overviewed using engagement theory. Finally, changes in achievement at transition are discussed. In all areas, after they change schools, children appear to suffer losses that can be related to transfer school environments. I discuss these relationships in order to relay why school transitions in early adolescence create academic risk.

Introduction

In the early 1980s, US psychologist Jacquelynne Eccles and colleagues set out to discover whether children's achievement motivation developed in response to the differences in school environment they encountered as they progressed through school. In a review of 23 studies, Eccles concluded that children's confidence and achievement declined across the school years, with a pronounced dip after transition to junior high school (Eccles, Midgley & Adler, 1984). The authors hypothesised that these declines were caused by a *developmental mismatch* between children's age-related needs and the features of school environment that changed over time. They called this theory *stage-environment fit* (Eccles & Midgley, 1989).

While she was writing the review, Eccles carried out a large scale empirical study of children's academic attitudes at school transition. These were mainly white children from low- to middle-income communities in Michigan, who moved from a single classroom teacher in the last year of elementary school (age 12), to subject specialist teachers in a larger middle school (age 13). The results published over the next decade revealed that children's needs for autonomy and social support from teachers were not being met in the transfer schools (e.g. Eccles, Wigfield, Midgley, Reuman, Mac Iver & Feldlaufer, 1993) and that these mismatches were accompanied by declining motivation and attitudes towards mathematics (Mac Iver, Klingel & Reuman, 1986). They also found that when classroom conditions improved after transition (e.g. when children moved to teachers who were more confident about teaching), children's attitudes improved (Midgley, Feldlaufer & Eccles, 1989).

This chapter takes stage-environment fit theory as a starting point for understanding changes in children's academic behaviour at school transition. It is underpinned by the idea that moving schools alters the conditions in which children seek to fulfil their needs for identity, self-esteem, autonomy, competence and social support, which in turn influences their motivation, engagement and achievement (Symonds & Galton, 2014). However, few studies make these connections explicit. More often they simply track changes in academic behaviour across transition. As a guide for educators, this chapter reviews the theory behind each area (e.g. what is motivation?) before summarising the relevant research at transition. It gives a good international overview of how motivation, engagement and achievement have developed and, where possible, refers to the features of feeder and transfer schools that were linked to these psychological changes.

Motivation

A good starting point for thinking about children's attitudes to learning is to consider *why* they want to learn. This is termed 'motivation', which in long hand is the '*energizing* properties that characterize various aspects of the self-system' (Roeser & Peck, 2009, p. 121) and in short hand is the answer for 'why does anyone do anything?' (Eccles & Wang, 2012, p. 142). Although there are countless elements to motivation, each with a special relationship to school achievement outcomes (Eccles & Wang, 2012), for decades psychologists have fixated on whether children are motivated more by the intrinsic value of mastering tasks and subject knowledge, or by their desire to perform according to external goals and standards (Ames, 1992). This mastery/performance distinction forms the basis of much motivational research.

Researchers have noted a link between mastery/performance motivations and the type of strategies that children use when they are learning. For example, children who strive towards mastery goals tend to use deep-processing strategies such as linking information, whereas those motivated by performance goals use surface-level strategies such as rehearsing subject content (Anderman & Patrick, 2012). Currently there is some debate about which motivational approach best predicts achievement, as many studies find that children do better at school when they strive to meet an external standard, rather than engage in learning for learning's sake (Anderman & Patrick, 2012). However, these studies looked at the effects of motivational approach on academic grades, whereas there may be stronger connections between mastery motivation and other types of achievements, such as contextual understanding and cross-referencing ability between subjects.

Internationally, researchers find that mastery motivation declines and performance motivation increases after children change to secondary school or the equivalent at age 11–12 years. The most in-depth study comes from Carol Midgley, a US psychologist. Midgley drew on work by Carol Ames, an educational psychologist working at the University of Illinois who wrote extensively about how teaching practices can influence different motivational styles (e.g. Ames, 1992). Ames advised that teachers should be able to promote mastery motivation in class by engaging children in tasks that were novel, varied, relevant and that offered opportunities for autonomy. She rationalised that children would focus less on performance if tasks could be completed through specific, short-term goals. Performance orientation would also decrease, she felt, if teachers stressed effort as much as ability and kept evaluations private. However, as Midgley recognised, Ames' recommended techniques for promoting mastery motivation were at odds with typical middle school pedagogy.

In her prior work with Eccles, Midgley discovered that teachers in middle schools wished to control children more and gave children fewer opportunities for decision making (Midgley, Feldlaufer & Eccles, 1988). She figured that these restrictions on children's autonomy would decrease the opportunity for them to independently master tasks. Also in her experience, middle schools promoted performance motivation by focusing more on relative ability than on effort in their grading practices, by streaming children and by giving special privileges to high achievers. In the early 1990s, Midgley studied students as they moved from 21 elementary schools to 10 middle schools in Michigan. In those schools, both teachers and students observed that performance goals were stressed more and mastery goals less, after transition (Midgley, Anderman & Hicks, 1995). In elementary school, teachers more often encouraged children to achieve for personal improvement, while middle school teachers talked about the benefits of getting good grades. Accordingly, middle school students were more concerned about doing better than other students, while elementary school students were more concerned with understanding lesson content.

Similar differences in motivational approach at transition are found in Europe, where 9-year-old children transferring into five Italian middle schools reported decreases in mastery motivation across a one-year period (Zanobini & Usai, 2002). Also in the UK, researchers found a decline in mastery motivation and an increase in learned helplessness (i.e. using the excuse of not being capable enough) at transition from primary to secondary school in the early 1990s (Rogers, Galloway, Armstrong, Jackson & Leo, 1994). Although there is no research on performance goals at transition in the UK, the ORACLE studies of children's classroom learning behaviours set in the 1970s (Galton & Wilcocks, 1983) and 1990s (Hargreaves & Galton, 2002) found that children put more effort into their schoolwork immediately after transition. This may reflect a similar scenario to the US, where children are encouraged by transfer teachers to focus on getting good grades. In Galton, Hargreaves and Pell (2003), children explained that this tied to them getting a better job when they were older.

School engagement

An area that crosses over with motivation is school engagement. 'Engagement' is a term that is used very broadly in the public forum. However, as Eccles and Wang (2012, p. 141) pointed out, 'to inspire policy makers and educational pundits, one needs sexy and overgeneralised core constructs. But to design effective interventions and move our theoretical understanding forward, we need to be much more specific.' To give some idea of how complicated engagement truly is, I refer readers to the *Handbook of Research on Student Engagement*, where Eccles and Wang made this comment. The book is 840 pages long and contains 39 chapters by researchers from locations as diverse as New Zealand and Germany. A large proportion of the book debates what engagement is, how it relates to motivation and how it can be studied. In general, there is very little consensus on what engagement actually is.

In the handbook, many researchers simplified matters by taking the perspective of Jennifer Fredricks and colleagues (Fredricks, Blumenfeld & Paris, 2004) that there are three types of engagement: emotional, cognitive and behavioural. The last two types cross over in a fourth type of engagement referred to as 'flow', which is a person's experience of being optimally engaged in the moment (Csikszentmihalyi, 1990). However, this has not yet been studied in the context of early adolescent school transition. Therefore, I use Fredricks et al.'s categories in this chapter. In their definition, emotional engagement is children's feelings about school; cognitive engagement is their application of cognitive regulation and learning strategies to a task; and behavioural engagement is their general participation in school and school activities. As readers will note, the last two types of engagement refer to activity as it is carried out in the moment, whereas the first comprises children's longer-standing mental states (i.e. attitudes) that are activated only in certain contexts.

The relationships between the three types of engagement and motivation are not clear-cut. In one perspective, being motivated to do well and enjoying school may energise cognitive and behavioural activity. However this pattern can be reversed. Children who concentrate and participate more may have greater opportunities to enjoy school and receive encouragement for their ambitions. Another point is that engagement types and motivation can be independent of each other. A simple way of putting this is that *some* feelings about school can motivate behaviour, but not *all* feelings necessarily do so. In a study of Year 7 children, I found that around a quarter valued school for their future career but disliked their overall school experience (Symonds & Hargreaves, 2014).

Finally, readers should note that researchers more often ask children to give retrospective accounts of their feelings, cognitive efforts and participation, rather than study these as they occur in the moment, like when doing a task in English. This presents a paradox, as this method turns the activity types of engagement (cognitive, behavioural) into memory schema that may in turn be influenced by children's attitudes. Researchers have done this because it is more difficult to assess children's emotions and cognitions during work activities than to gather their perceptions using a survey. Luckily, Galton and colleagues have conducted some high-quality observational research of 'in the moment action' that I review in the following sections.

Emotional engagement

Emotional engagement refers to children's emotional attitudes towards schooling. These attitudes assess school on the basis of emotion, such as whether children like or are frustrated by school (Symonds & Hargreaves, in press). Children's immediate emotional reactions to schooling, e.g. happiness and boredom, are better referred to as academic emotions (Pekrun & Linnenbrink-Garcia, 2013), as they are first order experiences that are later turned into these more ingrained attitudinal states. For example, a child might develop a negative attitude towards school if they feel constantly afraid of their peers. Although feelings towards schooling are often thought of as part of children's school motivation (e.g. Eccles, Adler, Futterman et al., 1983), children can feel positive towards schooling but put very little effort into it (Symonds & Hargreaves, 2014). This presents a need for studies that separate out the different criteria that children judge their school experiences by (e.g. liking, pride, value, interest) if they are to be of any use for understanding how children react to changes in school environment. Even in the field of emotional engagement, most studies have combined a range of children's feelings into an overarching emotional tone that changes at transition, as I explore below.

The general pattern across studies is that children's emotional engagement declines after school transition. In Leicestershire, children in the ORACLE and ORACLE replication studies felt less happy at school and enjoyed school less in the year after transition, with a sharp drop in attitudes occurring in the first transfer school term (Croll, 1983; Galton et al., 2002). This may have been part of a longer-term developmental pattern, for in the US researchers found that children's emotional engagement steadily declined across elementary school and middle school (Grades 5 to 8) (Li & Lerner, 2011), and across middle and high school (Grades 7 to 11) (Wang & Eccles, 2011), but suggests that something about changing schools precipitates a steeper decline.

These declines are also apparent if we look at children's attitudes towards individual subjects. In Leicestershire, UK (Galton, Gray, Rudduck, Berry, Demetriou & Edwards, 2003), and in Michigan, US (Wigfield & Eccles, 1994), children's attitudes towards mathematics dipped sharply after transition, then declined more slowly across the transfer year. In Michigan, children also reported a dip in liking English immediately after changing schools. However, in Leicestershire, children liked English more in their first term after transition, before becoming less enthusiastic. A similar pattern was noted for their attitudes to science, which were stable across transition but then declined rapidly by the end of the post-transition year. By comparing the end points of children's attitudes in both studies, through a new analysis that standardised the measures (Gray, Galton, McLaughlin, Clarke & Symonds, 2011), Galton and I found that having this 'honeymoon period' (Hargreaves, 1984) stalled the decline of children's attitudes so that, by the end of the first transfer year, they were less low in Leicestershire than they were in Michigan. So anything you can do in your school to prop up children's attitudes, even if this is only temporary, might have a positive effect on how their emotional engagement develops in the longer term.

There are few studies that connect these changes to specific features of feeder and transfer schools. In Symonds & Hargreaves (2014) we attempted this by systematically analysing children's statements about how they felt (e.g. 'I like school') in relation to their rationales for these attitudes (e.g. 'when my friends are not falling out with each other'). We found that 11- and 12-year-old children enjoyed school when they had positive relationships with teachers and peers, and lessons that were fun, relevant and gave them adequate opportunities for autonomy, reward and challenge. Conversely, they disliked school when they experienced conflict with teachers and peers, and when lessons were boring, irrelevant to their identities and made them feel incompetent. These feelings were the same for children regardless of whether they had experienced a school transition. Similar findings come from a study of around 3,000 15-year-olds across England (Gorard & Huat See, 2010), suggesting that these are widespread conditions for school enjoyment. However, children in our study who were in their first year of a transfer school also connected their feelings about school to a loss of emotional support from teachers and an increased focus on their personal identities and maturity status, revealing how their transition through the status passage and experience of teachers in transfer schools moderated their attitudes.

Cognitive engagement

The mental strategies that children use to engage in a task are referred to as cognitive engagement. These include learning strategies (e.g. rehearsal and summarising), controlling effort (e.g. persisting, avoiding distraction) and monitoring and evaluating progress (Fredricks et al., 2004; Markus & Wurf, 1987). Although not specifically a study of transition, research across the transition period with children in Washington, DC found they reported less cognitive engagement (how often they created links between information, made decisions on learning, and planned and checked their homework) as they moved through middle and high school (Wang & Eccles, 2011). However in the ORACLE replication study in Leicestershire, trained observers found that children paid more attention in class after transition than they did beforehand (Hargreaves & Pell, 2002). And, the percentage of children who were off task in lessons reduced from 23 per cent to 18 per cent. There, more boys moved into patterns of off-task behaviour than girls, while more girls switched to become concentrated workers. Possibly the different methods of these studies might explain their divergent outcomes, for children's retrospective accounts of their cognition might not match up to their behaviour in the moment. And, differences in educational context or cohort might have added to these variants.

There are many changes in school environment at transition that might influence children's cognitive engagement. First, children have reported an increased focus on achievement at secondary school (Symonds, 2009). As discussed earlier, if there is a shift towards performance motivation, possibly children might feel more under pressure to achieve in their new schools. Following a model of work-related stress (Demerouti, Bakker, Nachreiner & Schaufell, 2001), this may encourage children to engage more in work if they feel they are up to the challenge, but may cause others to disengage if they feel emotionally overwhelmed and under-supported. Second, as discussed in Chapter 6, some teachers begin the school year by offering basic tuition (i.e. starting from scratch) in order to enable children with less experience to catch up. This appears to work well for engaging less experienced children, but can frustrate more independent and advanced learners. Third, another type of intervention is when children are involved in learning skills programmes in the first year of transfer school (e.g. James, McCormick, Black, Carmichael, Drummond, Fox, et al., 2007). Children across the UK reported that these programmes made a positive difference to their learning, but some lacked the language for discussing learning skills and felt lost when required to conduct independent research (Deakin Crick, Jelfs, Symonds, Ren, Patton & Grushka, 2010).

Behavioural engagement

Behavioural engagement 'draws on the idea of participation; it includes involvement in academic and social or extracurricular activities and is considered crucial for achieving positive academic outcomes and preventing dropping out' (Fredricks et al., 2004, p. 60). This definition also covers misbehaviour and a lack of participation, i.e. truancy. Although there is conceptual overlap between cognitive and behavioural engagement (i.e. if children are concentrating on work, they are also participating in learning), one can parse out studies that focus on cognition versus other types of behaviour, such as being organised for school, turning up to lessons and taking part in extracurricular activities. The range of behaviours that fall under this definition makes it illogical to assume that behavioural engagement develops in a systematic way across transition. It is therefore surprising that the few relevant studies all show declines in children's behavioural engagement as they move through the secondary school years.

If we consider truancy as a measure of behavioural engagement in the UK, we can see that in 2011–12 the numbers of unauthorised absences were fairly low and stable at primary school, but rose steadily after Year 7 (Figure 9.1). There is little difference between absences in Years 6 (0.6 per cent of pupils) and 7 (0.7 per cent of pupils); however, this does mark the starting point of the increase in absences, indicating that there is something particular about

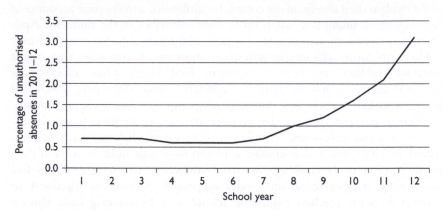

Figure 9.1 Percentage of unauthorized absences across school years

Source: compiled from open access data from the Department for Education (DfE, 2013).

secondary schooling (or being a secondary school student) that encourages children to truant.

In the US, researchers have studied behavioural engagement as children's reflections of how they have behaved in a set time period (i.e. recently, this year). In the 4-H Study of Positive Youth Development led by Professor Richard Lerner at Tufts University, around 2,000 children were asked each year whether they attended school regularly, went to school without homework completed and whether they brought books and other materials to school every day. Researchers used a clustering statistical technique to find four common patterns of behavioural engagement development, across Grades 5 to 8 (Years 6 to 9) (Li & Lerner, 2011). Most children were classified as having moderate stable engagement (62.2 per cent) or high stable engagement (18.4 per cent) across the period. However, two groups of children had decreasing behavioural engagement that either steadily declined across grades (4.4 per cent) or increased temporarily in the year after transition to middle/junior high school before continuing to decline (15.1 per cent). A similar-sized study (around 1,000 children) by researchers from the University of Michigan found an overall decline in children's behavioural engagement across Grades 7 to 11, when engagement was measured by how often children had got into trouble at school, been disruptive and had trouble getting their work done (Wang & Eccles, 2011). In both studies, declining behavioural engagement was associated with social and academic disadvantage, and with being male.

There are many ways that changing schools can shift children's patterns of behavioural engagement. First, children often report a decline in the quality of their relationships with teachers after transition (as covered in Chapter 6), as teachers become less emotionally supportive and more judgmental and strict (Benyon, 1985; Ferguson & Fraser, 1998; Midgley et al., 1988). This may account for declines in children's behavioural engagement, as researchers conducting a study of around 4,000 young people in Edinburgh found that children's misbehaviour across 13 to 16 years was more strongly predicted by the quality of teacher–pupil relationships than by gender, family and economic backgrounds, and emotional engagement with school (Smith, 2006). Also, children might be more likely to avoid school if they move to a peer group that is unsupportive, are bullied or make friends with others who encourage them to truant and misbehave. Their developing identities can also play a role, when becoming deviant is part of a strategy to obtain social status in the new peer group. Children may also avoid schooling if their new lessons make them feel incompetent (Smith, 2006), depressed or overly anxious (McLeod & Fettes, 2007), while others may pull away from school if they prefer to pursue interests outside of the school curriculum (Demetriou, Goalen & Rudduck, 2000; Symonds, 2009), as was the case with this author.

Achievement

A big question for policy makers is whether changing schools at age 11–12 years is detrimental for children's academic progress. If we follow the majority of research in this area, we can see this is the case for many schools in the US. Here, researchers find a general decline in grade point average (GPA) and in state-wide achievement tests across transition. This pattern is documented as far back as the late 1970s, in a study of around 1,000 children in Minnesota who made different types of school transitions (Simmons & Blyth, 1987). There, researchers found that GPA dipped sharply for boys at transition from middle to junior high school at Grade 7, then for both genders at a second transition to high school in Grade 9. These dips were not merely a continuation of a longer-term pattern, as children's GPA was fairly stable within each school level. Similar findings came from a recent study of transition to high schools in Los Angeles, where children's grades were fairly stable across middle school, but then dipped on entry to high school and declined in a linear fashion for the next two years (Benner & Graham, 2009). This pattern is not restricted to urban centres, as a third study presented almost identical findings from 16 schools in rural and small-town Missouri (Alspaugh, 1998). There, children generally made losses on state designed and administered annual tests at transition to middle and to high school in Grades 7 and 9. The researcher was able to demonstrate that these losses were larger at transition to high school, when roll size was bigger, and when schools took in children from multiple feeder schools (i.e. a pyramid system) compared to just one feeder school. In other words, the extent of the differences between school environments appeared to be a factor in the achievement loss.

There is less research on children's achievement and transition in the UK. This may eventuate from the UK not giving annual letter or numeric grades like in the US. The large gap in time between Key Stage 2 SATs scores in Year 6 and General Certificate of Secondary Education (GCSE) grades in Year 11 makes it impossible for researchers to trace any changes in achievement to school transition, even if comparing results across different school tiers, i.e. transition into high school at Year 9 versus into secondary school at Year 7. Also, when UK schools do give annual grades, these are teacher assessments, which is also problematic for research on school transition. Any changes in achievement based on teacher grades may reflect a change in grading practices, rather than a change in children's academic progress. Under these circumstances, the only valid ways of testing for change in children's achievement across transition in the UK are to analyse standardised Cognitive Ability Tests, which are rarely administered by feeder schools, or to administer one's own progress tests, which barely any research has attempted.

The one exception is the ORACLE studies of children in Leicestershire (Galton & Wilcocks, 1983; Hargreaves & Galton, 2002). There, researchers measured achievement in the third term before and after transition using abbreviated versions of the Richmond Tests of Basic Skills (France & Fraser, 1975), in the 1970s and in the 1990s. Each test in reading (vocabulary and comprehension), language (e.g. punctuation, spelling) and mathematics (concepts and problem solving) took around 30 minutes to complete. To assess progress, the researchers calculated whether children did better on the same tests after transition than in the year before. In the first ORACLE study, the majority of children made gains in achievement across the three tests (63 per cent), while a minority had stable achievement (7.4 per cent) or made losses (29.6 per cent) (Croll, 1983). A similar pattern was observed around 30 years later, with the majority of children making gains (60.1 per cent) and a minority being stable (6.1 per cent) or making losses (33.1 per cent) across all three tests (Galton et al., 2002).[1] In the 1970s study, more girls made gains than boys in mathematics (by 10 per cent), language (by 12 per cent) and reading (by 20 per cent), while in the 1990s study these gender differences were less apparent, suggesting an improvement in boys' progress at transition across the 30-year period. The central message from the ORACLE studies is that not all children experienced a decline in achievement after transition. In fact, around 60 per cent made academic progress. However, a significant minority (around 40 per cent) made no progress, which is not good news considering that all children should achieve more across school years.

There are several manners in which changing schools can impact academic progress. I summarise three of these below.

- *Changes in identity.* As discussed in Chapter 8, children can temporarily lose a sense of themselves as achievers when they are surrounded by unfamiliar peers, which can lead to a loss of academic self-concept. The new peer hierarchy may promote deviancy over conformity, which may encourage some children to reject learning in class. Also, many children feel more grown-up after transition, which may encourage them to seek new avenues for personal development that do not involve doing well at school. However, children may also work harder if they believe that their identities are being facilitated by getting good grades and by the curriculum. Also, new subject specialist teachers serve as role models for children's future careers, encouraging children to want a job in that subject.

- *Pedagogical continuity and discontinuity*. For a long time, educators and researchers have debated whether it is better to have a smooth transfer between units of work across transition, or whether children prefer more radical changes in work complexity and curriculum after changing schools. The influence of each strategy on achievement is discussed in detail in a series of reports by Galton and colleagues (e.g. Galton, 2009; Galton et al., 2003; Galton, Gray & Rudduck, 1999). These authors stress that too much continuity is a bad thing, as it fails to inspire children who are looking for new learning challenges after transition. However, it is also apparent that continuity serves the needs of lower achievers, and that starting from scratch advantages those who enter secondary school with little experience in that subject area (Symonds et al., 2011). What is clear, therefore, is that the success of either strategy depends on whether it meets children's needs for support and challenge. As Galton and colleagues recommended, a balance of continuity and discontinuity may help improve achievement after transition. I would add to this by stating that this balance must be carefully worked out based on the learning needs of children in each classroom.

- *Developmental mismatch*. Finally, returning to stage-environment fit theory, there are several characteristics of transfer schools that are a poor fit with children's needs for identity, self-esteem, autonomy, competence and social support. As discussed in the introduction and the preceding chapters, these characteristics can eventuate a decline in children's motivation and engagement, which may impact their achievement. Commonly, children report experiencing lower levels of emotional support from teachers, greater teacher strictness, increased focus on performance goals and assessment, and complain about learning activities that have no practical component or personal relevance in transfer schools.

Conclusions

In this chapter, I have illustrated how typical changes in school environment at transition can influence children's motivation and school engagement, and in turn affect achievement outcomes. Children are more positive about school and make better progress when they experience emotional support from teachers, a focus on mastery goals in lessons and assessment, interesting work and adequate learning autonomy, an appropriate amount of work consistency and a peer group that supports their academic achievements. In the US, children tend to have worse outcomes across the middle and secondary years of schooling, suggesting that these features of school environment are not readily forthcoming.

However in the UK, children's development is more mixed, suggesting that some features of transfer schools (such as moving to a more supportive peer group) are well suited to children's needs. On the one hand in the UK, children report enjoying school and subjects less, are less intrinsically motivated and are more likely to truant from school after transition. However, on the other hand they report more work effort and are observed to be more cognitively engaged in learning. Furthermore, school transition appears to act as a status passage, where children take school more seriously as a gateway to future career success. Unfortunately, children can hold this attitude while disliking school on a daily basis (Symonds & Hargreaves, 2014).

In general, transition appears to delay academic progress by disrupting children's academic identities, work trajectories and by creating developmental mismatch. Changes in the peer context are difficult for adults to control; however, they are a good topic for transition interventions that encourage children not to judge their achievements based on their classmates' progress, and to care less about how achievement might influence their popularity. In turn, this may help prevent children from disengaging and encourage a focus on mastery motivation. Teachers may also be able to reduce the delay in progress by creating a careful balance of continuity and discontinuity in children's learning – where the right balance should inspire children to achieve on tasks that are manageable for them. Finally, more attention to making work enjoyable may promote not only emotional engagement, but also children's desire to work, cognitive engagement and participation in school. In this way, school transition can live up to its potential for advancing children's progress, instead of causing the mixed reactions to schooling that we see today.

Note

1 These figures are a recalculation of data in Table 5.8 in Hargreaves and Galton (2002, p. 145).

References

Alspaugh, J. W. (1998). Achievement loss associated with the transition to middle school and high school. *Journal of Educational Research, 92*(1), 20–25.

Ames, C. (1992). Classrooms: Goals, structures and student motivation. *Journal of Educational Psychology, 84*(3), 261–271.

Anderman, E. M., & Patrick, H. (2012). Achievement goal theory, conceptualization of ability/intelligence, and classroom climate. In S. L. Christenson, A. L. Reschly & C. Wylie (eds), *Handbook of research on student engagement* (pp. 173–191). New York: Springer.

Benner, A. D., & Graham, S. (2009). The transition to high school as a developmental process among multiethnic urban youth. *Child Development, 80*(2), 356–376.

Benyon, J. (1985). *Initial encounters in the secondary school: Sussing, typing and coding.* Lewes: Falmer Press.

Croll, P. (1983). Transfer and pupil performance. In M. Galton & J. Wilcocks (eds), *Moving from the primary classroom* (pp. 63–94). London: Routledge & Kegan Paul.

Csikszentmihalyi, M. (1990). *Flow: The psychology of optimal experience.* New York: Harper & Row.

Deakin Crick, R., Jelfs, H., Symonds, J., Ren, K., Patton, A., & Grushka, K. (2010). *Learning futures evaluation report.* Bristol: University of Bristol/Paul Hamlyn Foundation.

Demerouti, E., Bakker, A. B., Nachreiner, F., & Schaufelil, W. B. (2001). The job demands–resources model of burnout. *Journal of Applied Psychology, 80*(3), 499–512.

Demetriou, H., Goalen, P., & Rudduck, J. (2000). Academic performance, transfer, transition and friendship: Listening to the student voice. *International Journal of Educational Research, 33*(4), 425–441.

DfE (2013). *Schools, pupils and their characteristics: January 2013. National tables.* Retrieved 5 August 2012 from www.gov.uk/government/publications/schools-pupils-and-their-characteristics-january-2013

Eccles [was Parsons], J., Adler, T., Futterman, R., Goff, S., Kaczala, C., Meece, J., & Midgley, C. (1983). Expectancies, values and academic behavior. In J. T. Spence (ed.), *Achievement and achievement motivation* (pp. 75–146). San Francisco: W. H. Freeman.

Eccles, J., & Midgley, C. (1989). Stage/environment fit: Developmentally appropriate classrooms for young adolescents. In R. E. Ames & C. Ames (eds), *Research on motivation and education: goals and cognitions* (Vol. 3). New York: Academic Press.

Eccles, J., Midgley, C., & Adler, T. F. (1984). Grade-related changes in the school environment: Effects on achievement motivation. In J. Nicholls (ed.), *The development of achievement motivation* (ed. University of Michigan, Vol. 3, pp. 282–331). Greenwich, CT: JAI Press.

Eccles, J., & Wang, M.-T. (2012). So what is student engagement anyway? In S. L. Christenson, A. L. Reschly & C. Wylie (eds), *Handbook of research on student engagement* (pp. 133–145). New York: Springer.

Ferguson, P. D., & Fraser, B. J. (1998). Student gender, school size and changing perceptions of science learning environments during the transition from primary to secondary school. *Research in Science Education, 28*(4), 387–397.

France, N., & Fraser, I. (1975). *Richmond tests of basic skills.* Windsor: NFER-Nelson.

Fredricks, J. A., Blumenfeld, P. C., & Paris, A. H. (2004). School engagement: Potential of the concept, state of the evidence. *Review of Educational Research, 74*(1), 59–109.

Galton, M. (2009). Moving to secondary school: Initial encounters and their effects. *Perspectives on Education 2: Primary–Secondary Transfer in Science, 2,* 5–21. London: Wellcome Trust.

Galton, M., & Wilcocks, J. (eds). (1983). *Moving from the primary classroom* (ed. University of Leicester). London: Routledge & Kegan Paul.

Galton, M., Comber, C., & Pell, T. (2002). The consequences of transfer for pupils: Attitudes and attainment. In L. Hargreaves & M. Galton (eds), *Transfer from the primary classroom, 20 years on* (pp. 131–158). London and New York: RoutledgeFalmer.

Galton, M., Gray, J., & Rudduck, J. (1999). *The impact of school transitions and transfer on pupil progress and attainment.* Norwich: DfEE.

Galton, M., Hargreaves, L., & Pell, T. (2003). Progress in the middle years of schooling: Continuities and discontinuities at transfer. *Education 3–13, 31*(2), 9–19.

Galton, M., Gray, J., Rudduck, J., Berry, M., Demetriou, H., Edwards, J., et al. (2003). *Transfer and transitions in the middle years of schooling (7–14): Continuities and discontinuities in learning.* London: DfES.

Gorard, S., & Huat See, B. (2010). How can we enhance enjoyment of secondary school? The student view. *British Educational Research Journal, 37*(4), 671–690.

Gray, J., Galton, M., McLaughlin, C., Clarke, B., & Symonds, J. (2011). *The supportive school: Wellbeing and the young adolescent.* Newcastle upon Tyne: Cambridge Scholars Publishing.

Hargreaves, D. J. (1984). *Improving secondary schools.* London: Inner London Education Authority.

Hargreaves, L., & Galton, M. (eds) (2002). *Transfer from the primary classroom: 20 years on.* London: RoutledgeFalmer.

Hargreaves, L., & Pell, T. (2002). Patterns of pupil behaviour in the transfer schools. In L. Hargreaves & M. Galton (eds), *Transfer from the primary classroom, 20 years on* (ed. University of Cambridge, pp. 159–184). London and New York: RoutledgeFalmer.

James, M., McCormick, R., Black, P., Carmichael, P., Drummond, M.-J., Fox, A., et al. (2007). *Improving learning how to learn: Classrooms, schools and networks.* Abingdon: Routledge.

Li, Y., & Lerner, R. M. (2011). Trajectories of school engagement during adolescence: Implications for grades, depression, delinquency, and substance use. *Developmental Psychology, 47*(1), 223–247.

Mac Iver, D., Klingel, D. M., & Reuman, D. A. (1986). Students' decision-making congruence in mathematics classrooms: A person-environment fit analysis. Paper presented at the American Educational Research Association, April. San Francisco.

McLeod, J. D., & Fettes, D. L. (2007). Trajectories of failure: The educational careers of children with mental health problems. *American Journal of Sociology, 113*(3), 657–701.

Markus, H., & Wurf, E. (1987). The dynamic self-concept: A social psychological perspective. *Annual Review of Psychology, 38*, 299–337.

Midgley, C., Anderman, E., & Hicks, L. (1995). Differences between elementary and middle school teachers and students: A goal theory approach. *Journal of Early Adolescence, 15*(1), 90–113.

Midgley, C., Feldlaufer, H., & Eccles, J. S. (1988). The transition to junior high school: Beliefs of pre- and post-transition teachers. *Journal of Youth and Adolescence, 17*(6), 543–562.

Midgley, C., Feldlaufer, H., & Eccles, J. S. (1989). Change in teacher efficacy and student self- and task-related beliefs in mathematics during the transition to junior high school. *Journal of Educational Psychology, 81*(2), 247–258.

Pekrun, R., & Linnenbrink-Garcia, L. (2013). Academic emotions and student engagement. In S. L. Christenson, A. L. Reschly & C. Wylie (eds), *Handbook of research on school engagement* (pp. 259–282). New York: Springer.

Roeser, R. W., & Peck, S. C. (2009). An education in awareness: Self, motivation and self-regulated learning in contemporary perspective. *Educational Psychologist, 44*(2), 119–136.

Rogers, C., Galloway, D., Armstrong, D., Jackson, C., & Leo, E. (1994). Change in motivational style over the transfer from primary to secondary school: subject and dispositional effects. *Educational and Child Psychology, 11*(2), 26–38.

Simmons, R., G., & Blyth, D., A. (1987). *Moving into adolescence: The impact of pubertal change and school context* (Vol. 2). New Brunswick and London: Transaction Publishers.

Smith, D. J. (2006). *School experience and delinquency at ages 13 to 16.* Edinburgh: Centre for Law and Society/University of Edinburgh.

Symonds, J. E. (2009). Constructing stage-environment fit: Early adolescents' psychological development and their attitudes to school in English middle and secondary school environments. Doctoral thesis, Faculty of Education, University of Cambridge. Available at: www.dspace.cam.ac.uk/handle/1810/223866

Symonds, J., & Galton, M. (2014). Moving to the next school at age 10–14 years: An international review of psychological development at school transition. *Review of Education, 2*(1), 1–27.

Symonds, J., & Hargreaves, L. (2014). Emotional and motivational engagement at school transition: A qualitative study of stage-environment fit. *The Journal of Early Adolescence, Online First* (Nov 3, 2014).

Symonds, J., Long, M., & Hargreaves, J. (2011). *Changing Key: Adolescents' views on their musical development across the primary to secondary school transition.* London: Paul Hamlyn Foundation. Available at: www.phf.org.uk/page.asp?id=1591

Wang, M.-T., & Eccles, J. (2011). Adolescent behavioral, emotional, and cognitive engagement trajectories in school and their differential relations to educational success. *Journal of Research on Adolescence, 22*(1), 31–39.

Wigfield, A., & Eccles, J., S. (1994). Children's competence beliefs, achievement values, and general self-esteem: Change across elementary and middle school. *Journal of Early Adolescence, 14*(2), 107–138.

Zanobini, M., & Usai, C. (2002). Domain specific self-concept and achievement motivation in the transition from primary to low middle school. *Educational Psychology, 22*(2), 203–217.

Chapter 10

Vulnerable children

Chapter overview

This chapter focuses on special groups of children, whose characteristics put them at risk for a more difficult transition. These are children with special needs, who mature earlier than their peers and who are an ethnic minority. Research finds that these children display typical patterns of emotional, personal, and social adjustment according to the qualities that set them apart from the mainstream. When adults are aware of these risk factors and put social and personal supports in place, this alleviates the children's chances of maladaptation. However, only special educational needs children are typically identified and catered to at transition, leaving large groups of vulnerable children unsupported.

Children with special educational needs

Children are thought of as having special educational needs (SEN) if they have a learning difficulty which sets them apart from their peers, or a disability which hinders their learning (DfES, 2001). These conditions include attention deficit disorder (ADD), attention deficit hyperactivity disorder (ADHD), autism spectrum disorder (ASD), Asperger's syndrome, behavioural, emotional or social difficulties, dyscalculia, dyslexia, learning difficulties that are specific, moderate or profound, hearing or visual impairment, multi-sensory impairment, and speech, language and communication needs. Often, children have sets of interrelated special needs.

In the United Kingdom if a child is thought to have SEN, they can be assessed informally by a special needs teacher at school, or by a formal assessment that their parents must apply for in collaboration with their school. This assessment determines whether they are awarded a statement of SEN, which allows educators and parents to track their progress across schooling and gives parents more options of where to send their child to school (gov.uk, 2014). Around half the children identified as having SEN in the UK are educated in special needs schools, although it is becoming more commonplace for SEN children to attend mainstream schools (Foundation for People with Learning Disabilities, 2014).

Most of the research on SEN and school transition has involved children who are integrated into the mainstream schooling system. These children make up 21 per cent of all students in state funded secondary schools, although only 2 per cent have statements of special needs which award them extra services (DfEa, 2013). The needs of SEN children are managed by the school's special educational needs coordinator (SENCO), and by learning support assistants (LSA), who are their primary 'go-to' person in lessons. At transition, children move to a different SENCO and LSA, unless their needs are severe, in which case the LSA may move with them (Maras & Aveling, 2006). Other children have lost their LSA provision after transition (Barnes-Holmes, Scanlon, Desmond, Shevlin & Vahey, 2013). In more positive cases, SEN children transfer to schools that have a learning support unit dedicated to serving their needs, which allows them to meet other SEN children, but requires them to attend the unit outside of normal lessons (Hannah & Topping, 2013).

Why SEN children are at risk at transition

SEN children typically have many risk factors for poor transition outcomes. These include low achievement, low self-esteem, problem behaviour and social difficulties (Barnes-Holmes et al., 2013). In comparison to children without SEN, SEN children have reported lower confidence in themselves (Forgan & Vaughn, 2000), less positive home and school friendships (Forgan & Vaughn, 2000; Martínez, 2006; Tur-Kaspa, 2002) and less support from classroom teachers (Martínez, 2006) in feeder schools, rendering them vulnerable before the move. Their teachers have rated them as having lower cooperation, assertion and self-control, and more internalising and externalising problems (Tur-Kaspa, 2002). Often, these issues are more prevalent for SEN boys (Martínez, 2006). These risk factors in tandem with children's special educational needs presents a complex scenario for teachers, parents and children to manage at transition. Below I explore what has happened to SEN children in mainstream school systems, during the different phases of changing schools.

How SEN children fare at transition

Preparation

Like most 11- to 12-year-olds, SEN children have worried about missing their primary school teacher, finding new friends, being bullied, managing harder work and finding their way around school, and have hoped for new and better resourced lessons (Barnes-Holmes et al., 2013; Pitt, 2012). However, what sets them apart from other children is that they have additional hopes and concerns that are specific to their special needs. For example, children with chronic physical illness in Australia (McMaugh & Debus, 1999) and boys with Asperger's syndrome in Scotland worried they would be victimised because of their disability (Hannah & Topping, 2013). Regarding schoolwork, the Australian children were concerned about keeping up after long periods of hospitalisation (McMaugh & Debus, 1999) and children with SEN in Northern Ireland were worried they would have more difficulty than their peers (Barnes–Holmes et al., 2013). In addition, SEN children have worried about whether to disclose their disability to other children, in the context of integrating into a new peer group (Barnes–Holmes et al., 2013; McMaugh & Debus, 1999). In contrast, other SEN children with Autism spectrum disorder have looked forward to transferring to a school with a special needs unit, where they could be educated in a more similar group of children (Hannah & Topping, 2013).

Because of their needs, SEN children are often better supported in the lead-up to transition than their peers. Marion Booth,[1] a SENCO in the east of England, described to me how she visited her incoming SEN children on several occasions at feeder school, to observe them in their pre-transition environment and to interview them with their parents, in order to know more about them. In other schools, children with emotional and behavioural difficulties, Down's syndrome and autism spectrum disorder were visited by their transfer LSAs to build their relationship before school transition (Maras & Aveling, 2006). SEN children have also been helped by attending more induction days and by having extra support on standard induction days that introduced them to their new school's layout, lessons, timetable and expectations. However, despite the extra provision for these days, SEN children have still wished for more time at their new school before changing, in order to familiarise themselves with new routines they might have trouble adapting to (Barnes–Holmes et al., 2013, Maras & Aveling, 2006).

Encounter

In the first few weeks of transfer school in the US (Knesting, Hokanson & Waldron, 2008), Australia (Pitt, 2012), England (Maras & Aveling, 2006) and Ireland (Barnes–Holmes et al., 2013), SEN children have spoken about taking longer than other children to adapt to new buildings and grounds, routines and organisational demands. They found it difficult to learn how to open lockers, find lessons, remember rules in different classes (Knesting et al., 2008), take responsibility for their own equipment (Maras & Aveling, 2006) and adjust to having multiple teachers (Barnes–Holmes et al., 2013). The new workload has been too demanding for them and SEN children have recommended a more gradual increase in work in order to help them cope (Maras & Aveling, 2006).

Adjustment

However, by the end of the first term, SEN children have reported that transition was not as bad as they expected (Barnes–Holmes et al., 2013; Hannah &

Topping, 2013). Many felt their initial fears about teachers, peers and work organisation evaporated after a few weeks (Barnes-Holmes et al., 2013), which has also
been the case for children without SEN (Gray, Galton, McLaughlin, Clarke &
Symonds, 2011). SEN children have been helped specifically by having an
enhanced transition programme whose activities helped them eliminate bad habits
and manage bullying, by meeting other children with SEN in support units and
by receiving support from external professionals (Hannah & Topping, 2013).

Six children with SEN in England were generally happy with their
friendships after transition (Maras & Aveling, 2006), as were children who
transferred to a special needs school in Australia (Pitt, 2012). However, this
perception of having a few supportive friends can be in contrast with SEN
children's general reputation within their peer group. In the Netherlands, a
survey of 39 hearing and 59 hard of hearing and deaf ('deaf') children found
that both groups reported that they were less popular after they moved
schools. However, the deaf children became far less popular across time. In
comparison, this decline was not apparent for SEN children transferring into
special schools, who instead had increased popularity and peer acceptance
(Wolters, Knoors, Cillessen & Verhoeven, 2012).

A particular social issue for SEN children is disclosing their special
educational needs to their peers after transition (Barnes-Holmes et al., 2013;
Knesting et al., 2008; Pitt, 2012). Even though in Knesting et al. (2008) several
children liked going to their SEN support centre, others did not use it, because
they were afraid of looking different in front of other children: 'Because if your
friends find out, they don't like you because you are different, stupid'
(p. 273). Unfortunately these fears may be well founded for some children, as, in
a study of around 500 children in England (Evangelou, Taggart, Sylva, Melhuish,
Sammons & Siraj-Blatchford, 2008), SEN children were 30 per cent more
likely to be bullied after transition.

The emotional adjustment of SEN children has been studied in Scotland,
for six boys with autism spectrum disorder (Hannah & Topping, 2013). After
transition, most of the boys had decreased symptoms of panic attack, agora-
phobia and separation anxiety, revealing a decline in anxiety tied to needing
familiar spaces and people. However, they became more anxious about physical injury and going to school in the mornings, perhaps because of threats
apparent in the social environment of their new schools.

School transition has also aggravated the symptoms of ADHD, which otherwise decline across late childhood and early adolescence (Langberg,
Epstein, Altaye, Molina, Arnold & Aveling, 2008). Using US data, these
authors found that parents rated their children as being more hyperactive,
inattentive and impulsive immediately after school transition. In comparison,
parents rated their children without ADHD as being stable on these criteria
as they moved schools. In relation to this, SEN children have reported that
having a dedicated room to cool off in, and where they could organise their
equipment, helped them control their feelings of stress and confusion in the

new school (Maras & Aveling, 2006), while others without this facility have desired it (Pitt, 2012).

Finally, there is little research on the changes in achievement of SEN children after transition. The only study that examined skills development noted that both SEN and non-SEN children had gains in reading the year before transition, but only SEN children had a loss in reading afterwards. In England, SEN children have reported being helped by their new LSA to adapt to the more complex timetable and work demands of their schools (Maras & Aveling, 2006), whereas in Australia a different picture emerged, where students struggled with the work and felt that in some cases their teachers did not cater to their special educational needs (Pitt, 2012). More study on SEN children and achievement at transition is warranted.

How can teachers help SEN children have a successful transition?

Despite the issues that SEN children face when changing schools, there is no framework provided to teachers by the UK government on how to help them. To address this deficit, the Foundation for People with Learning Disabilities, in collaboration with the Universities of Northampton and Cambridge produced a guide to help teachers with transition planning (Bryers, Fergusson & Davies, 2013) that is freely available online. The guide recommends that secondary schools identify SEN pupils as early as Year 5 and begin transition planning from then. It suggests that information about the children should be recorded using the same template in primary and secondary schools. The guide gives several ideas for how to create an enhanced transition programme – for example, by having secondary school SENCOs meet with parents and children at primary school, and by allowing SEN children more visits to their transfer schools and if necessary to give them a phased transition. Many of these recommendations were part of Marion Booth's work, which I explore more in Chapter 13.

A second issue is how to increase SEN children's resiliency to the challenges of school transition. Parents and teachers of boys with ASD have recommended that it is important to support and help improve the children's self-esteem at the transition period, so that they can cope better with the stressors involved (Jindal-Snape, Douglas, Topping, Kerr & Smith, 2006). These adults also stressed the benefits of having positive expectations and playing to each child's strengths when transition planning. Bryers et al. (2013) listed specific activities to help build SEN children's skills for managing transition, for example having a secondary school practice day at primary school, using a planner or diary at primary school, practicing buying their own lunch before changing schools and planning and running through their commute to school before they go there. SEN children may also be able to visit a website dedicated to helping them with their self-management and emotional needs at school transition, under construction at the time of writing by Dr Dianne Chambers at the University of Notre Dame in Australia.

Early maturing children

At 11 to 12 years old, most children begin to develop into sexually reproductive individuals (Coleman & Coleman, 2002) via three main types of pubertal changes. In gonadrache, the pituitary gland releases sex hormones, which travel through the blood to the testes and ovaries. There, the hormones stimulate gonad development and sperm and egg production (Sisk & Foster, 2004). In adrenarche, an increase in adrenal androgen spurs pubertal hair growth for boys and girls and facial hair for boys (Fechner, 2003). Third there is a growth spurt, which lasts a similar time for both sexes. Each event is governed by its own 'developmental clock' (Sisk & Foster, 2004), meaning that the three events can activate independently of each other generally after 6 to 8 years of age (Fechner, 2003). Normally they begin six months to 1 year earlier for girls (Fechner, 2003), which results in males being taller than girls in adulthood because girls begin their growth spurt from a shorter stature (Tanner, Whitehouse, Marubini & Resele, 1976).

There are several ways to measure pubertal development. The most common method uses a series of five line drawings or photographs of varying stages of pubertal development, and asks children, their parents/caregivers or medical practitioner to indicate which one best matches the child's physical state (Tanner, 1962). A second method asks children to report on their growth spurt, body hair, skin change, voice change, breast development and menarche using multiple-choice questions (e.g. Kaiser & Gruzelier, 1999; Petersen, Crockett, Richards & Boxer, 1988). Third, researchers have used children's height as an indicator of their pubertal development, which often matches with the self-reported physical changes gathered using the second method (Petersen & Crockett, 1985).

These pubertal data give researchers an idea of how developed a child is at a particular age, which is called *pubertal timing*. Also researchers consider how developed a child is in relation to their peers, by comparing the data for a particular age group and breaking it into categories of 'early', 'on–time' and 'late' developers (e.g. Petersen & Crockett, 1985). This is called *pubertal status*. Both measures are underpinned by a child's *pubertal onset,* which is the age they first begin puberty. Here we know that age of menarche is predicted by better nutrition (Dahl, 2004) and less physical stress (Graber, Nichols & Brooks-Gunn, 2010), perhaps as this allows the body to better support childbearing. Earlier menarche is also associated with lower-quality parenting (Graber, Brooks-Gunn & Warren, 1995), father absence (Susman & Dorn, 2009) and sexual abuse in childhood (Trickett & Putnam, 1993) because, in theory, girls who live in more stressful and dangerous environments need to have children earlier to maximise their chance of reproduction (Ellis, 2004).

Why early maturing children are at risk at transition

Studies of 10- to 14-year-olds find that children's perceived pubertal status associates more strongly with their psychological adjustment than does the raw age at which they began puberty (Ge, Conger & Elder, 1996). In particular, children who mature earlier than their peers have the worst psychosocial outcomes. The issue here is the mismatch between the group culture and the individual, for the typical development of that group is reflected in the social norms that group members and affiliated adults convey. Children who mature earlier than their peers are in violation of these norms and by default are associated with the social behaviours of an older group of children. These stressors may be taxing for the relatively undeveloped coping resources of early adolescent children, resulting in worse developmental outcomes (Ge, Brody, Conger, Simons & McBride Murry, 2002).

Because of their advanced physical stature, early maturing children have associated more often with older peers (Ge et al., 2002) and deviant peers (Ge et al., 1996). They have had accelerated transitions to dating (Simmons & Blyth, 1987), sexual activity and marriage, and more sexual partners (Seifert & Schulz, 2007). Maturing earlier in a mixed-sex peer group has predicted psychological distress for girls (Ge et al., 1996) perhaps because intensive interaction with boys and less developed girls emphasised issues of sexuality and body image for these children. Both issues were found to be more salient in early maturing girls (Simmons & Blyth, 1987; Petersen & Crockett, 1985), who have reported wanting to remain like children across school transition (Symonds, 2009). Perhaps because of these stressors, early maturing girls have exhibited more symptoms of depression, anxiety and eating disorders (Graber et al., 2010), while early maturing boys have been more vulnerable to depression and reported greater aggression (Ge, Conger & Elder, 2001). However, a major gender difference in adjustment is that early maturing boys have been more satisfied with their body image, whereas girls have been more uncomfortable with theirs, compared to their peers (Simmons & Blyth, 1987).

A second issue which might explain the worse outcomes for early maturing children concerns why they are more developed than their peers. As stated, harsher family environments predict earlier pubertal onset for girls (Graber et al., 2010). Typically, children in these types of families have more emotional and behavioural difficulties (Gore Langton, Collishaw, Goodman, Pickles & Maughan, 2011) and these may be exacerbated when children experience the stressors related with puberty (Caspi & Moffitt, 1991). Although entire peer groups may be from disadvantaged homes, even there some children will be from more stressful family backgrounds than others. Therefore early maturing children in any peer group might have experienced more background stress, and be more at risk of violating social norms and enacting more advanced adolescent behaviours. Accordingly, studies consistently find links between early pubertal status and risk factors associated with family disadvantage including lower achievement, lower impulse control and more psychopathology (Petersen & Crockett, 1985).

How early maturing children fare at transition

Despite the synchronised timing of school transition and puberty, there is little research on how early maturing children cope with changing schools, and the research that exists is limited to North America. In Michigan, Miller (1986) examined how satisfied girls were with their opportunities to make decisions in mathematics classrooms, according to whether their physical maturation was early (7.1 per cent), on time (81.4 per cent) or late (11.5 per cent) in comparison to their peers. Early maturing girls perceived a greater disparity between their needs and the school environment, which increased more greatly for them across transition than for their on-time or late maturing peers. In a study from Minnesota, researchers compared children transferring to junior high school to those remaining in a K–8 elementary school, across Grades 6 and 7 (Simmons, Blyth, Van Cleave & Bush, 1979). There, boys who matured earlier had increases in self-esteem only if they changed schools, suggesting they reaped the benefits of being more physically mature in a new social environment. In comparison, school transition coincided with a greater increase in dating for early maturing girls. In a second study of the same children, girls had lower self-esteem if they experienced a greater number of life transitions including school transition, dating, family mobility and menarche (Simmons, Burgeson, Carlton-Ford & Blyth, 1987). There, school transition acted as a risk factor for self-esteem loss if girls had also entered puberty. Finally, a study of Canadian youth found that changes in wellbeing were weakly related to experiencing a school transition or beginning puberty, but that there was no interaction between these two factors (Seifert & Schulz, 2007).

In conclusion, we know little about how early maturing children adjust to their new schools in comparison to their peers. Extant research indicates that early maturing girls are more at risk than are boys, perhaps because their physical development makes them more subject to sexual attention and violating social norms for 11- to 12-year-olds. In comparison, early maturing boys seem to fare reasonably well. Here, their tendency for aggression (Ge et al., 2001) and the strength implied by their advanced physique might act as protective factors, for these features are valued by the adolescent communities that quickly form after transition (Symonds, Galton & Hargreaves, 2014). However, putting on a tough front and being less gentle with peers can be detrimental to boys' academic success at transition (Measor & Woods, 1984). It may be prudent for teachers to monitor both early maturing boys and girls for their different predispositions to poorer psychological adjustment, and for these children to be offered additional support around the transition period.

Ethnic minority children

Ethnic minority children and transition in the United States

Most US research on ethnic minority children at school transition has concerned African American and Latino children (from Central and South America). Characteristically, these children come from homes with family incomes 40 to 50 per cent lower than those of white students (Wampler, Munsch & Adams, 2002). Accordingly, they are subject to the raft of risk factors that comes with poverty, including low achievement, single parent families, large household size, low maternal education, and parental mental illness and substance abuse (Burchinal, Roberts & Zeisel, 2008). Before transition to middle or junior high school, US ethnic minority children are found to have lower achievement (Wampler et al., 2002) and low levels of language ability (Burchinal et al., 2008), although their feelings about school are not necessarily more negative (Wampler et al., 2002).

Depending on the ethnic composition of their elementary school, moving schools can make African American and Latino children more aware of their status as an ethnic minority. This occurs when they move into a larger group of mainly white students and have few ethnic minority teachers as role models (French, Seidman, Allen & Aber, 2000). Based on the hypothesis that this experience associates with maladaptation, researchers developed a measure of ethnic incongruence by counting the number of same-ethnic peers in any given school. When children transferred to schools where they were an ethnic majority, there were no obvious negative consequences (Benner & Graham, 2007), However, if they became a minority in their new school they reported decreased feelings of school belonging, liked school less (Benner & Graham, 2009), had more work worries (Benner & Graham, 2007) and declines in achievement (Benner & Graham, 2009; Wampler et al., 2002).

African American children appear to be particularly at risk for these negative outcomes (Benner & Graham, 2007, 2009; Morrison Gutman & Midgley, 2000; Roderick, 2003; Simmons, Black & Zhou, 1991; Wampler et al., 2002), perhaps because this population has been subject to systematic disadvantage since their arrival in the US as slaves. Their development across transition is a portrait of how risk factors interact – for example, African American students living in poverty had difficulty with maths and reading, social skills and externalising problems at transition, augmented by their poor language skills (Burchinal et al., 2008). Black boys who eventually dropped out of middle school in Chicago attributed their post-transition failure to a lack of parental support and low educational expectations (Roderick, 2003), corroborating the results of other studies in this area (Morrison Gutman & Midgley, 2000; Wampler et al., 2002). Transfer teachers have also contributed to poorer adjustment for ethnic minority children through institutionalised racism, for they have rated African American children as less motivated, engaged and likely to go to college than their pre-transition colleagues, while their students thought their transfer teachers stereotyped them more, and paid little attention to boys who later dropped out (Roderick, 2003). Poorer adjustment at transition for African American children might also interact with typical changes in behaviour at puberty for this culture, for after transition African American boys have reported more involvement in peer conflict and dating in comparison to girls and white children (Simmons, Black & Zhou, 1991).

Ethnic minorities and transition in the United Kingdom

The picture is markedly different in the UK, where ethnic minority children are mainly from South Asia, in particular India, Bangladesh and Pakistan. Other prevalent minorities are black students from the Caribbean and Africa, and students from other Asian countries including China. In 2012, 24.2 per cent of students in secondary schools in England were ethnic minorities (DfE, 2013b). Since 1999, there has been a steady increase in the percentage of ethnic minority children in schools across England and more diffusion of ethnic minority children across the country. The largest increases have been in areas already densely populated with ethnic minority children such as London (Hamnett, 2011).

In the UK, ethnic minority children often start school at a disadvantage in relation to their white peers, due to having poorer English language skills and lower socioeconomic status (Dustmann, Machin & Schönberg, 2008). However, they soon catch up to the majority by the end of secondary school, often overtaking white children in work progress (Dustmann et al., 2008). Accordingly, there are few differences in achievement at the end of compulsory schooling between ethnic minority and white children in England (DfE, 2014). In 2013, more Asian (70 per cent) and mixed ethnicity (71 per cent) children, but fewer black children (65 per cent) obtained good grades (A*–C in their General Certificate of Secondary Education) than white children (69 per cent) (DfE, 2014).

The enhanced progress of ethnic minority children may be due in part to supportive parenting. In a national sample of ethnic minority and white children and their parents, around 15 per cent more ethnic minority parents expected their children to continue with schooling after age 16 (Strand, 2007). Similar findings emerge from the research on school transition, where ethnic minority children reported their parents regularly attending parents' evenings, helping with homework and having high expectations for academic success (Caulfield, Hill & Shelton, 2005). Perhaps because of their aspirations for their children, ethnic minority parents have been more likely to move their children to a secondary school that outperformed primary school, whilst white children's quality of schooling was more stable across transition (Dustmann et al., 2008).

In London and Glasgow, ethnic minority children have been more confident about their academic success than white children across school transition (Graham & Hill, 2003; ILEA, 1986). However, in reality, they had greater difficulty with their schoolwork. In Glasgow, fewer ethnic minority children reported good academic progress after transition (Graham & Hill, 2003) and in London their teachers rated them as performing worse than their white peers (Graham & Hill, 2003; ILEA, 1986). This temporary slight in progress was related to some children having difficulty speaking English (Graham & Hill, 2003; ILEA, 1986). Learning English as a foreign language (EFL) might be a particular issue at school transition, where children must adjust to the new voices of multiple teachers who use more complex terminology to describe subject matter. It might pose a particular difficulty for recent immigrants and Chinese children, who are more likely to only speak their mother tongue at home (Caulfield et al., 2005).

UK ethnic minority children have also had problems with social adjustment at transition. Although, in Glasgow feeder schools, ethnic minority children reported similar hopes and concerns to those of white children, they had an additional concern that there would be more racism in secondary school (Caulfield et al., 2005). After transition, ethnic minority boys did experience more peer violence. They were intimidated by groups of older children and noted that teachers were more sympathetic towards white boys in a mixed race fight. Often this was the boys' first experience of racism at school (Caulfield et al., 2005).

Although most ethnic minority children reported making mixed ethnic friendships after transition (Caulfield et al., 2005; Weller & Bruegel, 2006), around a quarter changed to socialising in same-ethnic groups, especially when their transfer schools had larger proportions of ethnic minority students. Children in these groups experienced more racism (Weller & Bruegel, 2006), as their status of being an ethnic minority was highlighted, encouraging out-group stereotyping and discrimination. In Scotland, children explained that they made same-ethnic friendships due to shared religious activities outside of school and to connections made through older siblings and parents (Caulfield et al., 2005), while in England they made same-ethnic friends, as they had little opportunity to socialise with white peers outside of school due to their parents associating mainly with other adults from their home culture (Weller & Bruegel, 2006).

Perhaps, for these reasons, fewer ethnic minority children have reported settling in well to secondary school than white children. Across studies they have felt less confident with their classmates, made fewer new friends especially just after transition, have had greater difficulty fitting in, felt less positive about school and evaluated their overall transition experience more negatively (Caulfield et al., 2005; Graham & Hill, 2003). However, the national picture of greater attainment at age 16 years for Asian and mixed-ethnic children attests to these difficulties being short-lived, at least regarding the extent that they influence children's academic progress. More longitudinal research is necessary to provide a fuller picture of these social and academic dips for UK ethnic minority children after transition, and the factors that contribute to their recovery.

Conclusions

The vulnerable children in this chapter have similar needs as other children for a successful transition. However, they have additional needs arising from their vulnerabilities that teachers can target in order to build their resiliency. Children with SEN need more help adjusting to their new school's routines, physical environment and increased workload. As discussed, teachers could address this by allowing them more frequent and extended visits to secondary school, implementing an enriched transition programme and providing extra education on how to manage themselves. Interventions that target the whole year group will also help build resiliency for vulnerable children. For example, any intervention that helps improve self-esteem and teaches skills in managing emotions and peer pressure will help steady the experiences of early maturing children who are thrust into an older peer group with more adult expectations of them, and of ethnic minority students who are made more aware of their ethnic identities after transition. Vulnerable children are also more at risk of difficulties with peers; therefore, anything that schools can do to help children make friends will be useful, such as ensuring a mixture of children in working groups and extracurricular activities. Vulnerable children would also benefit from encouragement to seek out provision for counselling and protection from bullying, given their tendency for lower self-esteem and experience of more hassles at school than other children. When talking with them about their needs, teachers can also draw attention to the strengths of being different, such as developing aspirations unique to their qualities, enriching the community through their differences and being ideally suited to mentor others like them.

Second, teachers can help vulnerable children by creating a school environment that embraces cultural, intellectual and physical differences. This may require whole school interventions that highlight personal differences such as maturation and SEN, and teach about stereotyping and its negative effects on personal and social development. These types of interventions will not only help children accept obvious physical and mental differences in their peer group, but should also promote more tolerance for subtle personal differences such as values and temperament, which are often at the heart of peer conflict. It is also important for vulnerable children to see that others like them have succeeded, and schools can help them do this by appointing staff members with disabilities and ethnic minority status, and by providing older peer mentors with similar experiences. Together these actions should help build a community that respects individual differences.

Third, teachers might want to pay closer attention to identifying vulnerable children before transition so that they can plan accordingly. Although feeder schools should be able to provide records of ethnic background and SEN, there may be clusters of vulnerabilities in your new cohort that feeder schools are unable to identify. For example, how many new entrants will be from the poorest families, or have a conglomerate of personal and social risk factors including low self-esteem, poor educational attitudes and uninvolved parenting? Which children have been bullied at feeder school, or are extremely anxious about the move? As part of their transition coordination plan (see Chapters 12 and 13), educators could survey children using a screening tool for vulnerabilities that would help them prioritise which types of interventions and support are most needed for each new cohort.

Note

1 This is a pseudonym for the teacher's real name. More about Marion Booth can be found in Chapter 13.

References

Barnes-Holmes, Y., Scanlon, G., Desmond, D., Shevlin, M., & Vahey, N. (2013). *A study of transition from primary to post-primary school for pupils with special educational needs*. Trim: National Council for Special Education.

Benner, A. D., & Graham, S. (2007). Navigating the transition to multi-ethnic urban high schools: Changing ethnic congruence and adolescents' school-related affect. *Journal of Research on Adolescence, 17*(1), 207–220.

Benner, A. D., & Graham, S. (2009). The transition to high school as a developmental process among multiethnic urban youth. *Child Development, 80*(2), 356–376.

Bryers, R., Fergusson, A., & Davies, J. (2013). *Moving on … Suggestions for busy teachers to support pupils with SEN moving from primary to secondary school*. London: Foundation for People with Learning Disabilities. Retrieved 21 April 2014 from www.learning disabilities.org.uk/moving-on

Burchinal, M. R., Roberts, J. E., & Zeisel, S. A. (2008). Social risk and protective factors for African American children's academic achievement and adjustment during the transition to middle school. *Developmental Psychology, 44*(1), 286–292.

Caspi, A., & Moffitt, T. E. (1991). Individual differences are accentuated during periods of social change: The sample case of girls at puberty. *Journal of Personality and Social Psychology, 61*(1), 157–168.

Caulfield, C., Hill, M., & Shelton, A. (2005). *The transition to secondary school: the experiences of black and minority ethnic young people*. Glasgow: Glasgow Anti Racist Alliance.

Coleman, L., & Coleman, J. (2002). The measurement of puberty: A review. *Journal of Adolescence, 25*(5), 535–550.

Dahl, R. E. (2004). Adolescent brain development: A period of vulnerabilities and opportunities. *Annals of the New York Academy of Sciences*, 1–22.

DfE (2013a). *Special educational needs in England: January 2013*. National Tables: SFR 30/2013. Manchester: Department for Education.

DfE (2013b). *Schools, pupils and their characteristics: January 2013*. National Tables. Manchester: Department for Education.

DfE (2014). *Level 2 and 3 attainment by young people aged 19 in 2013*. National Tables 6–14: SFR 10/2014. Manchester: Department for Education.

DfES (2001). *Special educational needs code of practice*. DfES/581/2001. London: Department for Education.

Dustmann, C., Machin, S., & Schönberg, U. (2008). *Educational achievement and ethnicity in compulsory schooling*. London: Centre for Research and Analysis of Migration, Department of Economics/University College London.

Ellis, B. (2004). Timing of pubertal maturation in girls: An integrated life history approach. *Psychological Bulletin, 130*(6), 920–958.

Evangelou, M., Taggart, B., Sylva, K., Melhuish, E., Sammons, P., & Siraj-Blatchford, I. (2008). *What makes a successful transition from primary to secondary school?* London: Department of Education.

Fechner, P. Y. (2003). The biology of puberty: New developments in sex differences. In C. Hayward (ed.), *Gender Differences at Puberty* (pp. 17–28). Cambridge and New York: Cambridge University Press.

Forgan, J. W., & Vaughn, S. (2000). Adolescents with and without LD make the transition to middle school. *Journal of Learning Disabilities, 33*(1), 33–42.

Foundation for People with Learning Disabilities (FPLD) (2014). Retrieved 21 April 2014 from www.learningdisabilities.org.uk

French, S. E., Seidman, E., Allen, L., & Aber, J. L. (2000). Racial/ethnic identity, congruence with the social context, and the transition to high school. *Journal of Adolescent Research, 15*(5), 587–602.

Ge, X., Conger, R. D., & Elder Jr, G. H. (1996). Coming of age too early: Pubertal influences on girls' vulnerability to psychological distress *Child Development, 67*(6), 3386–3400.

Ge, X., Conger, R. D., & Elder Jr, G. H. (2001). The relation between puberty and psychological distress in adolescent boys. *Journal of Research on Adolescence, 11*(1), 49–70.

Ge, X., Brody, G. H., Conger, R. D., Simons, R. L., & McBride Murry, V. (2002). Contextual amplification of pubertal transition effects on deviant peer affiliation and externalizing behavior among African American children. *Developmental Psychology, 38*(1), 42–54.

Gore Langton, E., Collishaw, S., Goodman, R., Pickles, A., & Maughan, B. (2011). An emerging income differential for adolescent emotional problems. *Journal of Child Psychology and Psychiatry, 52*(10), 1081–1088.

gov.uk (2014). *Children with special educational needs*. Retrieved 19 April 2014 from www.gov.uk/children-with-special-educational-needs/overview

Graber, J. A., Brooks-Gunn, J., & Warren, M. P. (1995). The antecedents of menarcheal age: Heredity, family environment and stressful life events. *Child Development, 66*(2), 346–359.

Graber, J. A., Nichols, T. R., & Brooks-Gunn, J. (2010). Putting pubertal timing in developmental context: Implications for prevention. *Developmental Psychobiology, 52*(3), 254–262.

Graham, C., & Hill, M. (2003). *Negotiating the transition to secondary school. Spotlight 89*. Edinburgh: SCRE Centre.

Gray, J., Galton, M., McLaughlin, C., Clarke, B., & Symonds, J. (2011). *The supportive school: Wellbeing and the young adolescent*. Newcastle upon Tyne: Cambridge Scholars Publishing.

Hamnett, C. (2011). Concentration or diffusion? The changing geography of ethnic minority pupils in English secondary schools, 1999–2009. *Urban Studies, 49*(8), 1741–1766.

Hannah, E. F., & Topping, K. J. (2013). The transition from primary to secondary school: perspectives of students with autism spectrum disorder and their parents. *International Journal of Special Education, 28*(1), 1–16.

ILEA (1986). *ILEA transfer project*. London: Inner London Education Authority.

Jindal-Snape, D., Douglas, W., Topping, K. J., Kerr, C., & Smith, E. F. (2006). Autistic spectrum disorders and primary–secondary transition. *International Journal of Special Education, 21*(2), 18–31.

Kaiser, J., & Gruzelier, J., H. (1999). The Adolescence Scale (AS-ICSM). *Acta Paediatrica Supplement, 429*, 64–68.

Knesting, K., Hokanson, C., & Waldron, N. (2008). Settling in: Facilitating the transition to an inclusive middle school for students with mild disabilities. *International Journal of Disability, Development and Education, 55*(3), 256–276.

Langberg, J. M., Epstein, J. N., Altaye, M., Molina, B. S. G., Arnold, L. E., & Vitiello, B. (2008). The transition to middle school is associated with changes in the developmental trajectory of ADHD symptomatology in young adolescents with ADHD. *Journal of Clinical Child and Adolescent Psychology, 37*(3), 651–663.

Maras, P., & Aveling, E.-L. (2006). Students with special educational needs: Transitions from primary to secondary school. *British Journal of Special Education, 33*(4), 196–203.

Martínez, R. S. (2006). Social support in inclusive middle schools: Perceptions of youth with learning disabilities. *Psychology in the Schools, 43*(2), 197–209.

McMaugh, A., & Debus, R. (1999). 'Just make friends, that's the most important thing!' School transition and making friends. The concerns and worries of children with illness and disability. Paper presented at the Annual Conference of the Australian Association for Research in Education, Melbourne, November.

Measor, L., & Woods, P. (1984). *Changing schools*. Milton Keynes: Open University Press.

Miller, C. L. (1986). Puberty and person-environment fit in the classroom. Paper presented at the Biennial Meeting of the American Educational Research Association, San Francisco, April.

Morrison Gutman, L., & Midgley, C. (2000). The role of protective factors in supporting the academic achievement of poor African American students during the middle school transition. *Journal of Youth and Adolescence, 29*(2), 223–248.

Petersen, A. C., & Crockett, L. J. (1985). Pubertal timing and grade effects on adjustment. *Journal of Youth and Adolescence, 14*(3), 191–206.

Petersen, A. C., Crockett, L., Richards, M., & Boxer, A. (1988). A self-report measure of pubertal status: Reliability, validity and internal norms. *Journal of Youth and Adolescence, 17*(2), 117–113.

Pitt, F. (2012). The experiences of students with mild to moderate intellectual disabilities as they transition from primary to secondary school. Unpublished PhD thesis. University of Wollongong. Australia.

Roderick, M. (2003). What's happening to the boys?: Early high school experiences and school outcomes among African American male adolescents in Chicago. *Urban Education, 38*(5), 538–607.

Seifert, T., & Schulz, H. (2007). The effects of pubertal timing and school transition on preadolescents' well-being. *Canadian Journal of School Psychology, 22*(2), 219–234.

Simmons, R. G., & Blyth, D. A. (1987). *Moving into adolescence: The impact of pubertal change and school context* (Vol. 2). New Brunswick and London: Transaction Publishers.

Simmons, R. G., Black, A., & Zhou, Y. (1991). African-American versus white children and the transition into junior high school. *American Journal of Education, 99*(4), 481–520.

Simmons, R. G., Blyth, D. A., Van Cleave, E. F., & Bush, D. M. (1979). Entry into early adolescence: The impact of school structure, puberty, and early dating on self-esteem. *American Sociological Review, 44*(6), 948–967.

Simmons, R. G., Burgeson, R., Carlton-Ford, S., & Blyth, D. A. (1987). The impact of cumulative change in early adolescence. *Child Development*, *58*(5), 1220–1234.

Sisk, C., L., & Foster, D., L. (2004). The nerual basis of puberty and adolescence. *Nature Neuroscience*, *7*(10), 1040–1047.

Stand, S. (2007). *Minority ethnic pupils in the Longitudinal Study of Young People in England (LSYPE)*. London: Department for Children, Schools and Families.

Susman, E. J., & Dorn, L. D. (2009). Puberty: Its role in development. In R. M. Lerner & L. Steinberg (eds), *Handbook of adolescent psychology*, Vol. 1, *Individual bases of adolescent development* (pp. 115–151). Hoboken, NJ: John Wiley & Sons Inc.

Symonds, J. (2009). Constructing stage-environment fit: Early adolescents' psychological development and their attitudes to school in English middle and secondary school environments. Doctoral thesis, Faculty of Education, University of Cambridge, UK. Available at: www.dspace.cam.ac.uk/handle/1810/223866

Symonds, J. E., Galton, M., & Hargreaves, L. (2014). Emerging gender differences in times of multiple transitions. In I. Schoon & J. Eccles (eds), *Gender differences in aspirations and attainment* (pp. 101–122). London: Cambridge University Press.

Tanner, J. M. (1962). *Growth at adolescence*. Oxford: Blackwell Scientific Publications.

Tanner, J. M., Whitehouse, R. H., Marubini, E., & Resele, L. F. (1976). The adolescent growth spurt of boys and girls of the Harpenden Growth Study. *Annals of Human Biology*, *3*(2), 109–129.

Trickett, P. K., & Putnam, F. W. (1993). Impact of child sexual abuse on females: Toward a developmental, psychobiological integration. *Psychological Science*, *4*(2), 81–87.

Tur-Kaspa, H. (2002). The socioemotional adjustment of adolescents with LD in the Kibbutz during high school transition periods. *Journal of Learning Disabilities*, *35*(1), 87–96.

Wampler, R. S., Munsch, J., & Adams, M. (2002). Ethnic differences in grade trajectories during the transition to junior high. *Journal of School Psychology*, *40*(3), 213–237.

Weller, S., & Bruegel, I. (2006). *Locality, school and social capital*. Families and Social Capital series. Swindon: ESRC.

Wolters, N., Knoors, H., Cillessen, A. H. N., & Verhoeven, L. (2012). Impact of peer and teacher relations on deaf early adolescents' well-being: Comparisons before and after a major school transition. *Journal of Deaf Studies and Deaf Education*, *17*(4), 463–482.

Part III

How to help them

Chapter 11

Interventions for wellbeing

Chapter overview

This chapter introduces the reader to school transition interventions, which are activities carried out by schools that address administrative, pedagogical, curricular, social and personal issues for children across transition. It discusses these using the framework of the Five Bridges (Galton, Gray & Rudduck, 1999), which has generated comparative data on which interventions have been most popular across different eras in the United Kingdom. The chapter also provides evidence on whether interventions actually support children's wellbeing, through a systematic review of intervention evaluations. It ends with a discussion on how interventions can support the five points of psychological wellbeing outlined in Chapter 2, by attending to these within each of the Five Bridges.

'Being *told* that there will not be any bullying is no substitute for experiencing a special first year playground with the head on duty, stopping fierce third years from stealing your crisps, football or comic' (Delamont & Galton, 1986 p. 35).

A transition intervention is any programme delivered in schools that aims to support educators and children in managing transition. Interventions can focus on educational and administrative practices, such as ensuring reliable data transfer, creating curriculum continuity and sharing good pedagogy across transition. They can also address children's emotional, personal and social adjustment – for example, alleviating pre-transition anxieties, familiarising children with their new schools, training them to cope with transition challenges and involving their parents in the process. As such, children, parents or teachers can be the intended target of transition interventions. Some interventions have become standard, such as induction days where children visit their new schools before attending, while others are more experimental, targeting specific groups of children or practices.

In the United Kingdom, transition interventions are funded by the government, local authorities (LAs) and schools. Recently the Department for Education (DfE) spent £50 million on summer schools aimed to help disadvantaged children adjust academically and socially at transition (Martin, Sharp & Mehta, 2013).

There, the DfE allowed schools to design and deliver the intervention to their own specifications, ensuring a more organic fit between the intervention and its recipients. In some areas LAs have led transition interventions by disseminating a set of materials for use in bridging units for example (DfES, 2004). However, these national and regional interventions are rare. More often, schools are independently responsible for coordinating transition interventions (Ashworth, Atherley & Chappell, 2011). In recent eras, they have had more freedom to do so as LA control over schools has loosened, and have done so more often in order to improve administrative procedures, attract students and support their wellbeing and achievement (Hargreaves & Galton, 2002).

Why transition interventions are important for children's wellbeing

As set out in the preceding chapters, transition creates many challenges for children's development. I have selected specific, salient problems that are observed across schools in the UK and the USA and have tabled these against the five points of psychological wellbeing outlined in Chapter 2 (Figure 2.1) so that teachers can consider these issues when designing transition interventions. It is becoming clearer to schools that not addressing these issues has negative repercussions. For example, when the transfer peer group bases popularity on female attractiveness and male strength rather than academic and humanitarian qualities, and when lessons are irrelevant to children's situational interests and aspirations, children can develop anti-learning profiles that quickly lead to a loss of achievement and support further deviancy amongst classmates (Measor & Woods, 1984). By designing interventions to support wellbeing, schools can increase children's chances of a successful transition, and in turn create a more positive school climate where there is social cohesion and respect for academic culture.

REVIEW OF EXISTING INTERVENTIONS

The Five Bridges

In the late 1990s, Galton, Gray and Rudduck (1999) worked with the Centre for the Study of Comprehensive Schools to survey 215 schools about their transition practices. The researchers devised five themes from the responses that best described common practices at the time. These were *administrative, pedagogy, curriculum, management of learning* and *social* (see Table 11.2). In an earlier study of transition set in the 1970s, Delamont and Galton (1986) observed transition activity occurring only in the social and pedagogy bridges. There, children were acquainted with their new school through short tours, whole days spent learning there, and by having their transfer teachers visit and teach them at their feeder schools. The schools also held parents' evenings. The programmes

Table 11.1 Key problems for children's psychological wellbeing at transition

Five points of psychological wellbeing	Key problem areas
Identity (interests, aspirations, roles, self-awareness)	Too much continuity can demotivate children who are seeking a status passage. Children are initially inspired by new subjects and resources (e.g. music), but can be let down when these don't live up to their expectations. Children configure their academic identities according to social stereotyping, their desire for popularity/safety, and on new information from teachers/peers and work experiences, which can be demotivating or misleading.
Self-esteem (positive perception of ego and other identities)	Girls' self-esteem is vulnerable at transition, especially if they mature early. Losing self-esteem in subjects through barriers to participation and failure configures identity (e.g. becoming non-musical) and impacts motivation.
Competence (skills, mastery, coping)	Children become anxious before transition when they are scared by transition myths, when they don't have enough information about the transfer schools and when they predict a negative social climate (e.g. bullying) and work that transcends their capabilities. Starting from scratch can demotivate high achievers who need more challenge. Children find it confusing having to adapt to multiple teaching styles. More disadvantaged children have fewer coping skills for positive personal and social adjustment.
Autonomy (matched to individual need)	There is often a lack of opportunities for leadership and decision making for Year 7 children in transfer schools. Some children dislike the move to a faster-paced environment where everything is regimented. Not all children can manage complete freedom in learning when opportunities to research and manage their own projects are offered as a post-induction programme.
Social support (underpins the other four points)	Most children make friends after the first term and expand their friendship group by the end of the year. However, this is the most frequent concern pre-transition. Vulnerable children may have more difficulty making friends. Year 7 children create their own value categories using stereotypes of male strength and female attractiveness that can limit their open engagement in educational activities and create a negative peer hierarchy of cliques and gangs. Year 7 children can feel at the bottom of the social ladder in the transition school. Older children offer valuable support as friends and peer mentors, but can also terrify younger children.

Table 11.2 The Five Bridges

Type of bridge	Description
Administrative	Communicating information about students including achievement, behaviour, special circumstances, school adjustment, home life.
Pedagogy	Sharing pedagogy for example through demonstration, observation, joint teaching and planning.
Curriculum	Curriculum based activities that support transition such as bridging units, summer schools, demonstrations of learning.
Self-management*	Enhancing children's learning, organisational and social skills necessary for them to become a 'professional student'.
Social	Allowing relationships to develop through for example induction days, recreational camp and celebration events.

Note
*In Galton et al. (1999) and other reports, this bridge is referred to as 'management of learning'. I have changed the title to incorporate schools' efforts to help children develop a wider range of skills (e.g. organisational, social) that help with their adjustment at transition. By positioning social skills here, the social bridge becomes more focused on building actual relationships, rather than on acquiring the skills to obtain these. From a psychological viewpoint, the self-management bridge is intrapsychic, whereas the social bridge is relational. This division also makes clear the different purposes of induction days (to educate children, to build relationships).

for children were designed mainly to relieve their anxieties about transition, but also to communicate the new school's rules and expectations.

These practices remained common in the 1990s, with all of the 215 transfer schools offering induction days and parents' evenings, and 20 per cent having their teachers teach in feeder schools (Galton et al., 1999). However, for the first time, researchers observed bridging units, where subject-specific activities were completed across transition as a collaboration between feeder and transfer schools (10 per cent of all schools surveyed), and summer training programmes for gifted or low achievers (5 per cent). Also, all schools employed heads of year in transferring data and managing the transition process (administrative bridge). These activities might have existed in the 1970s, but were not recorded by the researchers, who focused more on interventions to support wellbeing and learning. Finally, there was a little movement towards engaging children in managing their own learning (2 per cent of schools), for example through a 'Super Learning Day' where children discussed types of learning, their learning profiles and preferences after changing schools.

A new survey with 88 schools was conducted in the early 2000s (Galton, Gray, Rudduck, Berry, Demetriou, Edwards, et al. 2003). This documented the rapid uptake of interventions designed to promote curriculum continuity, such as bridging units. By this time, they comprised 46 per cent of all interventions across the five bridges. There were also more attempts to help children manage their learning (7 per cent of all interventions), which occurred mainly as post-transition induction programmes spread out over the first few weeks of school, a greater variety of social interventions, and increased focus on sharing pedagogy between schools (16 per cent of all interventions). A defining feature of this survey was the use of ICT to manage data transfer and to connect incoming students with transfer school peer mentors.

Even more recently, a team working on the Musical Bridges project funded by the Paul Hamlyn Foundation surveyed 168 schools about their transition programmes in music education. There, Ashworth et al. (2011) found similar patterns to Galton et al. (1999, 2003), with schools most commonly offering induction days and transfer teachers visiting and teaching in feeder schools, and fewer schools offering peer mentoring and joint musical activities. There, feeder and transfer schools rated the social bridge as being most important (72 per cent and 63 per cent of schools respectively), while the other bridges received similar, slightly lower rankings (e.g. pedagogy at 48 per cent of all transfer schools).

The following section uses the Five Bridges to demonstrate the range of existing transition interventions in schools in the UK and the USA. I have compiled lists of interventions from key reports (Evangelou, Taggart, Sylva, Melhuish, Sammons & Siraj-Blatchford, 2008; Fuller, Thomas & Horswell, 2005; Galton & Delamont, 1986; Galton et al. 1999, 2003; Sutherland, Yee, McNess & Harris, 2010) and books (Akos, Queen & Lineberry, 2005; Hargreaves & Galton, 2002). I also describe significant interventions in more detail and comment on contemporary issues facing each bridge.

Bridge 1: Administrative

Transfer of information from feeder schools including standard achievement test results, work habits, motivation, attendance, behaviour, friendships, record of SEN, medical information, extracurricular activities, educational history, defining aptitudes and home life. Scheduled meetings between senior staff, heads of year and subjects and Special Educational Needs Coordinators (SEN-COs), etc. Teams of staff plan, administer and evaluate transition interventions. Communication with parents. Manufacture and dissemination of transfer school information in booklets, etc.

The administrative bridge appears to be motivated mainly by transfer school staff. This might be self-imposed, historical or out of necessity, but regardless creates issues for feeder schools who are required to supply the information but otherwise can have little involvement in the administrative process. In the ORACLE replication study, feeder teachers were sceptical that the information they supplied to transfer schools was put to good use, as often it was kept by administrators and surfaced only when there was a problem with a child's learning or behaviour (Hargreaves & Wall, 2002). Furthermore, the portfolios of information were time-consuming to collate, during a busy year when feeder teachers were preparing for Key Stage 2 tests. In Sutherland et al. (2010), feeder school headteachers were concerned about the flow of information being only one way, as they wanted to evaluate their school's practice and extend their involvement in students' learning careers by being kept updated on their students after transition.

Feeder teachers' scepticism appears to have been well placed, as in numerous studies transfer schools have remarked on not trusting feeder school information as a reliable indicator of student progress (Ashworth et al., 2011; Evangelou et al., 2008; Galton et al., 2003; Hargreaves & Wall, 2002: Suffolk Local Authority, 2001). As one music teacher put it, 'Unfortunately, KS2 levels are often wildly inaccurate in our eyes – if a pupil has instrumental lessons, they are automatically given a level 5 in some schools. This means we end up with impossible FFTD [Fischer Family Trust] targets to reach in Y9' (Ashworth et al., 2011, p. 44). Generally transfer schools use achievement data to group children by ability in Years 7 and 8, so want this data sooner rather than later. However, Key Stage 2 standardised test results often arrive too late for schools to use these to set students in the first term (Suffolk Local Authority, 2001). The response from many transfer schools is to deliver their own standardised tests, either after the children arrive or at feeder schools as part of a transition intervention (Fuller et al., 2005; Hargreaves & Wall, 2002). Although this pre-transition testing is not yet commonplace, it could be a useful method for evaluating progress across transition if repeated across Years 6 and 7, and may ease the administrative burden for feeder teachers.

Bridge 2: Pedagogy

Exchange of pedagogy across school tiers. Transfer and feeder teachers teach individual lessons or a series of lessons in each other's schools. Use of team teaching and advanced skills teachers. Teachers and other staff observe lessons. Joint marking exercises. Shared teaching and learning policies. Training and planning sessions for teachers and headteachers on cross-tier pedagogy. Teachers visit children on both sides of transition to discuss changes in pedagogy. A common pedagogic language is developed and used in teachers' meetings and in classrooms.

Although teacher exchanges have been operating for 40 years or more (Delamont & Galton, 1986), it is only in recent eras that recognising, celebrating and learning from cross-tier differences has become part of the expected discourse of school transition (Ashworth et al., 2011). These teacher exchanges have been aided by the National Strategy, which gives explicit reasons for observing different types of Key Stage 2 and 3 teaching (DfES, 2004). However, some teacher exchanges happen only after the Key Stage 2 tests in feeder schools and once Year 11 students have gone on study leave from transfer schools. At this point, feeder schools concentrate more on enrichment subjects such as music and art after spending most of the year teaching English and other core subjects to their final year students. In these circumstances, transfer schools are unlikely to observe typical feeder school teaching (Galton, 2010), which could detract from the enterprise's value. In Hargreaves and Wall (2002), transfer teachers used language denoting the superiority of transfer schools, e.g. 'course structures filtering *down*' and 'coming *down* to the primary school' (p. 39) (italics added) when meeting feeder school teachers. This cultural stereotyping reminds us that although cross-tier differences have developed as independent historical approaches to pedagogy (Chitty, 2002), their teachers should be awarded mutual esteem (Department for Children, Schools and Families, 2008), which may make the task of adopting a common language for discussing schools, teaching and learning (Ashworth et al., 2011; Department for Children, Schools and Families, 2008) across transition all the more important.

Bridge 3: Curriculum

A focus on familiarising children with the curriculum of the transfer school, and on creating continuity and strategic discontinuity in the curriculum between Key Stages of learning. Joint activities across transition in specific subjects (English, mathematics, etc.) often formalised as bridging units. Transfer curriculum taught in the last term of feeder school. A two-year programme of work from Year 6 June to Year 8 May developed as a collaboration between transfer and feeder teachers. Summer schools for low achievers, gifted and talented, and children from rural areas. Demonstrations of children's learning, e.g. music performance, art exhibition shared across tiers. Taster lessons at induction days. Feeder children shadow transfer children to observe the curriculum. Training and planning sessions focused on cross-tier curriculum for teachers and headteachers can also be attended by LA representatives. Teachers observe curriculum being taught in each other's schools. Guidance session for incoming students to link subjects and learning to future careers.

Bridging units are the most popular initiative in the curriculum bridge, and have become widespread since the 1990s (Hargreaves & Wall, 2002). Typically they consist of themed learning activities (e.g. murder mystery, bridge construction) in a single subject (e.g. English, science) that are completed in a sequence across the adjacent terms of Years 6 and 7. The units have many functions. As a pre-transition activity they introduce the transfer curriculum, standardise children's knowledge and skills, familiarise children with transfer teachers and teaching styles (when taught by transfer teachers in feeder schools), increase children's awareness of knowledge and learning outside of their individual school, and can relieve children's anxieties about post-transition work. As a post-transition activity, they can be a useful tool for assessing children's attitudes, attainment and identities, a celebration of completing transition (Fuller et al., 2005) and a gateway to longer-term engagement when work is followed up. On both sides of transition they promote curriculum continuity, can help teachers get to know each other (Fuller et al., 2005) and understand each other's pedagogy and curriculum (Galton, 2010), and engage children by tapping into their local interests (Hargreaves & Wall, 2002) and desire to complete the transition.

However, researchers have observed many obstructions to bridging units achieving these functions. Where each feeder school contributed only a handful of children, the units became relevant to only a few children in each class; therefore, feeder teachers were less enthusiastic about delivering them (Hargreaves & Wall, 2002) and in these conditions children sometimes turned up to the transfer school without having done the unit, which caused problems for transfer teachers (Galton et al., 2003). Feeder teachers have also been reluctant to teach units in core subjects (i.e. English, mathematics, science) after spending most of the year preparing for national Key Stage tests. In the early days of bridging units, discrepancies in teaching across feeder schools caused further issues – for example, some teachers selected to teach only part of the unit (Galton et al., 2003), while others tailored it to their personal objectives (Hargreaves & Wall, 2002); both actions resulting in losing the common thread. In some transfer schools, opportunities to use units for grading and assessment were passed over (Galton et al., 2003), the value of doing the unit was restricted to individual subjects (Suffolk Local Authority, 2001), teachers were impatient to deliver the 'proper' Year 7 curriculum, there was no follow-through on learning and children were apathetic about continuing 'demeaning' work from feeder school (Galton et al., 2003).

While some of these issues were perceptual, others were tied to the content and structure of the units. In order to obtain real benefit from the units, schools can encourage children's engagement by making them relevant to local contexts (Hargreaves & Wall, 2002) and by creating systematic discontinuity so children feel they are making valuable progress. In a review of good practice, Fuller et al. (2005) made recommendations for raising the status of the units in the transfer school, including grading the work, putting the work on display in the hallways and sharing it with parents at parents' evening. No matter how many schools feed into the one transfer school, creating trust and respect across tiers is also key to delivering the units successfully. Here, perhaps ICT (e.g. online units, video conferencing) can solve some of the problems of delivering units to small clusters of children dispersed across a larger number of feeder schools.

A national survey of the DfE's summer schools programme found that children attending summer schools were more positive about transfer and felt more confident about their social and work skills than children not attending. This association was most significant for looked-after children, children receiving free school meals and those living in deprived areas (Martin et al., 2013). However, the survey did not establish whether these effects persisted across the first year of secondary school. Research on summer schools and taster lessons on induction days finds that, although these activities are enjoyable, they have a side effect of encouraging students to believe that learning will be far more exciting at the transfer school. As Matthew, a Year 7 student described to me, this could be misleading: 'I was really looking forward to it [coming here] because I went on a summer discovery school for science and maths … and we had to do a science poster and that was really fun and I have realised now that was not normal school and that was not how school is ever going to be.' Overselling science lessons on induction day is common across a 40-year period (Delamont & Galton, 1986; Galton, 2010; Hargreaves & Wall, 2002; Measor & Woods, 1984). For example, in a taster lesson where '[t]he Van der Graaf generator charged up two pupils so that their hair stood on end. Two more had their noses unexpectedly sucked into rubber tubing … The *pièce de résistance* was the discovery that science teachers could breathe fire' (Hargreaves & Wall, 2002, p. 50). The problem with this approach is that it leads students to expect a greater discontinuity in learning than they actually receive, which can encourage post-transition feelings of disappointment and boredom (e.g. Measor & Woods, 1984). This presents a complex challenge of striking a balance between novelty and realism when designing these interventions, in order to protect children's longer-term engagement.

Bridge 4: Self-management

> Helping children become a 'professional transfer school student' through understanding, managing and developing their personal and social skills. Educating children in learning metacognition (e.g. linking knowledge, concept maps), motivation and self-regulation techniques, knowledge awareness, study skills, goal setting, organisational skills (e.g. packing own equipment, timekeeping), social skills (e.g. how to avoid peer conflict, how to collaborate in lessons) and the new organisation and layout of the transfer school. This education occurs at the feeder schools (e.g. simulating transfer school organization), at induction days (e.g. a room scavenger hunt) and in extended post-transition programmes (e.g. 'learning to learn'). It is supported by having systems in place for children who require extra help and that encourage all children to ask for help, and by diagnostic testing that identifies children's strengths and weaknesses. The education is aimed at encouraging children to better manage themselves, and as such often involves children as active participants.

When Galton et al. (1999) devised this theme, they built on the concept of the *professional pupil* or student (Lahelma & Gordon, 1997), which outlines how children are socialised into their position as students of either feeder or transfer schools. This concept makes salient that teachers hold the responsibility for educating children on how to be effective students. It makes us think about which qualities are necessary for professional studentship in the present era, as schools incorporate more transferrable skills, including research, project management and collaboration, into their curricula. These skills require more autonomy than is necessary for more traditional modes of education, such as rote learning, and accordingly children's active involvement in self-management interventions is prized as a way to enhance both the authenticity of the intervention and their own learning.

Self-management in the transition context revolves around three types of skills that act together to increase children's chances of school success. The first is how to manage one's own learning, which was the sole focus of this bridge in other studies (Fuller et al., 2005; Galton et al., 1999, 2003). This is mainly taught at transfer schools, as is evident through the uptake of extended post-transition programmes on learning metacognition (Galton et al. 1999, 2003; Sutherland et al., 2010). Several examples come from the Learning Futures project (Deakin Crick, Jelfs, Symonds, Ren, Patton & Grushka, 2010), where schools implemented programmes on 'learning to learn' and independent research in the autumn term. Children's evaluations of these methods revealed that they enjoyed the investigation unit more if they were confident learners, and when they had plenty of support from their teachers. This was because children had little understanding of learning as a process, and many were not ready to strike out on their own, especially in a new school where their relationships with new teachers and classmates were uncertain. This variability in children's knowledge of learning suggests that there is much to be gained by starting these programmes earlier in feeder schools, and by integrating them into bridging units.

A second aspect of self-management involves organisational skills, as children are required to be more self-sufficient in transfer schools. There they must organise their own equipment, move between classes independently and use a planner to record homework and keep track of their obligations. This is a particular issue for children with special educational needs, who may be less capable in this domain than other children (Foundation for People with Learning Disabilities, 2014). Induction days familiarise children with some aspects of transfer school organisation, including the schools' layout, how to use lockers, lunchtime routines, the daily timetable, planners and expectations for children to be on time and self-organised. Recently, some feeder schools have been teaching these skills in advance by simulating the transfer school environment in the last few weeks or days of term (FLPD, 2014), which helps children learn in the comfort of familiar surroundings. In one school pyramid, transition took place in June, so that learning could begin in earnest in September, well after these organisational hurdles were overcome. This reportedly alleviated the dip in children's English and mathematic achievement (Sutherland et al., 2010).

The third aspect of self-management is social skills, which support both social and academic adjustment. Transition interventions that teach social skills aim to calm children's social fears as well as facilitate high-quality friendships after

transition (e.g. Bloyce & Frederickson, 2012). Social skills are an important component of being a professional student, similar to how adults use them in the
workplace to achieve effectiveness in relationships with colleagues, bosses and
employees. In schools, children need social skills to collaborate well with classmates (Demetriou, Goalen & Rudduck, 2000), to understand and appropriately
react to their teachers and to thrive in the demanding social arena of their peers.
In Chapter 8 on identity, children's desire to fit into their social group also
encouraged some children to put on a deviant front; therefore, training on resist-
ing peer pressure could help children retain a focus on their studies. Of course,
much of this is the focus of the Social and Emotional Aspects of Learning curriculum (SEAL) taught in feeder schools and in some transfer schools. However,
there are particular social issues surrounding transition, such as making new
friends, learning to collaborate with different children and negotiating a new
social hierarchy, that are an excellent subject for more targeted interventions.

Several types of transition interventions address all three areas of self-
management. These include induction days, although their provision is by nature
short term and therefore reasonably ineffective for creating longer-term changes
in behaviour (Galton, 2010). In the UK and the USA, researchers, educators and
funding organisations have delivered more complex extended pre- and post-
transition programmes that train children in academic, social and emotional
coping (Bloyce & Frederickson, 2012; Gonzales, Dumka, Deardoff, Carter &
McCray, 2004; Greene & Ollendick, 1993; Reyes, Gillock & Kobus, 1994; Shepherd & Roker, 2005); however, their attention is often focused on minority and
vulnerable groups of children. In Australia, Chambers and Coffey (2013) have
developed an open-access website to provide information to students with special educational needs on the social and organisational aspects of transition, while
across the internet there are websites and webpages dedicated to providing this
information to children transferring to middle, secondary and high schools.

Bridge 5: Social

The formation, strengthening and display of social ties that support children's
adjustment at transition. Opportunities for children to get to know each other
and their new teachers include summer school, pre-transition extracurricular
activities at the transfer school, induction days, recreational camp, joint activities
e.g. a cross-tier music performance, celebration activities, buddying/mentoring/
shadowing schemes with peers and adults, the 'blocking' of teachers and learning
groups after transition and programmes of relational support for vulnerable
children. Displays of social support – including buddies and teachers visiting
feeder schools, and of adults and older peers handling social situations respon-
sibly and intelligently – build children's confidence in the social atmosphere of
the transfer school.

Across studies, children have been most concerned about social issues at transition (Gray, Galton, McLaughlin, Clarke & Symonds, 2011). Accordingly, they have reported that getting to know new teachers and making new friends (Galton, 2010) and meeting friendly people who encouraged them to join the school (Evangelou et al., 2008) were the most important and welcoming features of their induction days. Induction days have become more social since the 1970s, with scheduled time for children to discuss their new school and meet new teachers and tutors (Galton, 2010). Like transition myths, induction days convey messages about the new social order, including who to respect, what the rules are and how to conduct oneself. As such they can be either an 'upsetting initiation into a new culture, or the beginning of a safe passage from one culture to another' (Hargreaves & Wall, 2002, p. 45). There, it is important for educators to set the foundation for good relationships by creating an environment of both perceived and actual social support, for, as my introductory quotation from Delamont and Galton (1986) observes, children need evidence to support their assumptions.

Being cared about by at least one person in particular is another important feature of social support at transition (Fuller et al., 2005). Many schools have addressed this issue by putting buddy systems in place, where feeder children are mentored by their older peers. Some programmes allocate buddies on the basis of shared interests, whereas others go by the older child's suitability as a role model for good work progress and behaviour. The degree of contact between feeder children and their buddies can vary, with schemes in the UK often using only written or email communication (Powell, Smith, Jones & Reakes, 2006; Sutherland et al., 2010), while in the USA activity is more elaborate, with longer-term programmes involving a buddy dance, watching a sports game with the buddies, and meeting regularly with buddies over the course of the pre- and post-transfer year (Akos et al., 2005; Reyes et al., 1994). A related activity is the support of learning mentors, who are adults employed by school pyramids, transfer schools and local authorities who stay with children as they cross school tiers and assist them with their learning (Evangelou et al., 2008; Sutherland et al., 2010).

In the USA, Felner and colleagues experimented with 'blocking' groups of students and teachers together, to augment familiarity and social cohesion in the first post-transition year. This can have additional benefits for learning by encouraging children's social confidence in lessons, creating more close-knit working groups and increasing teachers' knowledge of students. First, the researchers created a school within a school by blocking a subset of students into four tutor groups, who occupied nearby classrooms, liaised with each other, were in the same classes for core subjects and received enhanced support from their tutors. These students had higher, stable impressions of themselves, while the rest of the year group had declining self-perceptions on average across the post-transition year (Felner, Ginter & Primavera, 1982). Longer term, the intervention students were around half as likely to drop out of school and showed lower levels of social, emotional, behavioural and substance abuse difficulties than their peers, but had similar levels of achievement (Felner, Favazza, Shim, Brand, Gu & Noonan, 2001). The intervention also worked well for teachers, who reported lower levels of job-related stress and higher job satisfaction than their colleagues.

Similar projects have been instigated in England. In the southeast of England, one secondary school created a halfway house between itself and primary school in the first year, where children were taught literacy and numeracy in the same classroom, and had the same three teachers for all of their subjects (English/literacy, mathematics/French, science/humanities) (Association of Assessment Inspectors and Advisors, 2001). This technique was also employed by a technology college, where an experienced team of four teachers led by an assistant principal each taught English, history and geography across the year (Fuller et al., 2005). In both cases, the teachers felt that they had advanced their skills through teaching additional subjects, and that children's behaviour and engagement were better than that of the prior Year 7 cohort. Specifically in the first study there were 66 per cent fewer exclusions and a 67 per cent decline in serious behavioural incidents compared to previous years where children were taught by a different teacher for every subject. With regards to achievement, the technique appeared to most help children working at a very low level (Association of Assessment Inspectors and Advisors, 2001).

Perhaps the most intensive way to help new students get to know each other is by arranging for a recreational camp in summer or in the autumn term. A model of camp activity is given in Akos et al. (2005), where an incoming year group was split into four residential camps, each held over five days in the summer. Children were assigned to a social group for the week, with separate cabins for each group's boys and girls. In the morning, children attended educational sessions focused on their interests, such as jewellery making, model rockets and nutrition. In the afternoon, children did physical activities, including swimming, rafting and hiking. Teen mentors supervised the children and held evening campfire discussions on social and emotional issues. Camps such as these are observed to create better social integration after transition (Delamont & Galton, 1986) and have helped children become familiar with the protocols of the transfer school (Sutherland et al., 2010).

Home–school partnerships

In the Five Bridges, children, teachers and learning are the common focus of transition interventions. Parents have been involved less often, other than by attending the requisite parents' evenings and accompanying their children to open days (Hargreaves & Wall, 2002). This is an oversight, as parents have substantial personal resources, including emotional support and time to spend with their children, that when applied can have a positive impact on children's academic and social adjustment. Schools can tap into these resources by creating home–school partnerships (Osborn, McNess & Pollard, 2006) that pool parents, teachers and schools' resources and tighten the knowledge connection between home and school.

A common method of communicating with parents is to supply them with information about the transfer schools' curriculum, policies and requirements at open days and parents' evenings, in an attempt to recruit new students (Powell et al., 2006). Schools can also use transition to legitimate communicating with parents on how to manage their relationships with adolescent children, support their children academically (e.g. Gonzales et al., 2004) and take care of children's physical needs, such as nutrition (Evangelou et al., 2008) and sleep (Quach, Gold, Arnup, Sia, Wake & Hiscock, 2013). This information is often delivered as written material, at induction days or, in rarer cases, as programmes designed to support vulnerable students and increase parenting skills (Gonzales et al., 2004; Ralph & Sanders, 2003). Although there is evidence that the more intensive programmes do improve parent–child relationships across transition (e.g. Van Ryzin, Stormshak & Dishion, 2012), this practice still ignores the potential for parents to act as information sources for schools.

As there are so few examples of knowledge exchanges at transition, I have made some tentative suggestions below about how to create this two-way flow of information. Knowledge exchanges could occur as recorded question and answer sessions, as fun activities where parents discuss their children's characteristics in response to humorous prompt cards, as learning activities where parents rate their children using surveys that tell them something about their child's personality or needs, which can later be replicated by teachers and communicated back to parents to give an assessment of the child's behaviour at school, or indeed by involving parents as partners in designing, delivering and evaluating projects around transition. This evaluation strand should help ascertain the impact of transition interventions on children's home lives and may offer valuable insight from the family perspective (Akos et al., 2005). Building on Sutherland et al. (2010) and a Department for Education and Skills report on Key Stage 2 to Key Stage 3 transition (DfES, 2006) these exchanges could take place during open days, induction days, celebratory events such as a science fair, parents' evenings, parents' coffee mornings, whilst parents attend adult numeracy and literacy classes or take their children to extracurricular activities at the school, or via a parents' council. A final suggestion is for schools to create a secure portal where parents could view their children's data and teachers' comments and leave their own responses in electronic format.

What evidence is there that transition interventions work?

Although there are many examples of transition interventions, few evaluations of these exist in the public domain. Most are published in academic journals, and are interventions delivered by researchers to help improve children's wellbeing and achievement. There, researchers collect baseline and follow-up data to assess whether children have changed after the intervention was delivered. Often they compare children who received the intervention to a control group who were not involved, in order to tag any observed changes (or lack of change) to the intervention. In both types of study design, the pre- and post-tests are only proxy indicators of whether the intervention worked, because it is possible that the children would have changed in this way, even in their test and control groups, for some reason other than the intervention. However, this method provides us with better data than no data at all. A few studies interviewed children and their parents to ascertain the intervention's effects, and so provide evidence from the horse's mouth. However, because they only interviewed a small number of people, the comments might not reflect how the intervention was received in general. I have collated both types of information in Table 11.3, which houses the 14 evaluations that I identified by searching academic databases using the terms 'intervention', 'school' and 'transfer' or 'transition', and by limiting my results to children in mainstream schools without special educational needs (to give a general picture).

Of the 14 interventions tabled, twice as many were from the USA (n = 8), than from the UK (n = 4), and one each were from Canada and Australia. Of the USA interventions, 75 per cent were delivered to low-income, ethnic minority groups in urban areas, whereas only one UK intervention was aimed at vulnerable children. All the interventions surveyed the participants before and after the intervention, but only two did follow-up interviews. Six interventions were held in the pre-transition year and eight were held the year after, meaning that there were no cross-tier interventions. When interventions were given before transition, 66 per cent of studies returned to evaluate their participants after transition to estimate the interventions' effects.

The majority of interventions (n = 8) targeted children's self-management skills (i.e. the academic, organisational and social categories I outlined earlier) in general, without having a specific transition angle. Helping children adjust at transition, e.g. preparing for and settling into a new school, was a less common focus (n = 4). The other common foci were parenting skills (n = 4) and teacher support (n = 2).[1] Only Reyes et al. (1994) and Walsh-Bowers (1992) found no difference between the perceptions of the test and control groups, although in Walsh-Bowers (1992) parents and teachers gave the test group better ratings for behaviour and competence. Including these two studies, a total of seven studies found no test/control differences for certain outcomes. However, nearly all the interventions (n = 11) observed some positive changes in their test participants' perceptions of themselves, mental health and relationship quality.

If the survey data are to be believed as an indicator of effectiveness, then the trend is that parent–child relationships, children's self-perceptions and attitudes towards changing schools became more positive after treatment, while their perceptions of their new school were generally unaffected. On the one hand

Table 11.3. Transition evaluations

Study	Participants	Intervention	Evaluation	Results
1. Bloyce and Frederickson (2012)	351 test children 106 control children Mainly white, vulnerable children referred from 75 schools (test) and a normal opportunity sample from two schools (control) in the UK.	Six group-work sessions on how to cope with transition given by an adult transfer support assistant at the end of primary school (Year 6).	Children were surveyed in last term of primary school and first term of secondary school (Year 7).	Test children were initially more concerned about school, but this difference disappeared by Year 7. Both groups had reduced school, emotional and relationship problems, but worse behaviour after transition.
2. Elias, Gara, Ubriaco, Rothbaum, Clabby & Schuler (1986)	158 children receiving a full test (a, b) or partial test (a) and a control group (no numbers). Mainly multiethnic, working class, in New Jersey, USA.	Two-component social problem-solving skills programme in first year of middle school (Grade 6): (a) 20 lessons on social problem solving skills (b) weekly lessons to put skills into practice	Children surveyed in term one and term three.	Children's worries about adjusting to middle school and their negative rating of its stressful factors declined with a higher intervention dosage (control, partial, full).
3. Felner et al. (1982, 2001)	65 test children 120 control children Rhode Island, USA	Test children were grouped into four adjacent tutor groups, who attended the same classes in their first year of junior high school (Grade 9).	Children surveyed before and after the intervention in Grade 9.	Test children had higher, stable perceptions of themselves, while control children had lower, declining self-perceptions.
4. Gonzales et al. (2004)	22 families Mainly Mexican American, low income in urban southwest US.	Nine-week programme on parenting skills and child self-management in last year of middle school (Grade 6).	Children and parents surveyed before and after in Grade 8. Follow-up interviews with 10 families in first year of high school (Grade 8).	Parents had positive changes in mental health, parenting experiences and quality. Children had reduced depression. Families continued to use the skills after transition.

	Study	Sample	Intervention	Measurement	Results
5.	Greene and Ollendick (1993)	42 children receiving a full test (a, b, c) or a partial test (a). 24 control children. Mainly white, middle to low income, in southwestern Virginia, USA.	Three components given across 15 weeks in first year of middle school (Grade 6): (a) extra teacher support (b) peer support groups (c) extra parental support.	Children surveyed before and after intervention, and at the end of Grade 6. Achievement recorded five times across Grade 6.	Full test group had faster gains in achievement, declining depression and better behaviour across time than the partial test group. No self-esteem or school perception differences.
6.	Holt, Bry and Johnson (2007)	TBA 20 test children 20 control children Mainly ethnic minority, low income in an urban school in mid-Atlantic USA.	Adult mentoring intervention given across five months in first year of high school (Grade 9).	Children surveyed before and after intervention in Grade 9 with a follow-up survey in Grade 10.	Test children had stable perceptions of teachers and decision making, while control group declined in these areas. No differences in achievement, absences or discipline referrals between groups.
7.	Qualter, Whiteley, Hutchinson and Pope (2007)	191 test children 162 control children In a rural high school in northwest England. The control group transferred one year before the test group (two different cohorts).	Intervention on emotional intelligence in the first year of secondary school (Year 7) – information on coping with academic and social changes delivered by Year 10 peer mentors and Year 7 teachers.	Children surveyed at the start and end of Year 7.	Test group had increased perceptions of their personal and social capabilities. Emotional intelligence decreased for the control group and for most of the test group, but increased for low achievers there.
8.	Ralph and Sanders (2003)	27 test parents in Queensland, Australia.	Eight-week parenting skills programme in the first year of high school.	Parents were surveyed before and after the intervention.	Parents had less conflict with children and partners, overreactivity and laxness. Their self-efficacy, self-management and mental health increased.

(continued)

Table 11.3. Transition evaluations (Continued)

Study	Participants	Intervention	Evaluation	Results
9. Reyes (1994)	57 test children (a, b) 88 control children (a) Mainly Hispanic, low income from 2 schools in Chicago, USA.	Two-component programme in last year of elementary school (Grade 8): (a) high school orientation day (b) peer mentoring.	Children surveyed in terms one and three of Grade 8 and first year of high school (Grade 9) for self-esteem, school perceptions, school readiness and social support.	No intervention effects observed. Both groups had increased readiness immediately after transition, but declining perceptions of school climate after transition.
10. Rosenblatt and Elias (2008)	145 test children High (40+ lessons) Medium (21–39 lessons) Low (< 20 lessons) Mainly African American or Hispanic, low income in New Jersey, USA.	43 lessons given in last year of elementary school (Grade 5) on interpersonal skills, team work, problem solving and emotional regulation.	Children were surveyed in the last year of middle school and first year of high school (Grade 6).	Achievement declined for all groups, but declined less with a higher number of lessons, regardless of students' prior levels of emotional intelligence.
11. Shepherd and Roker (2005)	80 test children from eight primary schools in London, UK.	A series of 1.5-hour after-school sessions to alleviate transition fears and improve coping in the last year of primary school (Year 6).	29 children surveyed before and after the intervention in Year 6.	More children were positive about transfer, friendships, asking for help, and about their lives in general, after the intervention. Children were less fearful of being bullied and settling in.
12. Slater and McKeown (2006)	7 test children 7 control children In 2 different secondary schools in Croydon, southeast London, UK.	Peer mentoring programme in first year of secondary school (Year 7).	Children surveyed in terms one, two and three.	Test children had fewer personal problems and lower psychosocial stress across time, but a similar perception of friendship quality.

13. Van Ryzin, Stormshak and Dishion (2012)	386 test families 207 control families Mixed ethnic group from three schools in an urban area of the Pacific Northwest, USA.	Three-session parenting skills programme delivered to parents in middle school (Grades 6, 7 and 8).	Children surveyed across three years of middle school and after transition to high school (Grade 9).	Test children reported lower growth in family conflict, antisocial behaviour, involvement with deviant peers and alcohol use.
14. Walsh-Bowers (1992)	84 test children 20 control children Test/control in two different schools in southwestern Ontario, Canada.	15 small-group drama sessions focused on improving social skills and coping in the first year of middle school (Grade 6).	Children, teachers and parents surveyed before and after with follow-up interviews, all in Grade 6.	Test and control children's survey scores were similar. Parents and teachers rated the test group higher for competency and behaviour. The intervention reportedly helped children's empathy and problem-solving skills.

this makes perfect sense, as interventions aimed at improving the person are doing just that. However, theoretically children's school environments should improve if they enter them with enhanced social and personal skills learned in an intervention (Blank, Baxter, Goyder, Naylor, Guillaume, Wilkinson, et al., 2010). Possibly, children are working against a headwind of forces tied to the school's existing climate, that create fairly standard school perceptions no matter what interventions children receive to make them better students. This points to whole-school restructuring as being the most powerful intervention possible (Felner et al., 2001), as I discuss in my conclusions below.

How can transition interventions support wellbeing?

As the previous section showed, interventions that target children's personal and social skills and relationships can have a positive influence on wellbeing and adjustment after transition. These types of interventions address many of the key problem areas outlined at the start of the chapter. To recap, these include social and academic fears before transition, developing a social hierarchy that devalues academic achievement, reforming academic identity based on stereotypes and on misleading information from new teachers and peers, and being confused by multiple teaching styles and new, more challenging tasks. In these circumstances, having one's academic and social skills and metacognitive understanding of relationships (and stereotypes) enhanced by an intervention might help a lot. However, there are many niggling issues that these interventions do not touch, including students' longer-term boredom in lessons, losing self-esteem through barriers to participation, being demotivated by the start-from-scratch approach, having an inappropriate balance of autonomy and structure and being devalued as an incoming, younger child. These issues are more inherent to school structures and organisation but can still be addressed by even fairly simple interventions, as demonstrated in Table 11.4.

An important point to make is that interventions aimed at one area of well-being (e.g. self-esteem) can influence other areas, too (e.g. skills development, identity). The same point applies to the Five Bridges, as any type of intervention (even administrative) can impact children's wellbeing, if only indirectly. For example, by giving transfer teachers time to read administrative data about new students, those teachers can become more familiar with their students' identities which might help them resist the urge to stereotype new students in an effort to make sense of unfamiliar classes (e.g. Benyon, 1985). In turn, if teachers perceive them more accurately, children should receive better-quality feedback about their achievements, which might help them adjust academically. Below I give suggestions for how interventions across the Five Bridges and in the area of home–school partnerships can target specific transition issues for each of the five points of psychological wellbeing. This template could also be used to plan interventions or as an evaluation tool – for example, by

Table 11.4 Interventions to support wellbeing

	Bridge 1:Administrative	Bridge 2: Pedagogy
Identity	Gathering and sharing data cross-tier, e.g. teacher and parents' perceptions, children's written records or portrayals of their identity captured in another manner such as a photographic project (Osborn et al., 2006). Organise regular careers guidance sessions for incoming students.	Discuss academic, personal and social identities in training and planning sessions on pedagogy. Teacher exchanges gather information on children's identities through learning activities, teach units in a manner that elicits identity issues (personalised and exploratory), and encourage children's perceptions of moving into a more advanced student role through discussion.
Self-esteem	Gathering and sharing data cross-tier. Diagnostic tests to identify trends in the year group, and vulnerable children with low or artificially high self-esteem.	Give children praise, opportunities to ask and answer questions, encouragement on their work, realistic yet positive assessment, etc.
Competence	Gathering and sharing data cross-tier, including teacher assessments and Key Stage test results. Diagnostic tests pre- and post-transfer to identify trends in the (incoming) year group, progress across transition and children lacking in particular skills. This data may be especially useful for setting children, and for pitching work in the first term. Alleviate children's fears of transition by arranging interventions in feeder school, orientation days, providing maps, timetables, equipment guides, rule books, etc. ahead of time and in the first term.	Team teaching cross-tier can give teachers time to help individual students obtain skills. Focus on asking open-ended, discovery questions that allow students to display their knowledge and reach conclusions independently, as well as evaluate and consolidate knowledge through asking closed questions. Have discussions on children's hopes and fears and transition myths, to dispel these and create realistic expectations of the new school. Encourage children to try hard, but avoid pressurising them or creating the impression that the transfer school is going to be all about harder work. Ascertain each child's strengths and weaknesses (including motivation) and lean on this to encourage their learning.
Autonomy	Involving children in transition planning.	Facilitate children's autonomy through group work, project work, managing learning activities and by giving children responsibility for tasks, in cross-tier teaching.

(continued)

Table 11.4 Interventions to support wellbeing (Continued)

	Bridge 1: Administrative	Bridge 2: Pedagogy
Social support	Create personal files for each child that include information on aspects of identity, self-esteem, competence and background, and share these with feeder teachers for enhanced value of individual students. Diagnostic testing to identify trends in social support in new students and students who lack social support. Share information about social support with families.	Talk about children's 'whole-school value' in the classroom, cross-tier. Facilitate discussions about changing in role from being the oldest to the youngest students. Arrange lessons in a way that helps students get to know each other. Teachers could openly demonstrate their support of children as a group, and support individual children with discretion. Tutor groups, buddy schemes and other types of pastoral care allow for increased social support.

	Bridge 3: Curriculum	Bridge 4: Self-management
Identity	Use information about children's identities to structure units of work, and/or explore children's identities through these. Teach positive and realistic identity development, i.e. raise awareness of stereotyping, peer pressure, career pathways. Use the topic of 'becoming a secondary/middle/ high school student' as a basis for bridging units or post-transition programmes.	Link training given to children in academic, organisational and social aspects of self-management to their identity development, both in the short (i.e. becoming a professional student) and longer terms (i.e. acquiring skills for the job market, to protect mental health).
Self-esteem	Construct units based on small, achievable tasks for all children. Incorporate sessions on self-value into the curriculum.	Acquiring self-management skills should increase children's self-esteem, as found by the intervention evaluations.
Competence	Increase students' skills via summer schools for gifted and talented and low achievers, bridging units, teaching the transfer curriculum in the feeder school, preparing for transfer by increasing self-management skills and teaching these as extended post-induction programmes. Use transition myths, hopes and fears as a topic in bridging units or in pre-transition programmes, to dispel anxieties. Include appropriate discontinuities in the curriculum to increase children's skills, in mind of their ability to cope with these changes academically. Regularly review how children are coping with more difficult work in transfer schools.	Teach self-management skills in different areas to help children increase in a broader range of competencies (e.g. academic, social, organisational), within individual bridging units, intervention programmes, etc. and worked into the curriculum. Having greater self-management capability should relieve children's anxieties about transition, and help them cope with changes in the transfer school, as found by the intervention evaluations.

Table 11.4 Interventions to support wellbeing (Continued)

	Bridge 3: Curriculum	Bridge 4: Self-management
Autonomy	Implement a 'participation programme' where students choose from a selection of assignments that facilitate their active participation in school community, e.g. wellbeing evaluators (students gather and analyse data each term), entrepreneurship team (students plan and execute an entrepreneurship fair) and allocate weekly lessons for this. Implement project work in all areas of the curriculum.	Helping children to acquire academic, organisational and social skills should help them be more confident in managing their own learning and other projects.
Social support	Build relationships education into bridging units and other areas of the curriculum. Focus on meeting, evaluating and making friends with new people. Raise children's awareness of stereotypes (e.g. attractiveness, power) and ability to overcome these in their views of others. Emphasise the value of all children, and respect for others. Give training in avoiding peer conflict. The participation programme suggested for autonomy also facilitates children's value in the school community. Display work in school halls (as agreed by children), have work contribute to school decision making, future transfer management, etc. Raise the status of incoming students in the transfer school.	Learning social skills should help children make new friends, better quality friendships and a more pro-social and less judgmental peer network. Build opportunities for relationship development into self-management activities, e.g. peer mentoring, adult mentoring, small-group work, team exercises. Use a rolling system of teaching self-management skills to classes or smaller groups of children, then have these children teach the skills to others, so that all children can ultimately take on a mentorship and teaching role. Display and discuss work on self-management, for parents and the wider school community.

	Bridge 5: Social	Home–school partnerships
Identity	Use information about children's (and teachers') identities to improve the quality of teacher–student relationships. Match buddies/mentors based on children's identity-related interests. Use identity interests to organise social events.	Families and teachers swap information pertaining to children's identities. Joint initiatives on identity development, e.g. careers counselling at school, a unit on career pathways, and families follow this up by taking children to observe a job or talk to an adult with that career.

(continued)

Table 11.4 Interventions to support wellbeing (Continued)

	Bridge 5: Social	Home–school partnerships
Self-esteem	Give opportunities to master new things and receive praise and recognition for achievement at social events such as induction day, small-group programmes and residential camp. Give extra social support to vulnerable children identified by diagnostic tests or as communicated by feeder schools (e.g. SEN children).	Create programmes that incorporate or focus on managing children's self-esteem between parents and teachers. These could involve self-esteem training for parents, and helping parents develop schemes to support children's self-esteem at home.
Competence	Give opportunities to acquire new skills at social events, as for self-esteem. Build on cooperative work habits and skills, e.g. team work, group work, partnerships, leadership skills, etc. Identify friends that children work well with. Allow children to suggest their own seating arrangements. Older peer and adult mentors can help children acquire skills and knowledge.	Deliver training programmes to parents on how to support their child academically at home. Allow parents to extend their own academic skills by offering adult education at the school. Remove barriers to participation by offering free childcare for younger siblings, a family meal at the sessions and free transportation (Gonzales et al., 2004). Involve parents as 'consultants' on how to improve their child's competence.
	Provide fun but challenging social opportunities; this also helps with confidence building; e.g., assault courses, camp, drama, crafts. Have peer and adult mentors help children relieve their anxieties about transition.	Involve parents in planning sessions for interventions at transition that support children's motivation. Include parents in pre-transition interventions in order to relieve their anxieties, so that they can help their children be less nervous and more realistic about transition.
Autonomy	By helping supportive peer networks and high-quality friendships to develop, this should also support children's autonomy, i.e. confidence to try things independently, and manage learning/projects with their friends autonomously of adult supervision.	Assess how much autonomy children receive at home, in comparison to school. Use this as a starting point for making positive changes to school practices. Deliver intervention programmes that help parents better manage their relationships with children to enable their children's autonomy without reducing their support and monitoring.
Social support	Work discussion and instruction on social support (i.e. being a good friend, being non-judgmental, being a good team member) into social events, residential camp and in group work and team work activities.	Have discussions with parents on children's friendships and peer networks at home and school, to gather data. Involve parents in planning and delivering interventions that support children's pro-social friendships at home and school.

Table 11.4 Interventions to support wellbeing (Continued)

	Bridge 5: Social	Home–school partnerships
Social support	Use social events to highlight the value of exiting/incoming students to the school community. Give children opportunities to be valuable to their schools via group work, organising their own social events, etc.	Increase parents' value in the school community in ways that their children are comfortable with. This could occur on both sides of the transition through active participation, or family-honouring days/events/programmes. Help parents openly value their children at home, and use information they supply about children to help teachers value their students.

focusing across one or more rows (e.g. How can we improve students' value in our school community, through our administrative practices, pedagogy and the curriculum, etc.?) or columns (e.g. How can our administrative activities improve students' psychological wellbeing at transition?).

The timeline of transition interventions

The majority of interventions in this chapter were delivered in feeder schools or in the first transfer term. This is a fairly short-term perspective on when children need support for their adjustment, as remarked on by Galton (2010). Galton considers the occupational Transitions Cycle (Nicholson, 1987) in the school context, which has four defined phases of adjustment:

1. *Preparation.* Preparing to take on a new role in a new organisation (in this case, becoming a transfer school student).
2. *Encounter.* Making first judgments after transition, managing initial feelings, gathering information and exploring the new circumstances.
3. *Adjustment.* Changing both self and the environment to maintain wellbeing, i.e. the person-environment fit process described in Chapter 2.
4. *Stabilisation.* Achieving consistent personal and organisational effectiveness, by managing the environment's supports and demands.

Galton recommends that schools consider each of these four phases when planning how to manage transition (2010). In a recent study of children's feelings about school at transition, Linda Hargreaves and I identified specific ways in which children's psychology developed in the first three phases at school transition (Symonds & Hargreaves, 2014) which informed the model of transition phase psychology that I set out in Chapter 2. For example, the encounter phase is characterised by children's hopes and fears and transition myths, while children reconfigure their academic identities in the adjustment phase, after their initial encounters with the new school. Not only could schools design longer-term transition schemes crossing the phases, but also use interventions to address what happens to children in each phase, as I set out in Chapter 2 and as indicated in the key problems table in this chapter (Table 11.1).

In their book on managing transition, Akos and colleagues (2005) give examples of transition schemes that introduce a new component every month from the start of the pre-transfer year to the month after transfer. These examples begin by communicating with feeder schools, parents and children (e.g. October – send a Parent Teacher Association newsletter about transition), then gradually increase their active involvement in transition processes (e.g. January – transfer teachers first teach in feeder school; February – identify buddies and train them; March – implement buddy scheme). They are laid out in a monthly calendar developed by a dedicated cross-tier transition team. Galton (2010) and I suggest extending these activities across the post-transition year, in order to identify and arrest any declines in psychological wellbeing that might occur there. Components of activities, or an integrated series of activities, could gather information on children and help them adjust across at least a two-year period (one year pre- and post-transition). This information could be especially helpful for diagnostic purposes, such as identifying vulnerable children, and evaluating new interventions and student cohorts as the years go by.

Conclusions

In general, schools appear to be getting it right when designing interventions that support children's self-management, relieve anxieties and improve social relationships, as these have a knock-on effect across many of the five points of psychological wellbeing. However, a more targeted approach is warranted in some cases. Using the frameworks in this chapter, teachers can create interventions that address specific areas of wellbeing or address the full range of areas identified. They can also use these frameworks to evaluate existing practice, and as the basis for discussion with other staff, children and parents about how to manage transition. Interventions and transition schemes appear to be most effective when they are well planned and executed as cross-tier collaborations characterised by trusting and respectful relationships (Hargreaves & Wall, 2002). This team effort might consider a longer-term perspective on transition planning in order to address the ways in which children need support across the different phases of their adjustment.

A key issue in all of this is how to help children develop into positive, effective transfer school students. This is the central topic of the status passage discussed in Chapter 1, and the focus of many children's aspirations about transition (e.g. Measor & Woods 1984, Rudduck, Chaplain & Wallace, 1996). Galton and colleagues (2003) recommended that teachers create a careful balance of continuity (to relieve fear and facilitate work progress) and discontinuity (highlighting children's change in role, giving more complex work and responsibility) at transition, so that children move into this new role with ease, yet make visible progress there. Transition is a time of great excitement and progress for many children, and as such their change in status should be openly celebrated as well as supported by longer-term school practices. By helping children achieve effectiveness in their new role, transition interventions can motivate children and support their identity development, which should promote their mental health and engagement.

Felner et al. (2001) outlined three types of interventions that are relevant to those observed in this chapter. These are *first generation efforts* to improve conditions and self-management for vulnerable children, such as the interventions for low-income, low-achieving children in the USA and the targeted support for overly worried children from Bloyce and Frederickson (2012) in the UK; *second generation efforts* that target whole year groups of children to help develop their skills and resilience such as induction days, peer mentoring and extended post-induction programmes that comprise the bulk of interventions delivered by UK schools; and *third generation efforts* that change the ecology of the school environment for everybody – for example, by blocking teachers and students (Felner et al., 1982; Fuller et al., 2005) and by having children transfer in June (Sutherland et al., 2010). Although Felner et al. (2001) argue that third generation efforts should be the most effective, as they eventuate the most substantial change, I imagine that a combination of extra support for vulnerable children, self-management and social support interventions for cohorts of children and efforts to change school structures to create a more positive school climate would be a foolproof way to improve conditions at transition. At the end of the day, however, such efforts need a consistent cycle of planning, execution and evaluation in order to create sustainable programmes that are well matched to students' needs, as I explore more in the following chapter.

Note

1 Please note that some studies had more than one focus.

References

Akos, P., Queen, J. A., & Lineberry, C. (2005). *Promoting a successful transition to middle school*. Larchmont, NY: Eye on Education Inc.

Ashworth, D., Atherley, M., & Chappell, A. (2011). *Sound tracks: Supporting young people's musical progression from primary to secondary school*. London: Paul Hamlyn Foundation. Available at: www.musicalbridges.org

Association of Assessment Inspectors and Advisors (2001). *Crossing the bridge: Case studies in KS2 to KS3 transfer*. London: AAIA.

Benyon, J. (1985). *Initial encounters in the secondary school: Sussing, typing and coding*. Lewes: Falmer Press.

Blank, L., Baxter, S., Goyder, E., Naylor, P. B., Guillaume, L., Wilkinson, A., et al. (2010). Promoting well-being by changing behaviour: A systematic review and narrative synthesis of the effectiveness of whole secondary school behavioural interventions. *Mental Health Review Journal, 15*(2), 43–53.

Bloyce, J., & Frederickson, N. (2012). Intervening to improve the transfer to secondary school. *Educational Psychology in Practice, 28*(1), 1–18.

Chambers, D., & Coffey, A. (2013). Development of a mobile-optimised website to support students with special needs transitioning from primary to secondary settings. *Australasian Journal of Special Education, 37*(1), 79–91.

Chitty, C. (2002). *Understanding schools and schooling.* London: RoutledgeFalmer.

Deakin Crick, R., Jelfs, H., Symonds, J., Ren, K., Patton, A., & Grushka, K. (2010). *Learning futures evaluation report*: University of Bristol. Paul Hamlyn Foundation.

Delamont, S., & Galton, M. (1986). *Inside the secondary classroom.* London: Routledge & Kegan Paul.

Demetriou, H., Goalen, P., & Rudduck, J. (2000). Academic performance, transfer, transition and friendship: Listening to the student voice. *International Journal of Educational Research 33*(4), 425–441.

Department for Children, Schools and Families (2008). *Strengthening transfers and transitions. Partnerships for progress.* 00083-2008PDF-EN-1.

Department for Education and Skills (2004). *Curriculum continuity: Effective transfer between primary and secondary schools.* Nottingham: DfES Publications.

Department for Education and Skills (2006). *A condensed Key Stage 3: Improving Key Stage 2 to Key Stage 3 transfer.* Nottingham: DfES Publications.

Elias, M. J., Gara, M., Ubriaco, M., Rothbaum, P. A., Clabby, J. F., & Shchuler, T. (1986). Impact of a preventive social problem solving intervention on children's coping with middle-school stressors. *American Journal of Community Psychology, 14*(3), 259–275.

Evangelou, M., Taggart, B., Sylva, K., Melhuish, E., Sammons, P., & Siraj-Blatchford, I. (2008). *What makes a successful transition from primary to secondary school?* London: Department of Education.

Felner, R. D., Ginter, M., & Primavera, J. (1982). Primary prevention during school transitions: Social support and environmental structure. *American Journal of Community Psychology, 10*(2), 277–290.

Felner, R. D., Favazza, A., Shim, M., Brand, S., Gu, K., & Noonan, N. (2001). Whole school improvement and restructuring as prevention and promotion: Lessons from STEP and the Project on High Performance Learning Communities. *Journal of School Psychology, 39*(2), 177–202.

Foundation for People with Learning Disabilities (FPLD). (2014). Accessed 21 April 2014 from www.learningdisabilities.org.uk

Fuller, K., Thomas, F., & Horswell, C. (2005). *Key stage 2 to key stage 3 transition project.* Nottingham: Mouchel Parkman/Department for Education and Skills.

Galton, M. (2010). Moving to secondary school: What do pupils say about the experience? In D. Jindal-Snape (ed.), *Educational transitions: Moving stories from around the world* (pp. 107–124). New York and Abingdon: Routledge.

Galton, M., Gray, J., & Rudduck, J. (1999). *The impact of school transitions and transfer on pupil progress and attainment.* Norwich: Department for Education and Employment.

Galton, M., Gray, J., Rudduck, J., Berry, M., Demetriou, H., Edwards, J., et al. (2003). *Transfer and transitions in the middle years of schooling (7–14): Continuities and discontinuities in learning.* London: Department for Education and Skills.

Gonzales, N. A., Dumka, L. E., Deardorff, J., Carter, S. J., & McCray, A. (2004). Preventing poor mental health and school dropout of Mexican American adolescents following the transition to junior high school. *Journal of Adolescent Research, 19*(1), 113–131.

Gray, J., Galton, M., McLaughlin, C., Clarke, B., & Symonds, J. (2011). *The supportive school: Wellbeing and the young adolescent.* Newcastle upon Tyne: Cambridge Scholars Publishing.

Greene, R. W., & Ollendick, T. H. (1993). Evaluation of a multidimensional program for sixth-graders in transition from elementary to middle school. *Journal of Community Psychology, 21*(2), 162–176.

Hargreaves, L., & Galton, M. (eds). (2002). *Transfer from the primary classroom: 20 years on.* London: RoutledgeFalmer.

Hargreaves, L., & Wall, D. (2002). 'Getting used to each other' cross-phase liaison and induction. In L. Hargreaves & M. Galton (eds), *Transfer from the primary classroom: 20 years on* (pp. 28–53). London: RoutledgeFalmer.

Holt, L. J., Bry, B. H., & Johnson, V. L. (2007). Enhancing school engagement in at-risk, urban minority adolescents through a school-based, adult mentoring intervention. *Child & Family Behavior Therapy, 30*(4), 297–308.

Lahelma, E., & Gordon, T. (1997). First day in secondary school: Learning to be a 'professional pupil'. *Educational Research and Evaluation, 3*(2), 119–139.

Martin, K., Sharp, C., & Mehta, P. (2013). *The impact of the summer schools programme on pupils: Research report June 2013.* London: Department for Education.

Measor, L., & Woods, P. (1984). *Changing schools.* Milton Keynes: Open University Press.

Nicholson, N. (1987). The transition cycle: A conceptual framework for the analysis of change and human resources management. *Research in Personnel and Human Resources Management, 5,* 167–222.

Osborn, M., McNess, E., & Pollard, A. (2006). Identity and transfer: A new focus for home–school knowledge exchange. *Educational Review, 58*(4), 415–433.

Powell, R., Smith, R., Jones, G., & Reakes, A. (2006). *Transition from primary to secondary school: Current arrangements and good practice in Wales.* Swindon: National Foundation for Educational Research.

Quach, J., Gold, L., Arnup, S., Sia, K.-L., Wake, M., & Hiscock, H. (2013). Improving school transition by improving child sleep: A translational randomised trial. *BMJ Open, 3:* e004009. doi:10.1136/bmjopen-2013-004009

Qualter, P., Whiteley, H. E., Hutchinson, J. M., & Pope, D. J. (2007). Supporting the development of emotional intelligence competencies to ease the transition from primary to high school. *Educational Psychology in Practice, 21*(1), 79–95.

Ralph, A., & Sanders, M. R. (2003). Preliminary evaluation of the Group Teen Triple P program for parents of teenagers making the transition to high school. *Advances in Mental Health, 2*(3), 169–178.

Reyes, O., Gillock, K., & Kobus, K. (1994). A longitudinal study of school adjustment in urban, minority adolescents: Effects of a high school transition program. *American Journal of Community Psychology, 22*(3), 341–369.

Rosenblatt, J. L., & Elias, M. J. (2008). Dosage effects of a preventive social-emotional learning intervention on achievement loss associated with middle school transition. *Journal of Primary Prevention, 29*(6), 535–555.

Rudduck, J., Chaplain, R., & Wallace, G. (Eds.). (1996). *School improvement: What can pupils tell us?* London: David Fulton.

Shepherd, J., & Roker, D. (2005). *An evaluation of a 'transition to secondary school' project run by the National Pyramid Trust.* Trust for the Study of Adolescence.

Slater, P., & McKeown, M. (2006). The role of peer counselling and support in helping to reduce anxieties around transition from primary to secondary school. *Counselling and Psychotheraphy Research: Linking Research with Practice, 4*(1), 72–79.

Suffolk Local Authority. (2001). *Transfer review*. Available at: www.school-portal.co.uk/GroupHomepage.asp?GroupID=783552

Sutherland, R., Yee, W. C., McNess, E., & Harris, R. (2010). *Supporting learning in the transition from primary to secondary schools*. Bristol: University of Bristol.

Symonds, J., & Hargreaves, L. (2014). Emotional and motivational engagement at school transition: A qualitative study of stage-environment fit. *The Journal of Early Adolescence, OnlineFirst* (Nov 3, 2014).

Van Ryzin, M. J., Stormshak, E. A., & Dishion, T. J. (2012). Engaging parents in the family check-up in middle school: Longitudinal effects on family conflict and problem behavior through the high school transition. *Journal of Adolescent Health, 50*(6), 627–633.

Walsh-Bowers, R. (1992). A creative drama prevention program for easing early adolescents' adjustment to school transitions. *Journal of Primary Prevention, 13*(2), 131–147.

Chapter 12

Research and evaluation

> Without thorough evaluation it is often the case that the rhetoric of school-based initiatives outstrips the reality
>
> (Galton, Gray, Rudduck et al. 2003, p. 74).

Chapter overview

This chapter encourages readers to evaluate the experiences of children, teachers and the wider school community at school transition by doing systematic research. Evaluation of transition processes is important, because it enables people to develop better interventions and management techniques in the future. This chapter explains in simple terms what evaluation is, and how to research using questionnaires, interviews, audio/visual methods and document analysis. It discusses the role of teachers and children in research as active participants, and provides a guide to writing reports so that practitioners can keep and distribute valuable records of their evaluations.

Evaluation

1. What are the needs of children in your school and school pyramid at transition?
2. What type of transition intervention might work best for them?
3. In what ways does your transition intervention work and not work?
4. How could that intervention be improved?

Although there is a tremendous amount of good practice for supporting children at transition (see Chapter 11), there is less evidence of evaluating that practice (Galton et al., 2003; Sutherland, Yee, McNess & Harris, 2010). Often, the above questions are answered through educated guesswork or by consulting a small group of people who are easily at hand. Although a proper evaluation requires significant human resources, the payoffs are great, however. You will have hard evidence to support the design and administration of interventions, and will be confident that your interventions are working. Also, by harnessing the power of research, you will generate ideas for new and improved interventions that might have been unimaginable before. Using this evidence you can publicise your work to parents, staff and local authorities, share your story to help other schools and create a valuable record of children's adaptation and interventions to inform your future efforts. Indeed, given these benefits the bigger question is then, why wouldn't you evaluate?

Before you evaluate, it is important to consider the potholes you might fall into. First, do you have the time and resources to carry it through to the end? It is a great pity when effort is put into setting up an evaluation, that its bounty cannot be harvested. In Galton et al. (2003), schools were inhibited from evaluating their transition interventions because teachers were under pressure to meet assessment targets, in the middle of implementing an educational reform programme, and lacked the skills and knowledge to evaluate. Also, teachers have been unenthusiastic about being involved in evaluation, because they worried it might reveal sensitive and negative data about their teaching (Elliot, 1991). Local authorities have also been disinclined to help, because they were under pressure from OFSTED to dedicate their time and resources to failing schools (Galton et al., 2003). For these reasons, it is useful, before you begin, to create an action plan that maps the evaluation in time against your existing resources, limitations and need for skills development.

Second, who is going to help you evaluate? Evaluation is a team effort, no matter which way you look at it. As discussed in Chapter 11, transition interventions go well when they are managed by a team representing both feeder and transfer schools, and where there is mutual trust and respect of each other's priorities and availability (Hargreaves & Wall, 2002). The same goes for evaluation. Although you might be in charge of an evaluation, this doesn't mean you have to do it all by yourself. Even children can help you; indeed, they are key players when it is their views you are soliciting. If you view your school as a family, then naturally you might ask your children to help you evaluate the things you do together. Also, having others involved raises the chances of the evaluation being continued in years to come (Sutherland et al., 2010), making your initial time investment more worthwhile.

Third, will your evaluation capture a partial or a fuller picture of your children's qualities, needs and responses to intervention? Returning to the four questions above, in order to establish children's needs and their range of opinions, it is ideal to evaluate all children in a cohort, or a smaller *representative* group of children, as I discuss later in this chapter. We can find out how children responded to an intervention by asking them at the very end; however, we can only prove changes in experience by asking them at the beginning, too – that is, by involving both feeder and transfer schools in the project (Sutherland et al., 2010). The remainder of this chapter is dedicated to this topic – how to conduct good-quality evaluations through research.

Fourth, do you have clear criteria to use in the evaluation? Not being explicit about, or agreed on, what the evaluation is assessing can inhibit its success (Sutherland et al., 2010). It might be useful to use an existing framework or set of ideas as a starting point, and I have given a selection of these in Table 12.1. Or, you may want to design your evaluation to capture the priorities of children and teachers involved, then use these as your assessment criteria. This can involve doing a pilot study (a small investigation to set the stage for a larger evaluation) or having an emergent research design where these indigenous concerns surface close to the start of your study, then are worked into its structure. More on research design can be found in the next section.

No matter whether you use existing or novel assessment criteria, a useful distinction is to consider whether these evaluate the *merit* of the intervention as a success/failure and work in progress, or the *worth* of the intervention to its participants, the local community and wider society (Mertens, 2014). Also, are you assessing the qualities, needs and experiences of children and teachers to inform the initial and ongoing design of transition interventions (process focused assessment), or the effectiveness of an intervention on children's wellbeing and

Table 12.1 Examples of assessment criteria

Framework	Criteria
Child-centred frameworks	
Common Assessment Framework (Every Child Matters)[1]	• Be healthy • Stay safe • Enjoy and achieve • Make a positive contribution • Achieve economic wellbeing
Social and Emotional Aspects of Learning[2]	• New beginnings • Getting on and falling out • Say no to bullying • Going for goals! • Good to be me *Units focus on self-awareness, managing feelings, motivation, self-efficacy, self-esteem, social skills and empathy*
The Five-Point Star of Wellbeing (see Chapter 2)	• Identity • Self-esteem • Competence • Autonomy • Social support
Practice-centred frameworks	
The Five Bridges (Galton, Gray & Rudduck, 1999)	• Administrative • Pedagogy • Curriculum • Self-management • Social
Self-Evaluation Model (Sutherland et al., 2010)	• Shared practice across learning phases • Extended partnerships/community and other professionals • Shared vision and responsibility • Common framework/sustained collaboration and evaluation • Common assessment practices • Support for independent learning

teachers' practice (outcome focused assessment) (Elliot, 1991)? And, will your assessment seek to better understand the child, educational practice, or both?

Fifth, will your evaluation influence a change in practice? Here I refer to the tradition of action research, developed by psychologist Kurt Lewin (1890–1947). Lewin described how society uses research in the real world (i.e. outside of the lab) to make decisions and eventuate action. He refers to this as a 'spiral of steps' (Lewin, 1946/1948, p. 206), where a general plan is made, the first step is carried out, then it is evaluated. This leads to the planning of a second step and modification of the general plan, before repeating the cycle for a third step, and so on. Writing just before World War II, Lewin used the analogy of German air raids where the air force plan an attack, carry it out, then evaluate the effects before planning a second air raid. Elliot (1991) translates Lewin's cycle for the field of teacher-led research, adding that evaluation should comprise data analysis as well as gathering. The beauty of Lewin's idea is that it allows the assessment criteria (i.e. the general plan) to shift throughout the evaluation, as more information about the action steps emerges.

To clarify, I give an example of a rolling plan of research, intervention and evaluation at transition. First, you might sit down with your team and churn out a general idea about what it is you want to address. Together, you settle on children's wellbeing, and in particular their relationships with peers. The first step in your plan becomes to survey children before they transfer, in order to evaluate their social skills and discover their social hopes and fears. You design the questionnaire and deliver it in February well before transition, then analyse the data. Based on the results, you plan a second action step of developing a social skills intervention, which you administer in July before transition, and again in September after children transfer. You evaluate this intervention in October, using the same questionnaire that you used in February, to identify whether children's social skills have improved and fears have abated. You also interview a focus group of children who display interesting questionnaire results, on how the intervention did or didn't help them. Both types of data lead to ideas on how to modify the questionnaire and intervention for next year's cohort. You then repeat the entire process the following year, in a cycle of strengthening and extending your provision for children's needs.

Research

In order to evaluate children and interventions, we need to do research. Although Lewin visualised an ongoing spiral of action research, it is simpler to start out by focusing on just one of Lewin's action steps as a story with a beginning, middle and end. At the beginning, you to plan the research. In the middle, you gather and analyse your data. Then, you end by reporting your findings. Writing a report, or presenting your findings in some way, is critical, as there you synthesise what you have found, make sense of it for other people and create a record. You don't need to have special training to do basic research, although it may be helpful to engage a consultant or experienced friend to help you. In the remainder of this chapter I outline the types of research you might want to do. Further reading on each method can be found by looking up the references in those sections.

Research questions

Every good study begins with a question. You would be amazed at how many researchers can't narrow down their interests into a single sentence, until you try it for yourself and realize how tricky it can be. Yes you want to research peer relationships. But what exactly do you want to know? One way to identify a research question is to use an exploding spider diagram, creating tangents of your central interest that increase in specificity. This will help you look at your central interest in a more practical light, or you may find yourself focusing on one of the tangents as a road to a study. You can always ask more than one question, but ideally these should be sub-questions of a grander design.

Once you choose your question(s), it is time to pay attention to language. The words that you use in your research questions can set up how you do the research, so you must be careful. Asking about the *amount* or *extent* of something can lead you down the road to using numbers in your study, whereas process questions that ask *how* and *why* are best answered using participants' open-ended answers, as they hold the keys to perception and experience. Try writing your research question in different ways, until you get to a place that best expresses what you want to do in the study. A rule of thumb is that simpler is better – meaning, don't ask something complicated, don't ask too many things and don't ask more than one thing per question. You might wonder why and, at the end of your study you will know by experience that this is because even the simplest questions have complex answers.

Talk about the questions with your colleagues. Share them with children and ask if they make sense from the child's perspective. Sleep on it, then try writing them again. Ask whether the questions are going to provide valuable information for children, parents, your school and other schools. Think strategically about whether the questions will allow the study to be repeated, or might form a platform to extend your work later on. Know that careful questions make for a tight study. Simple questions bring in-depth results. Interesting questions can encourage an audience and funding. But lengthy, wordy and convoluted questions lead to irrelevant and confused work. Luckily, if your research is of good quality, you can change these later on and dismiss your earlier attempts as an exploratory first round of Lewin's action research cycle (the author winks).

Some examples of clear and useful overarching questions are:

- How do children's social skills change across transition?
- To what extent did children's social skills change in relation to the intervention?

- How did the intervention impact children's fears about making friends in their new schools?

But you might not want to lead a study with the following questions:

- What are children's friendships like at transition? (*Too vague, a lot of work!*)
- How do children make friends and think about their friendships, and does this have anything to do with learning? (*Double-barrelled, convoluted*)
- Did the social skills intervention change children's method of making friends? (*Too specific, requires a yes/no answer, better placed as a sub-question*)

Research design

Next, you can begin to plan your research. This involves thinking about how you are going to answer the question, in time and space. Who will be involved? What method will you use? (Methods are described in the following section.) What resources will you need? When will you instigate each step of the design? And, how long will it take? A good starting point for thinking about design is the notion of *focus*. Like a photographer, you might zoom in on what you are investigating, so that you get a good close-up picture (thus producing more detail). Or, you could capture a wider view of things, taking in all of the variation in the landscape. You might take just one picture, a snapshot of a moment in time or place. Or, you might take several pictures to reveal different angles of the view, or how the view changes over time. Like a cartographer, you can *triangulate* these pictures to ensure a more accurate position for your answer. But remember: the more pictures you take, the more time you will need to carry out the research. Sometimes it is better to stick to just one picture.

Another important element is *representativeness*. To what extent will your research represent the people or place you are studying? If you are studying children, you might want to include every child who is in the year group or the transition intervention. If you think of your research concern as mapping out a country, then the *population* are all of its inhabitants. But, it might not be practical to involve all of them in the study. Or, you might not be able to. In that case, your next option is to choose or make do with a *sample* of participants from the population. Ideally, they would represent the population on definitive criteria such as age, gender, ethnicity, family composition, free school meals, special educational needs and so on. If your sample is diverse enough, this will allow you to later look in depth at the experiences of a *subgroup* or *subsample*, say low-achieving females. Sometimes, it can be practical to work with a smaller number of people, who may or may not represent your population. If they work together, they are called a *focus group*. Or, if you are studying them individually, they become your *case studies*. It is important to note that if you are using a smaller group of people, your findings, no matter how detailed, cannot be generalised with any certainty to a wider population.

Third, you might wish to follow a traditional research design, or create one of your own. Traditional designs owe much to the foundations of different disciplines, including natural science, anthropology, sociology and psychology. And each has its own purposes and uses. They can be blended by containing elements of each other, inform each other when put in a sequence, or be stand-alone projects. But, as you might expect, simpler is better if you have never done research before. I overview typical research designs in Table 12.2.

Table 12.2 Research design examples

Design	Description
Cross-sectional study	Data are collected at one time point.
Repeated measures study	Data are collected at successive time points, using an identical method of data collection (e.g. the same questions are asked).
Longitudinal study	Data are collected at successive time points (may or may not be repeated measures).
Experiment	Data are collected from two or more groups using an identical method of data collection. At least one group is a 'control' group who lacks the 'treatment' of the 'test' group (i.e. participating in an intervention). Experiments often use repeated measures (e.g. a pre-and post-test).
Cross-over study	An experiment where the control and test groups cross over in their experience of treatment/no treatment, where the treatment is withheld temporarily from the control group, or where it is given in lagged moderated doses, so that eventually both groups receive treatment. This is an ethical manner of conducting an experiment in social settings.
Survey	Data are systematically collected from a population or sample of people, in order to canvass their perceptions and explore the study focus as it occurs within that group and subgroups therein.
Case study	Data are collected using multiple methods to give an in-depth picture of a chosen subject – for example, a school, a classroom, a student, a teacher. Often, several case studies are used for comparative purposes, or to illustrate different angles of experience. Case studies can be cross-sectional or longitudinal. They are often reported as narrative.
Ethnography	A longitudinal study of an 'object', usually a specific environment, group of people, and/or culture, where one or more methods are used to gather naturally occurring data (i.e. behaviour occurring in a natural setting) and where other types of less natural data (e.g. semi-structured interview responses, closed-ended questionnaire responses) can be used to complement this necessary base. Traditionally, researchers use participant observation in ethnography, where they immerse themselves as a participant in the environment in order to understand the experiences of the participants whom they study.
Action research	The process by which people research their own practice in order to improve it (see Lewin's action research cycle above).

Ethics

When conducting research in educational settings, it is critical to adhere to ethical guidelines in place to protect the rights of participants. These are set out for example by the British Educational Research Association (BERA, 2011) in an electronic document that can be freely downloaded from the Internet. BERA state that researchers must not discriminate against participants for any reason, such as their gender, ethnicity, special needs and so on. Participants must be given every opportunity to express their voluntary informed consent to participating in the research. This means you should make sure that they understand the purpose of the research, how they will be involved and who the research will be communicated to, before asking them if they want to be involved. Participants should also be made aware that they have the right to withdraw from the research at any point. It is essential to offer participants anonymity, or at least assure them that their privacy will be respected in research processes. Inversely, it is also their right to have their identity made known if it suits them. Participants may experience distress in the research process, and may be burdened by the research as it affects their working or workload. Researchers must do their best to minimise these discomforts. Finally, researchers are allowed to use incentives to encourage participation, but these must not be damaging to participant's health.

One way in which I have attempted to address all of these issues in my own research with children is to engage children as active participants. There, I typically run a participation workshop before the research commences, where children are taught about research methods, about their rights in research and about the specific research. Only then do I consider that they have enough information to make voluntary informed consent. Throughout the research children help me design the questionnaires and interview schedules, which helps me word questions in a way that is understandable and meaningful for them and allows them to point out questions they would be uncomfortable answering. When observing children, I have allowed them to read my notes on their behaviour, which helps correct my assumptions and gives them confidence that I am not writing nasty things about them. I have also let children go through their interview transcripts to indicate any information they would prefer to keep private. Finally, I have made children feel comfortable in the research setting by allowing them their choice of being interviewed alone or with a friend, by conducting interviews in places they are comfortable with, and by offering adequate refreshment when children are participating for longer periods. Readers are welcome to contact me for copies of Power-Point® presentations to teach children about research and research ethics.

Research methods

Once you have your question(s), you will need to choose a way to answer them. Research methods are the tools you can use for this. They are the means by which you gather information (or *data*) about your topic of interest. Several common methods are listed below:

- questionnaire (asking people to fill out a form)
- interview (asking people to talk about a topic)
- observation (watching people and the wider environment)
- audio/visual methods (capturing behaviour and the wider environment through, for example, photographs, video and selected sound recordings)
- document analysis (exploring and synthesising printed materials)

The most important thing to think about when choosing your method is what type of data it will produce. For therein will be the answers to your questions. A useful concept here is that of data being open-ended (unrestricted, allowed to flow naturally from their source, e.g. allowing a child to freely describe their day) or closed-ended (when you or a participant selects from one of several units of information that you have set up beforehand, e.g. a multiple choice question, a yes/no answer or a rating on a scale for observing behaviour). Each of the above methods can produce either type of data, as I describe below.

Questionnaires

Questionnaires can be printed or electronic, and administered in written or spoken form to participants. To collect closed-ended data, questionnaires offer a selection of alternative answers using a check box format (yes/no, multiple choice). These produce two types of closed-ended data. The first is called scale data.[3] Here, the idea is that the choices can be ranked according to value (e.g. bad/good, weak/strong, high/low, none/all). Each choice is assigned a number, visible or hidden to participants. These numbers can measure standardized, objective differences, such as inches or pounds, or number of cars in the household. This method is often used by census research.

Scales can also measure subjective differences, such as differences in attitude. Here you can break down attitudes – for example, enjoyment of mathematics – into a numeric scale (e.g. 1 = I don't enjoy mathematics at all, to 5 = I enjoy mathematics a lot). Often, people are asked to rate a covering statement (e.g. 'My teachers are friendly') according to a scale (e.g. 1 = none of the time, 2 = some of the time, 3 = most of the time, 4 = all of the time). Ideally, subjective scales should range from an absence to a total amount, have a similar distance between points, and measure at least 4 or 5 points, as this allows for more sophisticated statistical analysis and gives participants more freedom of expression.

Other closed–ended data do not have an actual or implied value – for example, being a boy or girl (there is no telling which is better), which feeder school children came from or transfer school they are going to. This is called categorical data (think value-free 'categories'). Like scale data, the answers to a categorical question are assigned numbers when they are inputted into a database. However, these numbers are not averaged. Rather, they are tallied, compared and used to split the participants into groups (e.g. boys, girls). Scale data can also be used for this purpose, but it is not restricted to it.

A second type of data is open-ended, and these can be gathered by asking people to freely write or speak their answers to an open question. The length of their answers in a written questionnaire will be determined in part by how much space you give them to reply. This produces valuable information about what people actually think, in contrast to what you assume they are thinking (e.g. by asking them closed questions). It allows for people to clarify their answer to a closed-ended question (e.g. 'Please explain why you chose that option'). But, if you ask open-ended questions, be prepared to spend several hours analysing the answers, as you have to read them, think about them and look for patterns in the data.

If you want to build a questionnaire, it is advisable to ask some demographic questions about people's age, gender, ethnicity, school and achievement. Measuring socioeconomic status is a little trickier, as there are many ways to conceptualise this (i.e. family income, mother's highest educational qualification, family assets). A good indicator is whether children are receiving free school meals. It is important to put these questions somewhere in the questionnaire where you feel they will be answered. Some researchers prefer to put them at the start to ensure this, or alternatively leave them until the end, when the participants have warmed up to the questionnaire, so that they will not be dismissed needlessly. In my experience, children's interest can fade quickly, so it is advisable to put your most important questions first. However, this must be balanced with putting sensitive questions later on in the questionnaire, so that children aren't put off straight away. Electronic questionnaires and questionnaires delivered in an interview are a great way to ensure that children complete the entire thing (e.g. you can request that the child complete a section before moving to the next one). Regardless of how you deliver it, your questionnaire will get a better response if it is fairly brief, and if it uses language familiar to the participants.

There are many excellent existing measures (e.g. sets of questions, for example, about children's motivation) that you might be able to access, if you ask the appropriate person for permission to use them. A quick search on Google Scholar for key terms (e.g. 'school enjoyment') might turn up an academic journal article that uses a measure which you can email the author to request, if they designed it themselves. However, some measures are copyrighted and you will have to pay to access them. It is sometimes more straightforward to design your own questions using a word-processing program, or an internet service such as Survey Monkey. Online services make things easy by giving you a choice of question types, saving your questionnaire to a server, allowing you to administer it to students online and by collating your data for you and returning it to you as a spreadsheet. This drastically reduces the hours necessary for inputting data from a paper questionnaire.

Interviews

Asking people what they think face-to-face has many advantages. You can see more of what they are thinking and feeling. You can reword questions so that they better understand. You can follow up interesting, hesitant or non-committal responses by asking more questions. You can let them speak in their own words, elicit their understanding of things and learn their mental language. And, you can use tricks of the trade such as pausing to encourage their response, and allowing them time to process what they are thinking, even in the middle of a sentence, in order to allow information to surface. Another advantage of interviewing is that you can ask participants 'What do you mean by that?', which can lead to a richer understanding for both parties.

However, people are often inhibited talking face-to-face. If you have a professional relationship with them, this can influence their disclosure. Being unfamiliar with your participants invokes a hierarchy where you hold the power, and they are the interrogated minor. Children have told me that interviewing in a comfortable place, sharing jokes and telling them about my life has helped them relax (and that was after we had spent a day together in an active participation workshop). Often, children are unaccustomed to sitting down and being questioned about their feelings. They have recommended walking around school and talking, and talking while doing something familiar (e.g. an art project) to help them forget about this power dynamic and the strangeness of it all.

When interviewing, it is also helpful to think about your body language and the way that you sound. Participants respond better when your tone is relaxed, informal and friendly. If you have your hands out where they can see them, if you are sitting casually (if it is a sit-down interview) and, if you smile a lot, that helps too. Unless you have a reason not to do so, it is courteous to let participants see the interview schedule before you begin, and to ask if they are comfortable with what you will be asking. Let them know they don't have to reply if they don't want to and, if they have nothing to say, that's OK, too. Encourage them to ask you questions, because this helps even out the power dynamic, and can lead to interesting lines of inquiry. Whether it is children, teachers or parents you are interviewing, any attempt to put them at ease should help to improve their experience, and your results.

There are three types of interviews commonly used, and people tend to stick to one in any given study, although you can use a mixture if you prefer. The first is the structured interview, which is where the interviewer reads a question-naire to the interviewee, and records their answers. Many studies are done this way in order to ensure that participants complete the questionnaire. The second is the semi-structured interview, where the list of interview questions (the inter-view *schedule*) is set beforehand, and generally prompts open-ended discussion. For example, you might ask teachers, 'What do you think was most successful about the intervention?' Then you might follow this up with open-ended prompts, such as 'Why did this work for you personally?' The third type of interview is unstructured. Here, researchers aim to have a naturally occurring discussion about a set topic. This allows for more nuances to emerge, such as how the discussants responded to each other and set each other up for a reply, who dominated the conversation and what their agenda was. Each type of interview can be recorded, ideally on a digital device, then you or a helper can listen to and transcribe those recordings word for word. Sometimes it is helpful to include things like pauses and vocal inflections, if you are interested in how people spoke, in addition to what they said. Bear in mind that it takes about three times as long to transcribe an interview as the interview took to conduct.

Observations

Here I describe three common approaches to observation, that can be stand-alone approaches or combined. The first is *participant observation*, where the researcher learns about participants by living as a member of their community. Participant observation stems from anthropology, where researchers have attempted to become a native amongst the foreign 'other'. Historically, the focus of the research has been pre-industrial society, such as tribal Micronesia (e.g. Brewis, 1996), but increasingly researchers use participant observation to understand microcosms of culture in their own countries. A concern of any participant observer is that they will contaminate the behaviour of that culture; therefore, the data that they gather will not be an accurate reflection. This is also an issue of reflexivity: the acknowledgment that personal perspective (and presence) can affect the results of our study. A second concern is that participant observers may lose perspective if they become so familiar with the culture that they cannot distinguish its characteristics as apart from their own, a state referred to as 'going native'. One way to address both issues is to observe the cultural proceedings from a distance (such as videotaping a lesson) or to have members of that community act as researchers, as they are less likely to upset the balance. But still, the people whom you are observing may act differently simply by knowing they are being observed.

The second approach is to observe a target, such as a person, group of people, item(s) or place. There you can study the target at different levels of specificity. At the broadest level, you can record what they do, or what happens to them in general. Or, you could focus on a more refined topic, such as the language that a teacher uses (e.g. Galton & Pell, 2002), or how attentive or distracted a child is in lessons (e.g. Hargreaves & Pell, 2002). Ethically, if your target is a person, then they must give voluntary, informed consent to being observed. And, as I described in the Ethics section, it sometimes helps to offer to share your observations with them. You can conduct targeted observation as part of being a participant observer. Or, you can work it into a more general observation schedule that involves watching the environment in general, and targeting certain aspects of it, without becoming a participant. Finally, if you are doing systematic observation (see below), you might choose one or more targets, thinking about how they represent their community and your topic of interest.

Systematic observation is where you rate what you see using multiple choice criteria. These can comprise rating scales to describe an action (e.g. she laughs a lot, a little, none) or different types of action (e.g. sits with friends, walks with friends, walks around alone). The trick is to mark off the behaviour at a specific time, such as the end of the observation (here you give a global, retrospective assessment), or at regular time intervals within the observation (say every minute). Galton and colleagues are well known for using systematic observation in the ORACLE (e.g. Galton & Wilcocks, 1983) and ORACLE replication (e.g. Hargreaves & Galton, 2002) studies of school transition. There, they marked the behaviour of a teacher or pupil on a checklist every 30 seconds. They did this for multiple targets (each observed in a different session), so they could compile a general picture of teacher and children's behaviour. There are several established coding schemes available – for example, in Hargreaves and Galton (2002) and Flanders (1970).

Audio/visual methods

If you are interested in the visual and audio world, you can gather data using sound recordings, photographs, video recordings, or by collecting images or webpages from the internet or printed images. Images and sounds are a critical part of our daily experience, and can be understood as a system of symbols that represent different layers of meaning in our social interactions and personal modes of thought and behaviour. Audio/visual research is rapidly progressing as digital equipment and virtual realities make new types of research possible (Pink, 2013). Audio/visual methods are attractive for school-based research, because of the abundance of visual material in schools, easy access to recording equipment and the opportunity for audio/visual collection to be done by children.

In the Learning Futures project (Deakin Crick, Jelfs, Symonds, Ren, Patton & Gurshka, 2010) we engaged schools in making a video presentation of their innovative pedagogy interventions that they carried out with teachers and children. The presentations involved children and teachers talking about their experiences, and exhibiting their schoolwork. These were analysed at the end of the project according to a set of themes. We also energised children to take photographs of meaningful places in their school, create a photo album and report on their findings. We also analysed these thematically. Third, we took photographs of the noticeboards in school hallways and reception areas that demonstrated (to us as researchers) the school's ethos and priorities for its students. Together these materials gave us a deeper understanding of the school cultures that permeated the design and eventual success of the innovative pedagogy interventions.

Document analysis

Documents are another great source of data, and some studies focus exclusively on printed or electronic text as representative of personal and collective action, organisational etiquette and ethos, and social history. Documents are often the primary source of data for historians, who piece together historical episodes and social change from letters, official records, logbooks and so forth. Ethnographers also collect documents and triangulate them with other data, to create a more comprehensive picture of school as a cultural microcosm. There are many uses for document analysis at school transition. For example, what do the promotional materials of the transfer school(s) tell us? What type of administrative records are collated by feeder schools, and to what effect? And, what printed information are children given about their new school, including calendars, timetables and maps, and to what extent does this information help or present challenges to their wellbeing?

Documents can be analysed using content analysis, where you focus on the communication, the sender(s) and the recipient(s). Some useful questions to ask of your document are: Who has written it? Who are they communicating with? What is the central problem, or message of the document? Why is this being conveyed? How is what they are saying influenced by public and/or institutional discourses? Which alternative discourses exist? Are these being considered and, if not, why not? And, what does a critical reading of these documents tell us (adapted from Jupp & Norris, 1993, p. 50)? Although these questions will produce open-ended data, you might also want to analyse your documents using numbers, for example, tallying quantitative assessments or how many times a phrase or word is used. You can find more on this type of mixed-methods analysis below.

Analysis

It is beyond the remit of this chapter to have a detailed discussion on methods of analysis. However, it is possible to convey the rudiments so you can think about how to interpret and communicate your data. Put simply, there are different methods of analysis for open- and closed-ended data. Closed-ended data are easily analysed using numbers and mathematics, i.e. *quantitative analysis*; and open-ended data lend themselves to *narrative analysis* – that is, if you have interviewed a person about their personal experience – and to *thematic analysis*, which is where you create themes that best describe the messages conveyed by all participants in your sample. If you categorise data thematically, you can also turn them into numbers by counting the number of data in each unit. And, you can analyse numbers thematically, by coming up with themes to fit numerical patterns into. You can analyse the same data in different ways, and compare your findings to create a broader picture. And, on the results of one type of analysis, you can create different analytical frameworks for other parts of your project. More on how to think about *mixed-methods* analysis can be found in Symonds and Gorard (2010), and a useful practical guide for all three analysis types is Creswell (2014). But, as I reiterate throughout this chapter, it is often simpler to choose one analysis type and do it well.

Analysing closed-ended data

If your data are in numbers or can be turned into numbers, they can be analysed quantitatively. A good starting place is to create some *descriptive statistics*. And often these are enough to answer your research question(s). Descriptive statistics involve creating totals, such as how many people answered each question, or picked each multiple choice answer in a questionnaire. There you can also identify what the most common answer was (the mode). If you have scale data, you can summarise the highest and lowest values that were checked for each question, and work out the average value (the mean) and the middle value (the median). If you have demographic data (e.g. gender, age, class, school) or other categorical data (e.g. children who are for, versus against, wearing school uniform), then you can work through the descriptive statistics for each group, then compare your results using tables and figures. For example, what percentage of girls versus boys rate their English lessons as quite or very enjoyable?

This brings me to *hypothesis testing*, which is often used to analyse closed-ended data. Here, you are considering the relationship between two or more items of interest, i.e. *variables* that you have measured, such as gender and children's enjoyment of English. Next, you create a statement that assumes a systematic relationship between those variables, e.g. 'On average, girls will enjoy English more than boys.' If your statement assumes there is no relationship (e.g. 'There will be no gender difference in enjoyment of English'), it is a null hypothesis. If you have access to a computer program for analysing statistics, such as SPSS, Mplus, MATLAB or R, you can also test hypotheses and explore questions using significance testing. There are different types of tests, depending on which question you ask, that check whether your results haven't arrived by random chance, and on generating the size of the effect that you have found, considering the potential biases in your data. You can also conduct parametric statistics, where you check whether two variables based on scale data are systematically associated with each other – i.e. 'Does enjoying English relate to level of achievement?'

Analysing open-ended data

Two common ways of analysing open-ended data are to employ narrative or thematic analysis. As stated, narrative analysis is where the data tell a story, such as a person describing an event, and you analyse it by linking pieces of the story together and perhaps focusing on the bits that are most important to your research questions. The other method of thematic analysis is where you categorise different data into themes. You are free to choose the extent to which these themes are derived from your own interests and priorities, or reflect the indigenous concerns and actions of those whom you study. Going back to the start of this chapter, you might be interested in coding data into one of the evaluation frameworks or, if you are analysing behaviour, you could code data using systematic observation schedules developed by other researchers.

If you prefer to code data according to how your participants personally construe and convey meaning, you might want to analyse your data using Grounded Theory. This method was developed in the 1960s by US sociologists Barney Glaser and Anselm Strauss (1967). Here I summarise the steps in Grounded Theory as it is perceived by Kathy Charmaz (2006). Before you begin, it is good to have a rough idea of what you are looking at. Is it people's attitudes? The way they make sense of an activity? Their emotional responses to learning? This will help you decide how to focus your attention on the text. Or, if you prefer to start with a complete blank slate, then Charmaz (2006) recommends identifying gerunds, that is verbs that end in '-ing', such as 'helping'.

With this in mind, consider a small portion of your data, such as the first few lines of text. Within it, identify any words or phrases that seem to capture the essence of what the person is saying (according to your interest). Mark these words/phrases and continue to the next portion of data. Read at least three transcripts using this line by line method and, as you go, consider whether those words/phrases that you have marked convey similar messages, such as 'frustration with time pressure'. These messages, or themes, become your codes. And, as you read and code more text, you can develop this system of *open codes* through expansion and refinement. The next step is to choose the codes that best represent your data, and to continue to code the remainder of your transcripts into these *focused codes*, developing them as you go. These two steps are often enough to answer your research question(s). If you like, you can stop here, and summarise the information within the focused codes. Or, you can continue with the next steps of Grounded Theory, which are to explore relationships between the focused codes (*axial coding*) and develop a theory from this process (*theoretical coding*) that explains, rather than describes, the action of participants.

No matter whether you are collating data into a pre-existing framework, generating a set of open or focused codes or attempting the entire process of Grounded Theory, you will find it much easier to manage your data using computer software. Although it is sometimes useful to code the first few transcripts as a hard copy (highlighters come in handy here), and to do this with a friend in order to share and test ideas, pretty soon you will end up with a floor full of notes and data that need to be sorted. I recommend searching the internet for the terms 'free', 'qualitative', 'document', 'coding' and 'software', to obtain a free program such as QDA Miner Lite. Or, you can purchase access to a specialist program, such as NVivo or ATLAS.ti, that are often used by researchers in universities. These programs are state of-the-art and you can use a trial version for a limited period, which might serve your needs. However, your data will be stuck in the program once the trial ends. In comparison, the freeware has fewer advanced features, so it really depends on your needs as to what you choose.

Reporting your findings

There is no point doing research unless you report it. At the end of a long piece of research, you may feel you have answered your questions, and your drive to research can slow. This is a signal to draw on your energy reserves to create the most important part: the report of your findings. Reports carry our messages across minds, schools, countries and eras. They help us gain perspective on our findings, and think more on how they can be useful. Report writing is a deeply satisfying process, for, like the cake coming out of the oven, it is the physical manifestation of all you have done. Reports are for sharing and, in addition to their intrinsic purpose of communicating information, they can help your career, attract parents and sponsors, and boost morale in your school. If you are brave enough to publish your report online, an intrepid educational researcher might find it and make it part of the broader story of what happens to children when they change schools. Or, it might be used to inform policy and the decisions of schools elsewhere.

There is no quick guide to how to write a report. However, I have summarised what usually happens in organisational reports in the following steps:

1. *Acknowledgments.* Thank your participants, your colleagues and any other source of support such as a sponsor or helper.
2. *Abstract.* Summarise the goals, topic, methods and findings of your research in a single paragraph.
3. *Key findings.* These should be no more than a page or two. You can come back and do this after writing the rest of the report. Or, you can stop here if you are writing a brief report.
4. *Methods and analysis.* Write a brief methods and analysis section. Mention the number of participants, their age and gender, the timeline of the research, the methods used and how you analysed the data.
5. *Results.* Cover your findings in depth. Here you can present those wonderful bar charts and line graphs you have worked so hard on, make a diagram of your codes, or put them in a table, and if you get creative you can draw concept maps of your conclusions. If you had a clear set of research questions, it is good to organise your findings by these. You might present your case studies here as narratives of identity or establishment. Or, describe the different angles of your topic as these have been explored using different methods of data collection, as in ethnography.

6. *Discussion*. This may or may not be relevant to the style of your report. However, if you want to make sense of your findings, put forward ideas supported by your findings to the reader, discuss your findings in relation to other people's work and relate them to important aspects of your school's work, then this is the place to do it.

7. *Limitations*. Spend a paragraph or two discussing the weaknesses of your study, and how it could be improved.

8. *Conclusions*. Focus on the key messages in your report, and summarise these. Consider how your findings might be useful to your school, other schools, the community and to policy.

Budget between four and ten hours to write your report, unless you are compiling a brief report, which will take less time. Share your report with a trusted friend or colleague, who can help you spot mistakes and point out where you have been confusing. Your report will make an excellent basis for an oral presentation and will help you narrow down what information to include in a slide show. Or, you might prefer to develop a slide show first, then write the report later on. Report writing is a cyclical process, as only after you have made sense of all of your findings through writing them down will you be able to give an accurate overview of the research. This is the gold dust that you can publicise on the school's website, and share with parents, colleagues and children as a flyer or email bulletin.

Participants as agents of change

In the 1960s, teachers led a grassroots action research movement into researching their own practice to make a positive change (Elliot, 1991). This was located by some educational researchers in sociological discourses of power: 'When teachers engage in collaborative reflection on the basis of common concerns and involve their clients in the process, they develop the courage to critique the curriculum structures which shape their practices, and the power to negotiate change within the system which maintains them' (Elliot, 1991, p. 56). Improving agency was not the only benefit; teachers also acquired research skills, gained insight into pedagogy and relationships, and developed their professional role through action research.

This was soon followed by efforts to increase children's agency as research participants. In the late 1970s, Andrew Pollard became a participant observer in the middle school where he taught. There he engaged a small group of children to assist him in the research. The student researchers became known as the 'Moorside Investigation Department' (MID) which 'generated a sense of self-importance' for them (Pollard, 1985, p. 227). Pollard noted that a sense of secrecy surrounded the group, which increased as they learned about confidentiality and immunity from teacher prosecution. Over the course of the year, the MID interviewed 90 pupils of their choosing, guided by basic suggestions such as 'What do you most like to do in class?' Pollard found that the children's involvement encouraged other children to accept and engage in his project. Also in interviews the children acted as 'checks, balances and prompts' for each other, enabling conversations to become 'part of their experience rather than a commentary on it' (Pollard, 1985, p. 229).

In the early 2000s, this activity blossomed into a more defined students-as-researchers practice (e.g. Fielding & Bragg, 2003; Kellett, 2005). Here, Michael Fielding wrote about student researchers as 'radical agents of change', who, rather than being passively consulted about their schooling for school improvement purposes, had power to research topics and use methods that were authentic to their age, maturity and interests (Fielding, 2001). My experiences of educating teachers and students to do their own research (e.g. MacBeath, Frost, Pedder & Frost, 2008) have taught me that this type of freedom, at least for children, needs a dedicated support person to guide children to make their own decisions, choose their methods and carry out the research, for children can feel lost and achieve little if they don't have prior research experience.

In my fieldwork I apply many of these principles to my treatment of research subjects. In the Ethics section above, I described how I involve children as active participants, by teaching them about research processes and by giving them power in the research, which facilitates their agency as the objects of inquiry. I have also worked collaboratively with 10- to 12-year-old children to design research methods that suit them developmentally. This was an interesting process that revealed children's responses are often biased by the researcher–participant power dynamic; that they are unfamiliar with many common research terms such as anonymity; that they prefer to do research with peers, yet desire space to express themselves independently; and that they enjoy dynamic and active modes of research the best, such as creating concept maps and making their own audio/visual recordings (Symonds, 2008).

If you are involving children or teachers as active agents in research, it is important to have conversations with them about power relationships, ethics and their responsibilities as researchers. Although it might be tempting to make decisions for them, remember that a major purpose of involving them is to facilitate their agency, and that means letting them move the research in their own ways. There are many ways that active involvement helps people's wellbeing: it offers opportunities for autonomy and competency development, it builds collaborative relationships, can improve self-esteem – as Pollard's work with the MID demonstrated – and can even be incorporated into people's identities when they feel more confident as participants, and think of research as part of their skill set. By blurring the lines between researcher and participant, you can also improve the quality of your data. Involving participants in research gives us insight into worlds only they can experience (Fielding & Bragg, 2003), and allows us to check and cross-reference our data with their inside view. Below I have tabled the three forms of improving agency in research discussed here. The references given for each category offer a practical guide.[4]

Table 12.3 Improving agency in research

Research type	Active participation	Students-as-researchers	Teacher action research
Uses	Participants gain power, agency, skills and confidence. They act as checks and balances for research processes, and help generate more authentic data.	Children research their experiences, and the experiences of others, to provide information to improve schooling.	Teachers research their own practice, with the goal of improving it.
Child's role	Participant	Researcher	Participant
Teacher's role	Researcher or participant	Facilitator	Researcher
Practical guides	Symonds (2009)	Fielding and Bragg (2003) Kellett (2005)	McNiff and Whitehead (2012)

Conclusions

Throughout this chapter, I have demonstrated how doing research can improve your understanding of children, teachers, pedagogy, curriculum and intervention. School transition is a critical period for children's development. By using research you can track their attitudes, participation, hopes and fears, and achievement across the move. Children and teachers' views and experiences can help you improve interventions for supporting wellbeing at transition. And, if these are gathered systematically, then this will generate better quality evidence than any casual conversation can provide.

Transition is a time of growth and movement. Just as your research might capture these personal and social changes, it should also be flexible to adapt to children and teachers' needs, as these shift between schools. Throughout, it is important to remember that children play an active role in their own adaptation by altering their environment and changing themselves. Therefore, at the heart of any intervention evaluation should be the interplay between children's needs, attitudes and coping at *that point* in the transition process, and the success of that intervention. Finally, it is useful to repeat your research annually in order to capture the experiences of new cohorts of children and consistently tailor your interventions into programmes that define the traditions of your school and its commitment to state-of-the-art care for children's wellbeing.

Notes

1 www.every-child-matters.org.uk/Framework_5_key_outcomes
2 http://webarchive.nationalarchives.gov.uk/20110809101133/http://nsonline.org.uk/node/66416?uc=force_uj

3 In statistics, the terms *scale* or *ratio* data are used to refer to the measurement of objective, tangible difference between categories, e.g. height and weight, and are contrast to *ordinal* data, which is the measurement of subjective difference, e.g. quite happy, very happy. In the United States, both types of data are referred to as *quantitative* data.
4 In Symonds (2009), readers need to skip to the methods section for examples of active participation techniques.

References

BERA (2011). *Ethical guidelines for educational research*: British Educational Research Association.

Brewis, A. (1996). *Lives on the line. Women and ecology on a pacific atoll*. Orlando, FL: Harcourt Brace & Company.

Charmaz, K. (2006). *Constructing grounded theory*. London: SAGE Publications.

Creswell, J. W. (2014). *Research design, qualitative, quantitative and mixed methods approaches* (4th ed.). Thousand Oaks, CA: SAGE Publications.

Deakin Crick, R., Jelfs, H., Symonds, J., Ren, K., Patton, A., & Grushka, K. (2010). *Learning futures evaluation report*. Bristol: University of Bristol/Paul Hamlyn Foundation.

Elliot, J. (1991). *Action research for educational change*. Buckingham: Open University Press.

Fielding, M. (2001). Students as radical agents of change. *Journal of Educational Change, 2*(2), 123–141.

Fielding, M., & Bragg, S. (2003). *Students as researchers, making a difference*. Cambridge, UK: Pearson Publishing.

Flanders, N. (1970). *Analyzing teacher behavior*. New York: Wiley.

Galton, M., & Pell, T. (2002). Teaching in the transfer schools. In L. Hargreaves & M. Galton (eds), *Transfer from the primary classroom 20 years on* (pp. 97–130). London: RoutledgeFalmer.

Galton, M., & Wilcocks, J. (eds) (1983). *Moving from the primary classroom*. London: Routledge & Kegan Paul.

Galton, M., Gray, J., & Rudduck, J. (1999). *The impact of school transitions and transfer on pupil progress and attainment*. Norwich: Department for Education and Employment.

Galton, M., Gray, J., Rudduck, J., Berry, M., Demetriou, H., Edwards, J., et al. (2003). *Transfer and transitions in the middle years of schooling (7–14): Continuities and discontinuities in learning*. London: Department for Education and Skills.

Glaser, B. G., & Strauss, A. L. (1967). *Discovery of grounded theory: Strategies for qualitative research*. Hawthorne, NY: Aldine de Gruyter.

Hargreaves, L., & Galton, M. (eds). (2002). *Transfer from the primary classroom 20 years on*. London: RoutledgeFalmer.

Hargreaves, L., & Pell, T. (2002). Patterns of pupil behaviour in the transfer schools. In L. Hargreaves & M. Galton (eds), *Transfer from the primary classroom 20 years on* (pp. 159–184). London: RoutledgeFalmer.

Hargreaves, L., & Wall, D. (2002). 'Getting used to each other' cross-phase liaison and induction. In L. Hargreaves & M. Galton (eds), *Transfer from the primary classroom 20 years on* (pp. 28–53). London: RoutledgeFalmer.

Jupp, V., & Norris, C. (1993). Traditions in documentary analysis. In M. Hammersley (ed.), *Social research: Philosophy, politics and practice* (pp. 37–52). London: SAGE Publications.

Kellett, M. (2005). *How to develop children as researchers: A step by step guide to teaching the research process.* London: SAGE Publications.

Lewin, K. (1946/1948). Action research and minority problems. In G. W. Lewin (ed.), *Resolving social conflicts* (pp. 201–220). New York: Harper & Brothers Publishers.

MacBeath, J., Frost, D., Pedder, D., & Frost, R. (2008). *The influence and participation of children and young people in their learning (IPiL).* Birmingham: General Teaching Council for England.

McNiff, J., & Whitehead, J. (2012). *Action research for teachers, a practical guide.* Abingdon: David Fulton Publishers.

Mertens, D. M. (2014). *Research and evaluation in education and psychology: Integrating diversity with quantitative, qualitative and mixed methods* (4th ed.). Thousand Oaks, CA: SAGE Publications.

Pink, S. (2013). *Doing visual ethnography* (3rd ed.). London: SAGE Publications.

Pollard, A. (1985). Opportunities and difficulties of a teacher-ethnographer: A personal account. In R. Burgess, G. (ed.), *Field methods in the study of education.* London: Falmer Press.

Sutherland, R., Yee, W. C., McNess, E., & Harris, R. (2010). *Supporting learning in the transition from primary to secondary schools.* Bristol: University of Bristol.

Symonds, J. (2008). Pupil researchers generation x: Educating pupils as active participants. *Research in Education, 80*(1), 63–74.

Symonds, J. (2009). Constructing stage-environment fit: Early adolescents' psychological development and their attitudes to school in English middle and secondary school environments. Doctoral thesis, Faculty of Education, University of Cambridge, UK. Available at: www.dspace.cam.ac.uk/handle/1810/223866

Symonds, J. & Gorard, S. (2010). Death of mixed methods? Or the rebirth of research as a craft. *Evaluation and Research in Education, 23*(2), 121–136.

Chapter 13

School transition leadership

Chapter overview

Every teacher has an important role to play in supporting transition. This can be helping students settle into their new classrooms, attending to the needs of vulnerable children across the move, participating in transition interventions and shaping the vision for transition in their school pyramid. This chapter reveals key messages about how to manage transition successfully that emerged from interviews with five teachers who were dedicated transition coordinators and a Special Educational Needs Coordinator (SENCO). It also shows how coordinating transition improved those teachers' personal and professional development. The findings suggest a need for educators and universities to help create a *culture* of transition to facilitate children's wellbeing and achievement. The chapter ends with suggestions on how to do this through education programmes for school leaders and teacher trainees.

Introduction

This last chapter of the book is dedicated to teachers. In my opinion, teachers are the most important people in the transition process because they have responsibility for shaping children's experiences. As I explored in Chapter 1, teachers can be responsible for setting the markers of the status passage: those activities that tell children 'You're becoming a transfer pupil', 'You're almost there', 'You've arrived'. Several studies have looked at teachers' perceptions of coordinating the transition process (Akos, Queen & Lineberry, 2005; Fuller, Thomas & Horswell, 2005; Powell, Smith, Jones & Reakes, 2006; Sutherland, Yee, McNess & Harris, 2010), and this chapter continues that tradition, to give educators ideas about how other people work, and tips from those at the frontlines of school transition.

Interviews with transition coordinators

The teachers whom I interviewed for this study were recruited from a national conference on transfer and transitions, and from my work with some of them in schools. They comprised four senior management staff, one head of department and one Special Educational Needs Coordinator (SENCO). All but the SENCO were responsible for the overall coordination of transition in their school. The transition coordinators had held their posts for three or more years, and were highly motivated to teach others about their role, evident in their presence as conference presenters. I have used pseudonyms for each teacher, and to preserve anonymity have adjusted their subject specialisms.

What do transition coordinators do?

Transition coordinators are school staff who have operational responsibility for transition. Typically they are members of transfer school senior management teams, such as assistant headteacher, head of year or head of department (Powell et al., 2006). They can lead a transition team made up of other staff in feeder and transfer schools, or have a more independent role, where they pool resources as necessary. Transition coordinators develop, administer and evaluate transition practices in their school. A selection of activities is given in Table 13.2, which is followed by two case studies of coordinating transition.

WHAT MAKES FOR GOOD TRANSITION LEADERSHIP?

Although we had very different conversations with no scheduled questions, the interviewees spoke on several common topics that were important to them. I have summarised these as an entry point to understanding what makes for effective transition leadership. Where possible, I have indicated similar issues arising in other studies. Three main themes emerged: working with people, having adequate resources and developing an identity for transition.

Working with people

Having a dedicated role for coordinating transition

All interviewees spoke about how important it was for schools to have a dedicated role for managing transition, so that one person was responsible for overseeing all the components involved. Those who had been in the role for several years or more felt that longevity was essential for networking and for improving the quality of relationships amongst colleagues who helped with the transition process: 'I know all my feeder schools and I know the people that work there, and I know the heads … and I've built up a positive trusting relationship … but it takes a long while to do it' (Marion). Being in the role for longer also helped the coordinators develop the role as a professional activity: 'I think you have to be continuous within this role to get the

Table 13.1 Teacher interviewees

Name	Teaching years	Role in school	Transition role	School type and percentages of children on indicators	English county
Sadie James	25	Assistant headteacher	Transition coordinator	Secondary school (11–18) 8% free school meals 8% special educational needs 2% English second language	East Riding of Yorkshire
Kira Hawthorne	15	Assistant headteacher	Transition coordinator	Secondary school (11–16) 20% free school meals 25% special educational needs 4% English second language	Devon
Eva Smith	10	Assistant headteacher	Transition coordinator	Academy (11–18) 40% free school meals 8% special educational needs 35% English second language	South Yorkshire
Ryan Andrews	10	Head of Science	Transition coordinator	Academy (11–18) 25% free school meals 15% special educational needs 55% English second language	London
Scott Ferrer	10	Assistant headteacher	Transition coordinator	Grammar school (11–18) 4% free school meals 7% special educational needs 1% English second language	Essex
Marion Booth	15	SENCO	Coordinates transition for SEN children	Secondary school (11–16) 10% Free school meals 25% Special educational needs 5% English second language	Essex

Note
Percentages of children are sourced from the BBC secondary league tables. SEN is percentage of pupils with a special educational needs (SEN) statement or on School Action Plus.

Table 13.2 Activities of transition coordinators

Type of activity	Specific activity
Management	Leads a team of transition coordinators, or delegates responsibility as necessary to teachers, children and other members of the community
Promotion	Promotes transition issues in schools and community
Communication	Liaises with senior management, feeder and transfer school teachers, SENCO, children's services, parents and children to arrange for transition
Administration	Responsible for, or helps with data on new pupils Uses this data to help design school timetables and class groups
Intervention	Designs and administers transition interventions, for example, bridging units, cross-tier teaching, induction days, post-induction activities, Year 7 camp and community activities
Documentation	Writes transition schedules and policies and communicates these to teachers, parents and children
Evaluation	Reviews existing procedures and policy, using research and evaluation methods
Wellbeing	Holds overall responsibility for the wellbeing of children transferring to the new school

Case study: Kira Hawthorne

Kira's approach to coordinating transition evolved from there being a disconnect between the significant minorities of disadvantaged and more advantaged children arriving into Year 7 each year. The first group of children were 'vulnerable for a whole variety of reasons'. When they entered Year 7, many found themselves educated alongside more affluent peers for the first time. With the threats of class differences and prejudice, and many children with poor coping skills to attend to, Kira's strategy was to instigate a blended self-management and social support programme that was applied in strong doses across the initial transition period, then in a lower dose throughout the transition year, so that these groups of children could become integrated.

First, she attended each feeder school with the head of Year 7 so that incoming children would recognise her, and know their head of year as a person to turn to for pastoral support. This activity stimulated the identity of the transfer school and the people in it for the children. Then Kira ran two induction days in July. In the first, children had a fairly standard induction experience where they met their new form teacher and classmates, and were introduced to school policy and lessons. This familiarised children with the administrative aspects of their new school. Second, Kira ran a whole-day Olympics, where children were mixed in teams across feeder schools, according to their previous choice of being in teams A, B or C. This event allowed children to develop relationships with others, in the spirit of team-building and competition.

These events were attended by teaching assistants from the feeder schools, who moved with children for the first few weeks of the autumn term. This helped children overcome the difficulties of adjusting to multiple subject specialists, by giving them somebody familiar to turn to in lessons. Kira ran 'Wonderful Wednesdays' each week across the year, where children worked in mixed-ability and socioeconomic groups that were decided at the start of the first term. They did project work on fun themes such as murder mystery, and trained in metacognitive skills including decision making and problem solving. This activity facilitated children's personal development, helped them make friends across class and ability tiers, and gave them a positive learning experience to remember, as Kira documented when Year 8 and 9 children asked for a return to Wonderful Wednesdays. Finally, at the end of the autumn term, Kira sent the children to a two-day residential camp, where they mixed across class and ability tiers, and engaged in team-building exercises. By the end of half-term, this set of activities created an 'incredibly bonded team of Year 7 pupils' who would define each other's school experience through successive years.

Case study: Marion Booth

Marion ran a dedicated unit for teaching SEN children in a medium-sized secondary school. I had taught at the unit for several days as a supply (substitute) teacher, and was impressed by the work that Marion and her colleagues were doing. Her coordination of transition was no less impressive. As the SENCO, Marion's contact with the children and parents began in Year 5, as soon as they elected to attend her school in Year 7. Then, Marion was involved in the Year 6 annual review of that child's special educational needs. In the final term before transition, Marion and the head of Year 7 visited the children at their feeder schools, to observe them in a comfortable and familiar place. This was followed up by interviews with children and their parents. Finally, Marion would have a detailed conversation with the feeder school SENCO to gather as much information as possible about each child. Marion collated her findings in a booklet that described each child on the special needs register, which she gave to every adult in the transfer school who was in regular contact with those children.

Marion ran an extended induction programme for the SEN children, where, in addition to attending whole school induction events, they had two more visits to the transfer school with their current learning support assistant. On those occasions they familiarised themselves with school buildings and grounds, took photographs to discuss later, practised navigating lunch queues and the playground, and attended lessons. For children, those experiences added to their meetings with Marion and the head of year in creating an atmosphere of familiarity before they transferred. Marion acknowledged that the activities were more intensive, and produced more information about individual children, than was typically the case for children without special educational needs. Her work serves an example of good practice for the transition of SEN children and of the type of attitude teachers could have towards obtaining information about every child before they transfer.

job satisfaction out of it, because it is such a big role, it's holistic, not only within your school, it's holistic within the primary schools and within the borough' (Ryan).

Being supported by the headteacher and the senior management team

Akos et al. (2005) recommended that headteachers delegate the roles involved in transition, including that of overall transition coordinator, to staff members. The transition coordinators all spoke about their headteacher as essential to their effectiveness in their role. Ryan's headteacher 'pushed him to grow' as a transition coordinator, and was a source of inspiration: 'He was able to give me my vision and he was the person to inspire me, and I think without him it could have looked different.' And, as Scott put it, 'if you haven't got the support of your headteacher you will not make progress with this, it will always be an added extra'.

Transition coordinators who were already members of the senior management team felt their seniority helped them secure resources for transition and popularise transition in their school. As Kira explained, 'It gives it status. You know you can push things forward, whereas somebody perhaps without that position would have to go through lots of channels.' This was certainly the case for Ryan, who had to market his work to obtain resources: 'I do strong visual projects, and I've put it out there ... and so it highlights the importance of transition. And so that gives me a sort of strength or the clout that I can move forward. And it's taken me really three years to get that, and it's been an uphill struggle at times, but it's been quite successful as well.'

Having a transition team

Effective organisations have strong leaders at every level, who sometimes put themselves in the chorus rather than out front (HMIE, 2007). This view fits the advice of Akos and colleagues to have a transition team of feeder and transfer teachers who 'share a common vision ... committed to serving students, create a positive school climate, nurture students' emotional and academic stability, encourage family partnerships; and establish high expectations for all students' (Akos et al., 2005, p. 72). Amongst my interviewees, several led transition teams that comprised a variety of people including SEN-COs, learning support assistants, teaching assistants, feeder classroom teachers, subject specialist teachers, heads of year, administrative staff and children: 'It means that nobody is exhausted by the process, because we all support each other' (Kira). Even when there was no official team, the set of people who helped with transition were viewed as a team by the transition coordinator: 'Personally from within my team it's just me, but I also work ... with the heads of year and the deputy heads of year. So there's myself within my team, but if you think about it, I've got a huge team' (Ryan). Although local authorities sometimes contacted schools regarding transition, none were actively involved in the transition process at this level.

Working collaboratively

The transition coordinators saw their position mainly in terms of relationships: of connecting people across school tiers and departments. However, this could be challenging when there was a lack of trust and respect across tiers: 'There's quite a lot of primary schools who think that secondary schools don't take any notice of what they do, that their job is less important than ours. And then a lot of secondary schools give out those vibes as well' (Marion). Sutherland et al. (2010) boiled this down to feeder and transfer teachers belonging to two different 'tribes' who lacked understanding of each other's professional role and contribution to children's learning. Similar issues were also noted in Fuller et al. (2005).

However, when trusting relationships were built across time, this under-pinned the success of much of the transition process: 'It's been a privilege to work with the primary colleagues because over the years we have built up such an amazing relationship that I feel that without anything obvious happening, the children coming to us ... we know a lot about them' (Sadie). The coordinators also spoke about the importance of having relationships with numerous stakeholders: staff, parents and children. This could help the coordinators by drawing in a wide range of expertise. For example, Ryan described how he worked closely with subject specialists from across departments to instigate bridging units. It also ensured that more people benefitted from the activity surrounding transition: 'When I first started out doing this, I was so keen to make it good at the school that I think you forget about the periphery of it, the parents and the primary schools' (Kira).

The coordinators also spoke about practical difficulties in establishing and maintaining relationships. In the East Riding school, attempts to engage feeder schools who contributed children from outside of the catchment area could be rejected: 'We can't say, "Would you like to do this piece of work?" because the answer would be, "Get out" (laughs)' (Sadie). The school's previous system of rolling heads of year also posed a problem: 'The primaries ... were reinventing the wheel for each new head of year' (Sadie) and inspired Sadie to fight for a permanent head of Year 7 post. Building relationships could also be hampered by a lack of time: 'It's getting across there, getting to know colleagues in the classroom and understanding what they're doing' (Scott).

Talking about transition with colleagues, parents and children

Hargreaves (2007) argued for more conversation about transition, as a means to helping children adjust. She put children at the heart of these discussions, either as active contributors or as the topic of conversation between teachers wanting to improve children's transition experiences. The importance of talking about transition was also stressed by the transition coordinators: 'Actually the most valuable thing was colleagues talking. And it was that simple' (Scott). Many said that without these conversations, they would have achieved far less. In East Riding, Sadie described the usefulness of talk as a means for passing on information about transition interventions: 'a teacher will be able to ask that colleague how do you actually run the unit, what happens, how does it work?' And, in Essex, talk played a major role in how Marion gathered information about SEN children: 'I have lots of detailed information ... because I get more information when I talk to somebody, rather than when they write it down. It's quicker to talk. You can say much more ... I think people are more cautious when they write things down because other people will see it' (Marion). Kira also used talk as a strategy to support her colleagues, by having an open-door policy in her role as assistant headteacher.

Having adequate resources

Professional resources

In addition to relational support, the coordinators spoke of their need for time and money to carry out their role. In the already demanding life of a teacher, time to build relationships, communicate and carry out transition activities was 'a major, major factor' (Scott). Other studies have suggested establishing protected time for transition coordinators and their team members to manage transition (Fuller et al., 2005). Time pressures meant that, for Eva, 'If a meeting's not strategic then there's no point in having it.' Scott also spoke of difficulties coordinating meetings and planning, when teachers' time for working on transition differed between the feeder and transfer schools. He described a situation where, because of time pressure, the benefits of working together did not achieve fruition: 'Because colleagues are busy, they avoid talking to each other, you know it is much easier to say, "Oh, can you come in next Thursday afternoon to deliver to Year 6? Great, see you then" – then the phone goes down … ' (Scott).

Money was another factor essential to the success of managing transition. Only one coordinator spoke of having adequate money to manage transition, and that was because, as assistant headteacher, she had ensured it was protected within the school's budget. The only non-senior management coordinator, Ryan, had to be resourceful to top up his 'minimal' budget for transition from the Parent Teacher Association by appealing to senior management for money to do special projects, and by combining his subject specialism with transition activities, thereby drawing money from that area. Eva also took a creative approach to funding transition from the money allocated to her school to become a specialist academy, by positioning transition under the requirement to work with the community (e.g. by collaborating with feeder schools and parents), which received a third of the funds.

Personal resources

The HM Inspectorate of Education for Scotland commissioned a report that acknowledged there was no one leadership style employed by good leaders. Rather, these people were characterised by being successful learners, confident individuals, effective contributors and responsible citizens (HMIE, 2007). The transition coordinators whom I interviewed had all presented their work at national conferences, and spoke to me about several personal qualities that allowed them to develop these examples of good practice. Confidence and determination were key to overcome the demands inherent in managing transition: 'Because I'm quite, how can I put it? A determined person. I don't ever let it drop' (Kira); 'I'm having to persuade people that this is important' (Scott); 'I can push, I can get people on board, I can work with primary schools, and a lot of my projects have gone through' (Ryan).

Coordinators also needed to be creative to design successful interventions and juggle the many components of transition in often challenging circumstances. As described, Ryan had a creative approach to obtaining funding. This method of making novel connections also helped him generate support and communication amongst colleagues: 'There's politics involved and I have to wangle myself a way through this. But because I have so many fingers in so many different pies, I get them all to work with each other, communicate with each other through the strategies' (Ryan). Creative thinking also helped coordinators develop their overall vision for transition, which was not 'short term'

(Ryan) but a long-term plan encompassing the family of schools and the wider community.

Two coordinators spoke about developing this plan by assessing prior models of transition and finding one that was a good fit to their school. Here they created vision through creativity, flexibility and attention to design. Kira described how she transformed her school's old induction day model by evaluating its worth and purpose against her goals: 'Let's look at the two days and say what do we really want out of it? Is it that we want to just get names and data, etc., or is it that we want those two days to be the start of the academic year? And that's actually what we wanted' (Kira). As transition coordinator for a three-tier grammar school operating on a split site, Scott found that many case studies of how transition was managed in the state system did not apply to his school. He felt that other schools might face the same issue of not having a blueprint for transition: 'What I would draw out more strongly is this issue of different approaches dependent on your school, therefore having a good framework for your own school' (Scott). Scott found that eliciting universal principles from case studies, and using broad frameworks such as the Five Bridges (Galton, Gray & Rudduck, 1999), helped him design a transition plan that fitted his school well.

Making transition part of identity

Raising the status of transition

In Fuller et al. (2005), and amongst the transition coordinators, there was a sense that transition was a low status topic. The coordinators gave several reasons for this. First, feeder schools were less concerned about transition because they were more focused on the Standard Attainment Tests (SATs). Second, transition was deprioritised because feeder schools had no official responsibility for students afterwards (although, as Eva pointed out, some feeder schools wanted to know more about their students in transfer schools). Third, some transfer staff didn't prioritise first year students or their issues, because they held the ethnocentric view that taking older students through school leaving and university entrance examinations was more important. Fourth, transfer teachers were not aware of the issues surrounding transition, and therefore did not think it to be critical: 'There are a large number of colleagues who have a patchy view on transition, because it isn't given priority' (Scott). As this book observes (and as Kira pointed out), a successful transition sets up the social and academic climate for the year group. This influences what they learn in their first year, which contributes to how well they do in their school leaving examinations. Therefore, schools who deprioritise transition are missing a serious opportunity for whole school improvement. Below, I turn to the transition coordinators for suggestions on how to address this misconception.

Creating a culture of transition in the family of schools

For the reasons explored above, it requires effort to put transition higher on the agenda of feeder and transfer schools. The coordinators who did this created a *culture* of transition, through their expectations of how transition should be valued. Eva's approach was to identify transition as 'a whole school family initiative', where her calendar of events strategically tied the family together so that 'it's not just a case of those students coming up in the summer term' (Eva). Sadie described transition as being part of the identity of schools in her pyramid in Yorkshire, which meant for greater collaboration: 'In London everybody says, "How did you manage to get primaries to work with you?" … well that's how we are, you know that's what we do' (Sadie). And Kira made transition part of the everyday language of Key Stage 3, by giving it 'lots of mentions. All the staff are informed every week, "This is what's happening in transition" in Monday morning briefing.' In comparison, Ryan advertised transition through his 'strong visual projects' that 'put it out there'.

Making transition part of your professional identity

Creating a culture of transition, and making the effort to raise its status, was underpinned by its importance within the coordinator's professional identities. Scott described how this happened for him, as a process of realisation: 'My response when I was first handed it, was that this isn't important, this isn't good for my professional development … I must admit I did feel like many secondary school teachers that Year 7 learning, and particularly Key Stage 2, was not really what I wanted to be doing. And over the three years that I did the job I was utterly persuaded by it. The first year I did it because I had to, the second year I thought, "This is really interesting", and then the third year where we did some work together I thought, "You know this is not just interesting, it's crucial"' (Scott). Like the other transition coordinators, Scott had been described as a 'transition expert' by colleagues. No longer was transition just an issue to be dealt with; it had become part of who the coordinators were, thereby encouraging them to put more energy into it.

How coordinating transition can help you develop

Even though managing transition could be challenging, it also added a great deal to the coordinators' quality of life. As Ryan described, it had helped him 'emotionally … academically and environmentally, because I've been able to get out to all these amazing institutions, been able to get out and speak to all these wonderful pioneers in transition, and really grow within who I am and the way I perceive the education within this country. I'm very proud to be part of it, it means the world to me' (Ryan). Similarly, transition had increased Kira's social consciousness: 'It really opened my eyes to my idea of the whole school approach, about the community that we live and work in ... not only the community within the school and all the people here, but outside the community as well, the parents' (Kira).

Several of the coordinators attributed part of their promotion to assistant headteacher to the work they had done on transition. For Sadie, this involved her close relationship with the feeder schools and parents of children who transferred. These were significant resources that she brought to the post, and that helped her carry out her new job. Scott thanked transition for its 'addition to my understanding of teaching and learning ... and passion for it', which 'helped me to get this job'. And Ryan had once applied for an assistant headship 'solely with the confidence that transition had given me'. These comments revealed how coordinating transition helped teachers develop their emotional, personal and social resources, which helped them become better educators and advance in their career.

Conclusions

As HMIE (2007) observed, there was no one approach to managing transition amongst the coordinators that I interviewed. Rather, they achieved success by finding methods that fitted their individual context (as Scott emphasised). Across their approaches, having a strong transition programme rested firmly on the extent and quality of their relationships with colleagues in feeder and transfer schools. The coordinators also spoke of actively involving parents and children in transition activities, although not in planning which I would recommend to do, in order to design programmes that better fit the entire transition community. Coordinating transition is a challenging task, and the interviewees needed significant professional and personal resources to make it work – most evidently time, money and determination. They found that obtaining external resources was easier when there was a culture of attending to transition in their school pyramid, and that, by making transition part of their personal identities, they became instrumental in creating and maintaining that culture.

Although this chapter might be useful for teachers coordinating transition and those aspiring to this position, it also holds messages for universities. Because it is critical to school effectiveness, and has such important implications for children's wellbeing, transition and its management should be a prerequisite in postgraduate leadership programmes. It also makes an excellent case study of leadership that can be taught on these programmes. By educating school leaders about transition, universities can encourage those leaders to provide transition coordinators with the resources that they need and improve the culture of transition by transmitting its value through authority figures. As transition becomes part of the professional identity of those leaders, they take it wherever they go, which might eventuate in transition becoming more of a priority in local authorities and government.

Universities can also help improve transition for children by working it into programmes for teacher trainees. As Howe (2011) pointed out, programmes that train teachers as middle years educators (such as the one I attended) require trainees to teach both primary and secondary curricula. In doing so, these programmes produce educators that have a more balanced view of teaching across the transition years, rather than ascribing to one of the 'two tribes' of teaching (Sutherland et al., 2010). As Howe (2011) also observed, these middle years programmes are in the minority; therefore, it is important to dedicate time to issues of transition and curricular tribalism in primary and secondary programmes, so that transition between schools and curricula becomes foundational knowledge for all educational professionals.

References

Akos, P., Queen, J. A., & Lineberry, C. (2005). *Promoting a successful transition to middle school.* Larchmont, NY: Eye on Education Inc.

Fuller, K., Thomas, F., & Horswell, C. (2005). *Key stage 2 to key stage 3 transition project.* Nottingham: Mouchel Parkman/Department for Education and Skills.

Galton, M., Gray, J., & Rudduck, J. (1999). *The impact of school transitions and transfer on pupil progress and attainment.* Norwich: Department for Education and Employment.

Hargreaves, L. (2007). Let's talk transfer: Smoothing transition throughout secondary school. *Curriculum Briefing, 5*(3), 3–10.

HMIE (2007). *Language for learning: The challenges of leading in a time of change.* Livingston: HM Inspectorate of Education.

Howe, A. (2011). Managing primary–secondary transfer: Lessons learned? In *Bridging the transition from primary to secondary school* (pp. 153–165). Abingdon and New York: Routledge.

Powell, R., Smith, R., Jones, G., & Reakes, A. (2006). *Transition from primary to secondary school: Current arrangements and good practice in Wales.* Swindon: National Foundation for Educational Research.

Sutherland, R., Yee, W. C., McNess, E., & Harris, R. (2010). *Supporting learning in the transition from primary to secondary schools.* Bristol: University of Bristol.

Index